FIRST CUT 2

First Cut 2

More Conversations with Film Editors

GABRIELLA OLDHAM

UNIVERSITY OF CALIFORNIA PRESS

Berkeley   Los Angeles   London

University of California Press, one of the most distinguished
university presses in the United States, enriches lives around the world
by advancing scholarship in the humanities, social sciences, and natural
sciences. Its activities are supported by the UC Press Foundation and
by philanthropic contributions from individuals and institutions. For
more information, visit www.ucpress.edu.

University of California Press
Berkeley and Los Angeles, California

University of California Press, Ltd.
London, England

Library of Congress Cataloging-in-Publication Data

Oldham, Gabriella.
    First cut 2 : more conversations with film editors / Gabriella
Oldham.
        p.   cm.
    Includes bibliographical references and index.
    ISBN 978–0–520–27350–4 (cloth, alk. paper)—
ISBN 978–0–520–27351–1 (pbk. : alk. paper)
    1. Motion pictures—Editing.   2. Motion picture editors—
Interviews.   I. Title.

TR899.O44   2012
777'.55—dc23   2011046243

Manufactured in the United States of America

21   20   19   18   17   16   15   14   13   12
10   9   8   7   6   5   4   3   2   1

In keeping with its commitment to support environmentally
responsible and sustainable printing practices, UC Press has printed
this book on 50# Enterprise, a 30% post consumer waste, recycled,
de- inked fiber and processed chlorine free. It is acid-free, and meets all
ANSI/NISO (z 39.48) requirements.

Contents

Acknowledgments

Great thanks to all the film editors who gave of their time to participate in these interviews (as well as for their many kind words about the first *First Cut!*). I remain in awe of their creativity, their artistry, their process, and most of all, their kind and compassionate spirit.

A special acknowledgment and tribute to Sally Menke, who graciously agreed to be interviewed before her untimely death. Her extraordinary experience working with Quentin Tarantino and other directors would have greatly illuminated this book.

To the many editors of *First Cut: Conversations with Film Editors* who responded to my letters of inquiry more than twenty years later, supplying encouragement and contacts to jump-start this second volume. I am especially grateful to Paul Hirsch for his insights, assistance, and support in the early stages of this book.

To Mary Francis of University of California Press for her sage advice, enthusiasm for pursuing a "sequel," and unwavering confidence in this and future projects. I am also most grateful to Kim Hogeland, Cindy Fulton, Andrew Frisardi, and all at UC Press who worked on this book.

To Fabiana—when *First Cut* (the first) came out, you were three years old, too young to understand film, but mature enough to know a good thing when you saw it! Here's the "sequel" and you're twenty-two—little did I know that my wistful hope for you to *"be a film editor when you grow up"* would become reality. Immerse yourself in film. Study the best, learn from the worst, love the process, and discover your voice. Let film be your world and the world, your film.

To Raoul, I know you would have liked a doctor or lawyer in the family, but thank you for supporting your daughter's aspirations. One day you will be proud.

To Petunia, I hope she knows why I remain grateful for her presence.

To my mother, who believed I could write even when I doubted. All that I am is because of what you have given me, and for that I am so rich and deeply grateful.

Introduction

Twenty years may seem endless, but they may also feel much like the blink of an eye.* In the twenty years since the publication of *First Cut: Conversations with Film Editors,* this duality of endless/instant has come to characterize everyday twenty-first-century life, not to mention the evolution in the techniques of filmmaking, and of film editing in particular. Before looking at editing specifically, however, a snapshot of the twenty years that led to this second volume, *First Cut 2: More Conversations with Film Editors,* may illuminate this duality that both intimidates and exhilarates.

During the late 1980s, when I was seeking editors to interview for the first volume, I had no such tools as Yahoo, Google, IMDb, or any other database that is at one's fingertips today. I had chanced upon a book at the Coliseum Bookstore in New York City that happened to list the credits of most working and retired editors of feature films from the golden age of Hollywood to the 1980s—and, unbelievably, their home addresses and telephone numbers. Subsequently, I mailed letters requesting interviews, and each editor graciously answered using my return self-addressed stamped envelope. To screen films for my interviews, I rented ten or more VHS tapes each weekend from local video stores, to the wide-eyed wonder of attendants behind the counter. I recorded all interviews on audiotapes, vigilantly watching the turning wheel of the cassette to make sure the fragile tape did not catch in the recorder's mechanical jaw. Via snail mail

---

* In editing, this phrase has special meaning. Not only does this natural flutter of the eye permit the optical illusion that is film, but it is also the title of a classic book, *In the Blink of an Eye* (2001), by veteran film editor Walter Murch, who was a pioneer in the "digital revolution" that is frequently referred to in this set of interviews.

again, I forwarded transcripts to each editor who added, deleted, and reworded their thoughts in meticulous longhand directly on the pages, and posted them back so I could enter them on, yes, a computer, but without today's bells and whistles. This revision process flew cross-country between us several times, every change documented in the editor's fine penmanship. Had there been a speedier way to execute this routine, I did not know or did not care to know. The "slow way" created my rapport with the editors as well as the quiet enthusiasm I savored in producing my first book.

Twenty years ago, life seemed slower anyway. Although progress was percolating in fits and starts, there was still no rampage of cell phones, faxes, Internet, CDs, DVDs, HDTVs, laser disks, laptops, tablets, apps, iPods, iPads, iPhones, Nooks, Kindles, Tweets, Twitters, high-speed modems, and high-def lifestyles too complex to describe. Film editors were slowly transitioning as well to using new technology. Their world had long operated with hand-cranked reels, Moviolas, Steenbecks, flatbeds, grease pencils, tape, hot splices, and scissors. It was all in a day's (and night's) work for editors to dash dailies to laboratories for every print and to imagine in their mind's eye "special effects" (dissolves, fades) that they would mark on the celluloid for the labs to create. Despite the tedious *hand*-craft that ruled the editing room from the onset of filmmaking until the 1980s, editors created masterpieces that broke new ground and set cinematic standards that reflected changing mores and expectations. They did it the "hard way" because that was the way they learned how to do it, and they did it extraordinarily. The slow pacing of many golden age films yielded to the flash-cutting of wild car chases and acid trips in the 1960s and 1970s, but the physical labor of cutting prevailed and succeeded, regardless of rhythm. The so-called tedium, in fact, prompted greater contemplation and reflection on the film's characters, stories, and emotions. The slowness of editing both invited and compelled editors to think deeply about every cut *because* it was labored as well as a labor of love.

First Cut, then, became a time capsule of this slower history of an industry witnessed by editors who worked with *film*. Not long after the book's release, however, even the shadowy film strips featured on the cover were already becoming passé, with video dominating the field. When University of California Press suggested the idea of revisiting the first volume for a new age, it was our quick consensus that the text should remain intact, without revision or update. Rather, a whole new second book would pick up where the first left off. We were now in a time of sprocketless film, cut nonlinearly by editors who had had to rattle their comfortable cages and leap into new technology, or who had grown up with technology and knew little else. Call it destiny or miracle, but the first volume ended at a point in time when a radical movement in editing was stirring but had not yet burst full-blown on the horizon. Rumblings of this movement were evident in the first volume, and it was not entirely embraced with glee. I still recall one editor from *First Cut* who nostalgically glanced at a tall green piece of equipment sitting in the corner of his cutting room. "We call it The Fern," he said wistfully of the Moviola, as he proceeded to slide levers and punch keys on the more formidable Avid to demonstrate the new wave of editing.

Flash-forward twenty years. The Coliseum Bookstore selling the volume of editors' home addresses was gone; production books now featured agents' contacts. Video stores were dropping like flies, but the ones that survived Amazon and Netflix were now renting DVDs. I myself was long past being impressed with technology, which had become both a blessing and a curse. It had become second nature to expect instant contact with anyone via Myspace, LinkedIn, YouTube, you-name-it; privacy was essential, yet everything seemed blatantly in one's face(book). I worked on higher-speed computers nearly 24/7 and learned to calculate time-zone differences to ensure immediate e-mail responses. Finding data on films was a mouse-click away: typing in a title on a search engine yielded synopses, credits of cast and crew, biographies, and useful links. Having crossed a threshold of no return, the world had shrunken to the dimensions of a computer screen for everything from tech support in distant countries to arcane knowledge in distant libraries. Much like the editor with The Fern, however, I felt twinges for an age of innocence when instant gratification for output and impatience with slow machinery were rare. Nostalgia for vestiges of another day vied fiercely with a determined, fast-paced mindset that no longer had room or time for it. I found odd comfort in purposely recalling some incident from the "old days," such as the moment when coworkers and I huddled around our first fax machine, silently awaiting the slow squeal of communication from "the other side" and confirming that we had bridged time and place in seconds. It was humbling yet powerful—much as I imagine prehistoric peoples must have felt when discovering fire. These days, many may forget humility and focus on power instead, but one point remains certain: of all the inventions the world has known, those of the past twenty years have surpassed (not always reasonable) expectations and are, in a hyphenated word, mind-boggling.

Standing like a wobbly Colossus of Rhodes, with each foot planted on a different shore, I tried to access the best of two worlds. Hoping to revive a personal approach in an age of impersonal technology, I rummaged for ways to "meet" a new group of editors whose words would become *First Cut 2*. I dug out from my files a twenty-year-old, yellowing piece of paper with the addresses of editors from the first volume. Sadly checking off those who had passed on, I snail-mailed letters to the rest, trusting their addresses were still viable and that they could offer personal referrals. Instead of a self-addressed stamped envelope, though, I supplied my e-mail address. I also enclosed a brief questionnaire to probe the editors' sense of the new directions that editing was inevitably following in both fiction and documentary films. My own life these twenty years had also been filled with inevitable twists and detours, and I had fallen off the editing loop. I had hoped that the success of *First Cut* would encourage these editors to share with me their thoughts to jump-start this endeavor at film editing redux. What had changed? What, if anything, had remained the same? Were these changes for the better or worse? Who was the editor today and how was he or she faring in a brave new world of technology? Within days, several editors e-mailed me their perspectives of where editing was headed and new concerns engendered by new expectations. One editor used a term that virtually bounced off my computer screen—a term which, in retrospect, was hardly surprising or novel, likely not even a term he had coined. But for me, it became the core that guided the purpose and development of *First Cut 2*. Editing had undergone a "digital revolution," he said. Of necessity and by force, I concluded, film editing would not be the same. But part of me, of course, hoped that it would.

. . .

The digital revolution did not happen overnight, as its name might imply. All seismic phenomena brew and bubble for decades or longer, before they erupt on a mostly unsuspecting world (except for those who anticipate the rumble). Television, for example, had its initial trials as early as the first decade of the twentieth century before sweeping the country in the 1950s. So too, nonlinear editing took its first crawl as early as 1971 with the CMX 600, a collaboration between CBS and Memorex. This technological "editor" could access analog video in "skip-field" mode, drawing on disk packs said to be as large as washing machines. On the work console, a human editor could cut on a "preview" monitor using a light pen, while screening the edited version on a second monitor. Its technical intricacies are beyond the scope of this introduction, but suffice it to say that this dinosaur reflected a "bigness" in both physical size and concept. It introduced a nonlinear mindset that would change a hundred years of editing.

Nonlinear editing is, in simple terms, the ability to avoid searching *linearly* or sequentially through footage in order to reach a desired point. Now, not only did editors not have to endure playing material from the beginning to the intended spot, but nonlinear also meant noncutting, as in chopping prints or negatives. Random access made an editor's search for footage quicker and less labor-intensive. The actual term *nonlinear* became common parlance in 1991 with the classic text *Nonlinear: A Guide to Digital Film and Video Editing*, by Michael Rubin, but it was already in the vocabulary of those designing and witnessing these developments.

The 1980s introduced computers with multiple laser disks or VCRs. The most famous (and certainly most endearingly named) was the Edit-Droid, developed by George Lucas of *Star Wars* fame, and a comparable sound system, the SoundDroid. This featured timeline editing and clip bins, both of which would become staples of all nonlinear systems. Full-fledged nonlinear editing with computers was introduced in 1989, first by Editing Machines Corporation with the EMC2 editor, and literally a few weeks later by Avid introducing its Avid/1, based on the Apple Macintosh platform. Although video quality was only comparable to VHS tapes, the Avid Media Composer series would soon become the most popular editorial system, formally launching the digital revolution.

These innovations were initially functional for small projects, given their limited storage capacity, but by early 1993, a team at the Disney Channel introduced a system that could hold over seven terabytes, enabling feature-length motion picture editing to become fully nonlinear digital. Together with Avid as its manufacturer, this system within one year supplanted the entire history of 35mm film editing equipment and, despite competition from other developers, Avid became the leader in the field.

"Bigger" and "better" set off an inevitable race with each other throughout the 1990s, as issues and concerns were addressed with greater refinements: storage, memory capacity, security, image resolution, upgrades, flexibility, data transfer, high definition, compression, film (twenty-four frames per second) and video (thirty frames per second) compatibility, and so forth. Avid's staunchest rival has been Final Cut Pro, released in 1999 by Apple and receiving a Technology and Engineering Emmy Award in 2002. Avid, Apple, and Adobe (which produced Adobe Premiere in 1992) have been dubbed the "A-team," and together have virtually controlled the options of nonlinear editing, both professionally and on the home-front. While professional editors were readjusting to new modes of working, novice and aspiring filmmakers were now offered unprecedented opportunities to create movies right at home. "Desktop" democratization opened the doors to amateurs who could shoot and edit right on their computers in their own basements or bedrooms, with increasingly professional quality at a fraction of earlier film costs. Many personal computers are now automatically supplied with free basic nonlinear video editing (iMovie, Windows Movie Maker), guaranteeing the appearance of everything from dancing cats and dogs to award-winning films on YouTube, other Internet venues, and independent film festivals. In a sense, the digital revolution has leveled the playing field for all, providing affordable, time-saving, quality tools to anyone with a cinematic vision.

As with any radical transformation, initial resistance was inevitable—and some filmmakers still revert to old ways. It has been said that Steven Spielberg, Alan Parker, and David Lynch have continued to cut on film and, according to Walter Murch, Spielberg has a team of technicians on call to keep his collection of Moviolas fully functional. The editors in *First Cut* presented vivid rationales for why hands-on-film was vital to the editing process—for most of them, it was the only way they knew how to cut. The sensory interaction with film strips, manipulated by hand via reels and spools or streaming through one's fingers, was the entrance to a world of unanticipated connections among image, music, words, sound, and silence that surfaced through the tactile spark. It was for many a terrible thing to lose, and even today—as accustomed and resigned to the distance between themselves and the film created by keyboard and computer screen—many editors still miss it.

The enormous benefits of working with computers now "go without saying," but Murch in his book *In the Blink of an Eye*, has calculated a purely mathematical rationale for why using computers makes sense, editorially speaking: ". . . a scene made up of only twenty-five shots can be edited in approximately 39,999,999,999,999,999,999,999,999 ways. In miles, this is twenty-five times the circumference of the observable universe." Of course, precomputer editors were faced with comparable exponential challenges and entered the fray undaunted. Murch himself recalls the "1.2 million feet of workprint, almost seven tons of film and sound" for *Apocalypse Now*, which he and three other editors cut on Moviolas and KEM "8-plates."

Despite the ease of managing all this video footage today, the technology has spawned new and unforeseen dilemmas, imposed on editors across the board. With enormous storage capacity in editing software, directors can shoot unlimited footage to their hearts' content—even as deadlines are shortened. Translation: editors are now expected to wade through endless hours of dailies and weed out shots that are unusable and unnecessary, but nonetheless present to be screened and evaluated. The tendencies toward excess—simply because the technology permits excess—have also backfired in some cases. Eagerness to update, upgrade, and outdo may produce bigger, but not always better. In 2011, editors across the country expressed outrage over the release of Apple's new version, Final Cut Pro X, which—despite incredible speed and other useful features—they say has stripped the software of many of the basic functions they require to do their work. Editors in fact have fought technology with technology: according to *Variety* of June 29, 2011, "An online petition from 'editors and affected filmmakers' asking Apple to restore previous versions of [Final Cut Pro] and declare the new version a 'prosumer' app had more than 3,700 signatures."

The repercussions of new ways of working inevitably trickle from the editing room to the outcome of all that work. As Matt Hanson writes in *The End of Celluloid* (2004), "Filmmaking in the digital age allows us all to create and experience fantasy worlds that are as real as the world we live in. . . . Moving image is being morphed, bent, and warped along x, y, and z-axes." Special effects—not only in science fiction and disaster films, where one would expect them, but even in traditional dramas and comedies—are de rigeur. But one may ask how necessary these breathtaking visuals and optical tricks are to engage an audience, weave a scenario, create an art form. Has good storytelling itself improved with progress and grown with spectacle? Has great acting been helped or hampered by technical wizardry? The effects of *A Trip to the Moon*, fashioned by Méliès in 1902, may not hold a special FX candle next to *Inception* in 2010, but is it any less of a good tale or milestone for its time as well as all time? Both have their place, and feed each other in remarkable ways. It can seem, though, that dazzled by the bright shine of progress, it is easy to overlook the precedents and reach past the essentials.

. . .

With the term *digital revolution* whirling in my head, I set about meeting each of the editors for *First Cut* 2 via e-mail. The letters that I would have snail-mailed on textured paper were now sent within seconds and several were answered within hours of receipt. I was gratified to know that a number of the editors were familiar with the first volume and considered it an honor to participate in its "sequel." I arranged to interview New York–based editors in their cutting rooms or an occasional Starbucks, and those living out of town or country would be interviewed by telephone—and I still used audio-cassettes! Once potential editors were on board, I

"IMDbed" their credits and immediately acquired DVDs for all films that would be the basis of our conversations. The remarkable advantage of DVDs was the wealth of "bonus features" ranging from "the-making-of" featurettes, to outtakes, to commentaries sometimes spotlighting the editors themselves, and all of this priceless background knowledge filtered into my questions—and consumed far more viewing time than anticipated. The rigorous reality was that while technology had filled life with perks and bonuses, it unfortunately had not yet determined a way to compensate by adding more hours to the day.

To achieve a good balance of interviews for the book, I found it imperative, not only to find editors who work on a diversity of films, but to reopen the discussion—as I had in *First Cut*—to both documentary and fiction film editors. *First Cut* had been a pioneer in juxtaposing editors from both fields, since audiences, students, and even professionals tended to conjure up only "Hollywood" when thinking of filmmaking and—if they even included editors in their consideration—of editing itself. Twenty years ago, the conversations with documentary editors revealed richly complex understandings of the key differences between documentary and fiction film editing. Usually lacking any kind of a script, documentary editors face sifting through hundreds of hours of interview, archival, reenactment, sound, and music material to discover the spine of the story and all the character and plot arcs radiating from it. Documentary editors in essence become scriptwriters as they assemble the evolving film, shot by shot and scene by scene. By contrast, fiction films are sprung from a script, although all editors working in this domain will readily admit that the end result may sometimes deviate radically and of necessity from what the screenwriter originally envisioned, as what looks good "on paper" does not always translate well to the screen. Set side by side, the examples and insights of both fiction and documentary editors in *First Cut* finally offered a holistic understanding of *editing* in a multitude of facets for creative expression and articulation. The need to continue including both "forces" in *First Cut* 2 was a given; in fact, I considered it even more vital in this book to balance documentary with fiction film editors and highlight the unique stance of an *independent* filmmaker-editor. It was also important for me to include a sense of history in the various conversations, so *First Cut* 2 features veteran editors as well as "new kids on the block." This sense of history is even more poignant when one contemplates that the "old days" now refer to the 1970s and 1980s, not the 1930s and 1940s as they did in my original volume. Yet, preserving this sense of history remains vital, as it is often one of the essentials that is bypassed with the speed of progress. Today's wide availability of technology, the growing number of venues to present "homemade" films, and especially the expectation that we must be "global citizens" with a broad exposure to history and multicultural knowledge makes it impossible to continue having a myopic view of film as only of "Hollywood" or only of "today." Once again, the editors here provide the threads that weave this rich tapestry of twenty-first-century life.

Inevitably, however, some editors who would have made excellent contributions could not join in because of time constraints; in a tragic turn of events, Sally Menke, who had agreed to participate, died not long before I could schedule what might have been her last interview. As time and responsibilities continually threatened to overwhelm my progress on the book, I knew it would become ever more important to focus on quality over quantity. The lens would become the *person* of the editor, more than the process, as my way of making up for the limited face-to-face time we would spend with each other, and because most of our work would be exchanged through electronic means. *First Cut* had chronicled the process of twenty-three documentary and fiction film editors through a thematic deconstruction of the various steps and considerations that comprised this art and craft. *First Cut* 2 would turn more to the *doing* and *being* of the editor. Having only twelve longer, more in-depth interviews permitted the leisure to explore these editors' thinking processes as well as more of their personal views: how they respond to film, what they value, how their lives inform their work, and what *being* an editor means today.

The stereotype of the editor as "just a pair of hands" for the director, or as a murky figure in a darkened room spinning reels of film, was already broken twenty years ago—especially once editors' names could be spotted on posters without a magnifying glass and award shows recognized best editing as more than a mechanical skill. Yet, the pressures and expectations that the editors ultimately revealed in the conversations in this book continually threaten the balance between their being indispensible to the film's success and their still feeling isolated and invisible.

I too wanted to strike a balance between exploring the digital revolution and discussing the art and craft of editing, albeit in a new century. The conversations did not springboard into the pros and cons of Avid versus Final Cut Pro (or, for that matter, Final Cut Pro versus Final Cut Pro X). For editors, decisions along those lines are often dictated by on-the-job contingencies and editors learn what they must to do—and keep—their jobs. What was more critical to my balance between the old and the new was to see how old and new worked together, played off each other, built on each other, and existed individually and symbiotically. The editors' willing engagement in these conversations lay in the fact that they were, once again, happy to be asked to articulate their intuitive sense of what makes a film good, great, or, yes, even bad—because of and despite technology. As key figures in postproduction, editors would know first-hand both the technical *and* artistic aspects of the questions I would ask, and would offer answers they considered appropriate from their eagle-eye perspective.

The topic of technology thus tended to weave subtly in and out of the conversations. The bottom line was that speaking about editing was a continual reaffirmation of the editor's role in understanding what makes a film succeed or fail. As every editor concurred, there is no film without story, and all visual effects, Sensurround sound, IMAX, 3D, 4D, or other razzle-dazzle can still bomb, despite budget and zeal, without the archi-tecture of a story to support it. Likewise, the "tools of the trade"—at least theoretically—might not matter if the story-heart of the film pumps with strong characters and emotions that resonate for an audience. That said, would editors revert to scissors and glue? No way . . . but if every com-puter on earth crashed because of viruses, editors could probably still find a way to cut their film.

These conversations also echoed the aforementioned universal despair of increasingly overwhelming amounts of footage, compressed schedules, and tightened budgets. Wistfully longing for a director who would preweed the footage, these editors acknowledged that such exigencies have always been part of their "job description." Hand in hand with the overwork, however, does come a persistent sense of isolation—not just isolation imposed by outsiders who do not understand what editors do, but isolation even within the editing room. The capacity of the software to complete an unprecedented range of tasks—such as designing special effects and opti-cals, laying in sound and music tracks, or correcting color—has given the editor greater autonomy than ever before. Where previously it was critical to hand off the film to specialists like sound and music editors and to labo-ratories, the so-called "picture" editor is now able—even expected—to carry out many of these tasks alone. There are fewer hands to help along the way, so the job occasionally feels lonelier. At times, as well, directors may be away for long stretches, leaving the editor alone to make the best decisions about the film. The other, creative side is that the editor is con-sidered powerful enough to decide when and how help is needed. Count-less anecdotes reveal the close, sometimes decades-long relationships between editors, directors, cinematographers, sound editors, and assistants that are nurtured from film to film. Because of film's collaborative process, postproduction experts often become involved in much earlier phases of editing, working as a team to shortcut problems, assemble needed materials, and condense work efficiently. Technology has offered new opportunities for editors to befriend those who speak computer-ese to troubleshoot or translate technical jargon. To paraphrase one editor, there is no such thing as a stupid question about computers in this day and age, especially when making a multimillion-dollar film.

As naturally reflective personalities, editors appreciate both the isolation and the socializing that the process entails, and they find ways to work productively at both ends of the spectrum. One universal concern stemming from nonlinear editing, however, is that time is a scarce commodity, and levels of reflection formerly lavished on each cut have been threatened. The end of the sensory experience of film that characterized the "dark ages" or "old days" has virtually eliminated the editor's kinetic interrelationship with film—or conversely, has driven the search for new relationships with digitized film. Each shot must still be considered for purpose, placement, impact, length, and necessity in a scene, each scene within a sequence, each sequence within the film. What may have been a slow glide into a creative trance through the feel of film has morphed into kicks of adrenalin pulsating from every keystroke and mouse click. Both states of being can, in their own ways, be ripe for finding connections. As the editors point out, it is as possible to obsess for hours over two frames on a computer screen as it was on a Moviola.

Perhaps the issue is not whether "fast" or "slow" or "old" or "new" leads to greater creativity—especially for those who have worked in both camps—but rather whether those who have never known how to savor a cut on film can understand the gift of slow thinking. Will there be compromises to the potentials of a film that are often discovered with time, over time? Will haste engender waste? Or does it all, once more, fall to human resilience, adapting in new ways to new demands with even better results?

Understanding the tenets of creative excellence in editing seems to be a timeless quest that transcends (and transforms) the tools with which editing is accomplished. One tenet for these editors is to love and immerse oneself in film, and to allow film to be the vehicle of one's self-expression. The editors all point to a sense of urgency to be of and in the world, especially as the industry itself has become globalized, with unprecedented opportunities to connect peoples and countries with a common cause to produce uncommon films. They stress learning about all that comprises the human experience: music, art, history, psychology, science, language, family, pets, nature, love, hate, fear, compassion. Immersion in film is the way to open the mind to impulses that foster creativity, build intuition, and cultivate motivation each day. It was gratifying, and not entirely unexpected, that the editors voiced hard-earned pride in their work and often echoed—some without knowing the first volume of *First Cut*—the precise allusions that their predecessors used to describe editing. For both present and past editors, editing was alchemy, painting, psychology, and music. It involved finding the film's heart, keeping the beat, and choosing the "good stuff" to "make it work." Significantly, the editors rarely if ever referred to *technological* metaphors in describing the nature of editing. In short, while editing is highly complex, it is at its core an intensely human process, shared by all editors across time and space.

In a daring and precarious era, it was a comfort to know that the person of the editor had remained unscathed by technology, while also becoming all the more powerful and creative because of it. Editors may well be the last stronghold and filter in the filmmaking process to render quality control, understand both director and audience, and extend their feelers into the future without losing touch with what grounded them in the past. *First Cut* 2 is likely to become another time capsule of this age, only a stone's throw ahead of its predecessor. Perhaps in another twenty years, progress will have once again exceeded the great expectations that are today's baseline. Or perhaps these expectations will, of necessity and by force, become simpler in unimaginable ways. Editors will likely never return to the old tools of cutting. Yet . . . who ever thought we'd see vinyl records again? Whatever the next twenty years will bring, editors will still be around to tell the story.

1. Keeping Beats

MARK LIVOLSI

2001 *Vanilla Sky* (coeditor), dir. Cameron Crowe

2003 *Pieces of April,* dir. Peter Hedges

2004 *The Girl Next Door,* dir. Luke Greenfield

2005 *My Suicidal Sweetheart,* dir. Michael Parness

2005 *Wedding Crashers,* dir. David Dobkin

2006 *The Devil Wears Prada,* dir. David Frankel

2007 *Fred Claus,* dir. David Dobkin

2008 *Marley and Me,* dir. David Frankel

2009 *The Blind Side,* dir. John Lee Hancock

2011 *The Big Year,* dir. David Frankel

2011 *We Bought a Zoo,* dir. Cameron Crowe

AWARDS

2006 Eddie Award (ACE) nomination, Best Edited Feature Film—Comedy or Musical, *Wedding Crashers*

2007 Eddie Award (ACE) nomination, Best Edited Feature Film—Comedy or Musical, *The Devil Wears Prada*

With a computer screen glowing off to the side of his New York cutting room, Mark Livolsi spoke of some of the box office smashes he has edited, including *Wedding Crashers, The Devil Wears Prada*, and *Marley and Me*. Livolsi peppers his comments with some essential metaphors (playing jazz, handing off batons, making a stew) that many editors here, as well as in the first volume of *First Cut*, have evoked in discussing their art and craft, establishing the multilayered nature of being an editor. In addition to metaphors, Livolsi offers practical illustrations of the many day-to-day decisions and pressures that an editor in the twenty-first-century cutting room faces, including the need to work faster because of tight schedules, excessive amounts of dailies, and "infinite" possible edits that the new technology facilitates. As Livolsi also notes, technology has finally eliminated the physical tedium of splicing film and the clatter of sound cuts that were prominent in editing on celluloid. However, the fundamental principles of editing—to find the story, tap into emotional truth, and present the material for maximum impact—remain key editorial responsibilities, as they have since the beginning of narrative cinema.

Because many of Livolsi's films to date have been comedies, he offers a strong analysis of the editorial necessities of that genre, but he has also been extending himself beyond comedy to explore other types of film. Cutting across all genres, however, is perhaps editing's greatest challenge: discovering the "story" and its related concerns with pacing and rhythm. Livolsi reflects enthusiastically on how actors' improvisations, special effects, and the occasional "crane shot" can impact his efforts to pull the most effective story out of the chaos of feature filmmaking.

When did you start editing?

I started when I was a kid. My father had an 8mm camera and shot home movies and I was fascinated by them. One day I found his camera in the closet, and I bought film and started to shoot. It slowly occurred to me that movies—which I loved—were something I could make as well. I started with little zombie movies. Back in the seventies, I was obsessed with George Romero and *Night of the Living Dead,* and zombie movies seemed easy to make. I was also into theatrical makeup, especially scars, so it seemed like the way to go.

Just you and your friends?

And my brother, Tim. In one film, I had my next-door neighbor attack and eat my brother! I have that movie somewhere in the attic, and my brother still talks about how I forced him into it. (*Laughs.*)

Did you edit in camera?

I did, actually. In fact, I remember the moment when I first made an edit in camera. It literally was a shot of my brother walking down the driveway, holding a BB gun, and I shot it in a wide. Then I paused my brother midaction and grabbed a medium shot from another angle. When I got the film back from the lab and looked at it, here was this professional piece of work! It actually told a little story in two shots and that fascinated me.

Did you have any editing equipment at the time?

I had a small hand-cranked splicer. My dad used it to cut out all the overexposed bits of film. I used it primarily to watch those old Castle Films, which were eight-minute condensations of my favorite movies.

How about scripting?

I'd say my movies were done on the fly, although I did write some scripts, but silly ones that were ten, twelve pages long involving massive special effects and alien invasions. I remember showing one script to my art teacher who remarked, "It's a good script, but I think you bit off more than you can chew!" He was right because I never shot it. The planning, the coordinating, the sheer magnitude of what it took to actually *make* a film was to me so painstaking and daunting that very few of my epic projects ever left the planning stages. I was beginning to realize that each shot is a setup that has to be lit separately. Before that, I thought you'd just run out there and grab it like in a documentary, right? And then I realized, my God, you mean each of these shots has to be created separately and you have to move the camera here, move it there, set up lights? Forget that! I'll wait till it's all in the can and *then* work with it.

Aside from wanting to avoid those filmmaking logistics, why did you gravitate to the editing process itself?

I found I had a natural inclination for editing when I was in college. I tried everything at Penn State, which had a wonderful, very small film program. It was amazing because I had the opportunity to use equipment as opposed to competing for it. I learned how to write screenplays, direct actors, record sound, edit . . . but of all the filmmaking crafts, the only one that came easy to me was editing. In fact, with editing, I could get lost for fifteen, sixteen hours in the basement of the film department and just create, you know, put the film together. It was clear to me and it was clear to my girlfriend, Maria (who later became my wife), that editing seemed to be the right direction for me.

Did the detailed nature of the work appeal to you?

I think there was an obsessive component, a need to make order out of chaos. The chaos of infinite options, of infinite ways of cutting, of infinite performance choices, and what seemed like an infinite amount of dailies and turning it all into one final, decisive piece of storytelling. It was all instinctive. I never sat down and said, "This is what I like." I just did it and didn't think twice about it. When I got out of college, I focused on that. I said, "Okay, I'm not going to try to be a director or a writer. I know I'm good at editing and I'm going to get in there." And that's what I did from day one.

Did the chaos of editing ever overwhelm you?

To be honest, in college, you never have an overwhelming amount of footage. You barely have enough footage to tell a coherent story! But certainly in the professional world, there can be an overwhelming amount of footage, and, yes, I have been overwhelmed at times. That's when you hire second editors to come in and help you out. As much as possible I try to tackle these situations by myself. It becomes a personal contest. But at a certain point, you risk undercutting the project because of your inability to look through all the footage and give it careful attention.

I imagine that if you parcel out work to others, you still have to oversee it.

Absolutely. It's my responsibility as the editor. I like to delegate creative work to my assistants, who benefit from the chance to flex creative muscles and hone their abilities. In return, I get the benefit of their opinions and the wider perspective that collaboration brings. But this mostly happens during shooting, before the director walks in the door to begin his director's cut. From that point on, it's mostly between the director and myself.

Are you partial to editing any particular genre—besides zombie movies?

Yeah! No, I love all movies. I started with horror films as a kid, and blossomed into a little bit of everything. I love noirs, Westerns—I was a big holdout against Westerns for a long time, but finally fell under their spell a few years ago. Comedies, especially the classics, Marx Brothers, Buster Keaton. But that's just as a viewer. As an editor, I think challenges are to be had in any genre, and I would love to work in all genres. My goal is someday to cut a musical, a thriller, a drama—whatever. It's really immaterial because I think telling a story well is the great challenge of editing, just creating effective storytelling and doing the best work I can on any film. But it seems like all I've done so far is comedies!

I was just going to say that.

Well, that happens. You do one comedy film, somebody sees it and thinks you did it well, and that leads to another comedy film, and the next thing you know, you're being stereotyped as a comedy editor. That certainly doesn't preclude you from being able to do other genres, though. One of the main reasons I recently did *The Blind Side* was to try my hand at drama.

You made an interesting point that each genre poses its own set of challenges. However, since your overarching concern for all films is story, what are different editorial challenges within each genre?

Well, the prime directive of comedy is to make people laugh and to tell a story entertainingly. I think, then, that issues of rhythm and pacing in a comedy are different than they would be in a drama or horror film. You certainly have to present the material in a way that achieves maximum impact, but a brisk comedy won't necessarily have the same presentation as a thriller.

By pacing you mean . . .

A combination of length of shot, rhythm of cutting, number of cuts, connections.

And use of sound and silence?

Exactly. The kinetic qualities that are either within the frame or imposed on the film by the editor, by the editing itself.

Marley and Me *has both comedic and dramatic scenes in it. Can you speak of that film as an example to compare the pacing of each?*

Marley and Me begins as a comedy and gradually morphs into a drama. The first half of the film is generally briskly paced. We never outstay our welcome in those early scenes. And that, I think, is one of the mandates of editing comedy. People become invested through laughter, through enjoyment of the experience of watching comedy. The minute they become bored or the film loses its focus, you risk losing them and it becomes that much harder to get the momentum back. If a scene wasn't funny enough or slowed down too much, David Frankel, the director, would toss it out. This cut-and-dry approach was a little more complicated in the later, dramatic scenes. Audience investment wasn't dictated primarily through pace and laughs, but through investment in the characters and their problems. It was often a hard call to make: is a scene too long or just right? The third act wasn't terribly plot-driven, each scene being a beat in the declining years in the life of a dog. We went back and forth on the length of many of the later scenes, as well as removing and reordering them.

When you say that each scene is a "beat," are you referring to the action within the scene or the rhythm of how the shots are cut together?

A beat is like an ingredient. It could be small, a moment within a scene, or it could be a whole scene when looking at an entire film. When I'm looking at a film overall, I tend to think of it as a sort of stew, and you need many different ingredients. Like you can't leave out the salt—you need a pinch of salt here, a dash of something else there. *Marley and Me* is sort of a tone poem, more about emotion than plot. In fact, there's very little plot. It's very episodic. So when the plot especially in the second, more dramatic half is not advancing at a breakneck pace, then the film becomes all about the little emotional beats and what adds up to make the best stew. What is the best recipe? Well, you figure that out by trial and error. So for instance, toward the end of *Marley and Me*, when the dog is very sick, Owen Wilson's character talks with the dog as they're walking up a hill, asking Marley to let him know when "it's your time to go." The next scene shows Owen finding Marley lying near the fireplace, too old to climb the stairs. We removed this scene, but found that suddenly the *next* scene, where Marley is dying at the vet, came too soon. We needed the fireplace scene as a bridge to make clear that time had passed, that the scene on the hill and the dying scene weren't happening one right after the other. That was a necessary beat.

So the beat or scene of the dog by the fireplace served to transition between the beat of the sick dog on the hill and the beat of the dying dog at the vet.

Yes, it was a transitional point. In a film where we deliberately avoided referencing the passage of time with titles, we needed to show the passage of time in subtler ways. That scene represented a necessary space. In that way, you don't think it all happened from one day to the next, but you have the opportunity to think it's more gradual.

The beat of that scene also reinforced Owen's connection to the dog—

Which I felt was solid throughout the film. The dynamic was clearly between Owen and the dog. The triangle between Owen, Jennifer Aniston,

and Marley was not a perfect triangle in that sense. A scene that we ultimately took out might have helped to balance the triangle—but maybe not,
because it happened too late in the film. It was a scene where Jen has a
private moment with Marley under a tree. It would have been interesting,
but again for pacing reasons, we were cognizant that we had to honor the
progress of the dog's decline and death, while also being aware of not overly
methodically pacing it by including *every* beat we had. Also, when we
previewed the movie, some of the audience commented that the film was
too sad for too long. Some things had to fall by the wayside.

But the ending had to be sad. Moreover, it was a true story.

Yes, it was based on John Grogan's book. Many people commented on
how obvious or manipulative or whatever it was to kill off the dog at the
end. Never mind that it actually happened!

*Still, because the first half of the film was so bouncy and comedic, and
the second half depicted such a sad reality, the film almost splits in two.*

I do feel that the transformation is gradual, though. Yes, it is a very
different film in the first act than it is in the third act, and juxtaposed side
by side, they seem black and white. But the second act I consider a baton
handoff, so that the film morphs into more serious material. In the beginning, it's all very cute and sparkling and hilarious. Then it starts to become
serious in the second act, dealing with real issues such as when Jen has a
miscarriage and she and Owen fight a lot, but there are still comedic
moments. By the third act, I can safely say there is no comedy. Now,
Wedding Crashers has the same sort of paradigm, although not as extreme,
where we start out as a crazy-guys comedy and then suddenly it's more
serious, or at least more like a romantic comedy, with the emphasis on
romantic. Again, there's a baton handoff that I find interesting, with the
comedy between Vince Vaughn and Owen Wilson turning into Owen's
more serious romantic story. I remember when we got to the postprocess
on that film, a twenty-something-year-old guy working at a video facility
was watching the movie as he was turning out reels. He was laughing his
head off at the beginning, and then about halfway or two-thirds through,
he looked up and said, "Hey! This is a chick flick!" He was completely
confused. It snuck up on him that the movie was suddenly trying to be
something else.

*In the opening montage to the song "Shout!" when Vince and Owen are
crashing several weddings and picking up girl after girl after girl, you*

sense Owen is unhappy by the end of it. It was almost foreshadowing that Owen was facing a major life change, unlike his buddy Vince.

That's right. I think any film that doesn't really "feather in" those sorts of turns is the poorer for it.

In Wedding Crashers, *I noticed another comedy-genre device not seen much anymore—wipes!*

Yes, wipes can live in a comedy environment because they're whimsical, like a page turning. They're punctuation marks, so to speak. A dissolve usually means "later on, that same day." A fade-up and -out could be "later on, that same year." A wipe is "meanwhile, in the next room," or some such. In *Wedding Crashers,* since parallel stories were going on a lot, especially when Vince was trying to win over Isla Fisher and Owen was in a parallel circumstance trying to win over Rachel McAdams, I saw opportunities to wipe from one to the other. I had absolutely no predisposition to use wipes. In fact, I usually try to avoid that sort of thing. But the footage guided me and, in this case, wipes seemed best.

Not to stereotype you further, but I notice that montages seem to be something of a trademark for you. Wedding Crashers, Marley and Me, *and* The Devil Wears Prada *all had them.*

I know. They get thrust upon me! (*Laughs.*) They're in the script, of course. *The Blind Side* had two of them practically back-to-back.

Montage has been the cornerstone of editing, from the days of Sergei Eisenstein. What are the purposes of your montages here? To enhance comedy? Compress time? Tell visual stories? Substitute for long dialogues?

The answer is "all of the above." I can think right off to the "James Holt sequence" in *The Devil Wears Prada,* where Miranda Priestly, the Meryl Streep character, goes to the James Holt showroom to view the latest fashion and disapproves of everything she sees. The dailies rolled in and I spent the better part of that day cutting that scene. It was clearly going to be way too long if it played in real time. At one point, I got up to clear my head and said, "This just has to be montaged." I thought I was being brilliant till I reread the script pages, which described the scene as a series of quick cuts—something I had missed the first time around. So much for brilliant! But the lesson is still there: creating the *impression* of something is oftentimes much more satisfying than sitting through the real thing. So in that case, a montage was an expediency. The whole point of that scene was that there is a fashion presentation and Miranda is unhappy with it. It was a no-brainer then to take *all* those shots and do what montages tend to do, which is distill an idea into its purest essence and make it move as fast and entertainingly as possible. Montages can be strategically placed to provide a jolt of energy at a certain point when you feel you need it. A montage in *Marley and Me* takes place at the end of the first act, with shots of the dog's antics set against music, and it was specifically placed to propel you into the second act as well as convey the passage of time. And the opening montage of *Wedding Crashers* was obviously trying to reduce the concept of many weeks, many weddings, many girls, many experiences into one single entertaining, organic entity.

In itself, it told a little story of the guys' lifestyles, too.

Yes, it told a whole story with its own arc and provided enough energy and sex and good will to keep you going through the next part of the film, which was the inevitable setup for the story itself. In fact, the next scene after the montage is a quiet dialogue scene, so hopefully the residual energy from the montage carries you through that scene to the next one and beyond.

I have to say that the Wedding Crashers *montage was such high energy I was almost palpitating by the end of it!* (*Laughs.*)

Thank you!

Yet nothing like that reappears in the film, which slows down, by contrast, almost to the point of somberness. Is it a risk to create such energy so early in a film and not revive it later?

It would have to be considered on a case-by-case basis. In that situation, the idea was that people wanted to see Vince and Owen as wedding crashers—it is the name of the film, after all. Let's get all the crashing out of the way so we can have the story we want to tell, which ultimately became a romantic comedy—again, emphasis on romantic. Actually, there is another montage later on that I call the "sad-Owen montage," when he's lost everything important in his life. It's a visual storytelling device for passage of time. It's there for a very specific reason: to show him bottoming out. And to go back to your question of beats, each shot in that sequence or montage is a beat. We structured the "sad-Owen montage" so that each beat felt like it was in the right place for his descent, lower and lower. Some beats were stronger with a little comedy; other beats emphasized his character's sadness. Feathered within that was a parallel story—Rachel McAdams's growing uncertainty over *her* future. Ultimately, each beat was juxtaposed to show these two people going on separate minijourneys—Owen disintegrating and Rachel questioning. This transitional montage sets these characters up for their decisions in act three.

When you say you structure a montage to accomplish x, y, *and* z, *do you mean literally mapping it out shot by shot on paper or just in conversation with the director? And how long does it take you to cut a montage like that?*

It varies. Cutting the wedding-crashing montage was done in bits and pieces and fits and starts throughout the shooting process because the crew would pick up little pieces of weddings when they could. It wasn't like all the film for that came in over a one- or two- or three-day period and suddenly that was my next scene to cut. The opening "Shout!" montage was scripted as such, and the director, David Dobkin, had a very specific idea for it. We used the Isley Brothers version of "Shout!" where the song would slow down and then pick up again. David wanted to see that musical breakdown translated into a montage. Side by side, he and I built the montage. We would cut the music together to achieve that sort of shape and then start to put pieces in. We would go through the footage, David would find pieces he responded to, and then sometimes he would leave the room and I would do the roll-up-your-sleeves work and give it its visual rhythm. Sometimes at the end of a day, when I was tired of working on a regular scene, I would play around with the montage. It's very important when you work on a montage to stay fresh, and for me, it works best to spend an hour here, an hour there, maybe devoting a whole Saturday to it, scheduling it outside everything else. I think that is key for editing in general—to keep it fresh, go back to it at different times. You can develop a tendency to work a scene to death and obsess over a cut. I mean *obsess* for hours over a cut.

Editors have often mentioned that tendency.

Here's an example from *Wedding Crashers.* Rachel McAdams is sitting on a sailboat. She gets up to join Owen, so I needed to—I mean, I obsessed about cutting from a close-up of her to a wide shot as she stands to walk across the sailboat. I just couldn't get it right. I spent *hours.* Then I got it to a point where I could live with it. I didn't love it, but I could live with it.

What was wrong?

It just wasn't a perfect match. Rachel was not in the same position in both shots, so finding that key point where you could get away with it was eluding me completely. I reached the moment where I thought I could live with it. Then a few days later, I went back to the scene and realized it didn't *matter* how good or bad the match was. It took too long for her to move, so I just took out the whole middle and had her spring up instead. And you know what? It looked fine! It didn't match exactly, but you don't notice it in real time, and it achieved a greater good—better pacing. So coming to it fresh is really important. I know a lot of editors who will cut a scene and put it away immediately, then revisit it the next morning and see something that wasn't apparent before.

Do you feel the need to break with principles of matching that are fundamental to "good editing" and jump cut instead wherever it makes sense?

In editing and working with dailies, you juggle so many balls at one time. You deal with rudimentary issues like matching an actor's movements or performance, or the overall direction of the scene, or the placement of shots into a scene, or the position of a scene in the context of a film. You have to continue thinking about the whole, though.

So in the "Shout!" montage, with hundreds of jump cuts from close-up to long shot and everything in between, what principle guides cutting those shots together? Can you achieve seamlessness by jump cutting?

Yes, in that you're matching *motion*. You're not matching reality, you're matching energy, and that's my consideration. When I cut a montage like the "Shout!" one in *Wedding Crashers*, I tend to defocus my eyes, watch the overall motion of what's going on, and feel my way through the montage. I defocus my brain in a way and edit from a place in the back of my brain. It's instinct, but then again not entirely, because when you're juggling all those balls, you're dealing with some very front-of-brain stuff—story, dialogue, and so on. However, in editing, you are also dealing with much that comes only from a gut place and a rhythmic place, so in cutting something like a montage, I go into a bit of a trance state. That's the best way to describe it. I guess I'm not alone in approaching it that way. You end up *feeling* and can't necessarily intellectualize about it. It's a process of trial and error. Is the shot too short? Too long? Should it be two shots earlier? Or three shots later? If it's a shot where you're trying to match movement or create a general pattern through energy, you can sometimes tell where the shots should be, but it still boils down to playing with it, trial and error.

In other words, you can achieve a working trance, but something that isn't "right" in the film can jolt you out of it.

It could jolt you out of the trance and you either make a mental note as you're watching or you stop dead right there to fix it. In my own process, I prefer to smooth the wrinkles out on the bed as I go along, so to speak. When I'm watching a scene back for the first time—not necessarily a montage, but any scene—the moment I hit something that seems wrong, I'll stop and fix it. Then two seconds later, there might be something else wrong and I'll start from the beginning again and fix it until I've completely smoothed the bed sheet and taken it all the way down and it's perfect for me. If that's ever possible!

Does music help you to make bits and pieces come together in a montage?

Definitely. As I said, the "Shout!" montage was scripted to use that song. The opening montage in *The Devil Wears Prada* was a different situation. We initially didn't have a song in mind. The point of that montage was to show the world of high fashion opening up, and bring it back to Anne Hathaway's plain character through comparing and contrasting images.

Yes, that montage is full of quick-change surprises. For example, Hathaway's character puts on a plain shoe, then her shoe cuts to a fashionable high heel, which belongs to a glamorous model we didn't expect to see, and so on.

That was the overall idea. Once I found the right piece of music for it, the montage came together really fast. Initially, again, the film pieces would come in scattershot over three months of shooting, and if I found two or three shots that could go together, I would make a tiny sequence of them and store them in a bin in the Avid. Then I'd come back to it bit by bit. One day, I realized I had to face this thing and finally put it together because I seemed to have all the pieces I needed. When I'm putting together my first cut of a film, I need to add music, whether it's temp score or songs, and everyone gets to participate in the search process. My assistants and I initially look for music, along with the help of a music supervisor, and finally a music editor. In the case of *Prada*'s opening title montage, one of my assistants, Amanda Pollack, happened upon KT Tunstall's song "Suddenly I See," which was at that point brand new and relatively obscure. As soon as I heard it, I knew it was perfect for the scene. It worked so well with the images that the scene pretty much flew together in a few hours—it was a pleasure to cut.

How do you handle music on a sequence that isn't meant to be a montage but rather a straight performance?

My instinct is to use restraint as much as possible in dramatic scenes because they can become very maudlin with music. *The Blind Side*, for example, could have gone over the edge and off the cliff if the music wasn't restrained. The plot was dramatically ripe enough as it was, and if the music was too emotional, it would have been manipulative in a bad way. John Lee Hancock, the director, and I were very aware of this fine line, and in defining the tonality of the score, we'd occasionally find that no music worked best of all. The scene where Sandra Bullock's character, Leigh Anne Tuohy, gives Michael Oher (played by Quinton Aaron) a bed for the first time was clearly a place to avoid music and allow the actors and the charged moment to carry the scene. Overall, the power of music can help me as the editor understand a scene and begin to see the finished product in my mind's eye. But, bottom line, I don't want to *create* emotion with the music as much as I want to underscore and uphold the emotion that hopefully is already in the footage.

Speaking of withholding music, another film you edited, Pieces of April, *has hardly any music in it at all.*

Yes, and it was always intended to be music-free, with the exception of the ending, because the emotional release of the film was to occur at the very end of the film, when the mother and daughter characters reunite for the first time. That release was to be underscored by the music which, again, reinforces what I was just saying. That is a sort of textbook-y case of music used in an extreme way—withholding, withholding, withholding, allowing the film to build up dramatically *without* music, then letting go at the very end with music full force. That was the original intention, although after I was off the film and on to other projects, the director, Peter Hedges, decided to put snippets of score throughout the film in small transitional scenes. It was just enough to allow the music at the very end to feel organic to the film and not a complete left turn for the audience. Again, it's a question of feathering elements into a film. The music is feathered in enough so that it becomes part of that film's world and doesn't come out of nowhere at the very end. It seemed like the right choice for a film that had an "indie" feel. It was shot for very little money on video in like two weeks with a purposely gritty, vérité style. I think it just proves that you don't have to have a polished style to tell a story effectively if the screenplay, characters, and acting are all good.

Thanks for the lead-in to talking about a polar-opposite film like Fred Claus. *How did those high-budget computer-generated special effects affect your editing process?*

They affected my whole life! (*Laughs.*) It's such a huge undertaking to work on a film like that. In some ways, you have to be more proactive, with an eye toward the finish line. You need to fine-tune cut scenes much earlier so that you can turn them over for visual effects, which can take a long time to generate. One of the primary reasons I took on that film was because I wanted the challenge of trying something new. To tie back to the earlier question about different genres, I always welcome working on different types of films. I never want to do the same thing twice if I can help it.

Even though Fred Claus *was another comedy?* (Laughs.)

Yes, it was another comedy, but there was a new angle to it—big special effects. That aspect of that film attracted me primarily. Plus it was a Christmas film and I'm kind of a Christmas guy, so I wanted to play in that sandbox for a while.

Describe what you actually got to cut since so many special effects were added in after the editing.

Well, the effects were feathered in during the process. We're given temp versions of visual effects to pop into the film at various points in postproduction. The film kind of evolves. Individual shots, the building blocks for any scene, need to exist in some form. Whether it's a previsualization or storyboard or actors standing in front of a green screen, you need something to convey the idea of a scene.

Does having a green screen in the images throw off your editing judgment?

No, it really doesn't. It's surprising to me how easily I adapted to that style of filmmaking. I was able to look past all that. However, one thing I can't look past is bad sound. Most often, fortunately, the sound is workable, but shooting on locations like a beach or near a highway can make the tracks very hard to smooth out. If I hear bad audio edits or obvious tone shifts, my rhythm is thrown off. So I have to try to cross-dissolve sound or, worse case scenario, play the scene so that it's barely audible and then I can judge the visual rhythms. In general, I tend to cut for dialogue, so sound is of huge primary importance. I will listen to the scene, I will listen to the dialogue, I will listen to the performances, but I will often *not* look at the screen. Initially I'll just stare at my keyboard and listen to how it's playing. Later, I'll make the picture work, figure out where the splices go, where the cuts are, where things need to be opened up or compressed. That's how I tend to cut dialogue, unless the blocking is complicated. It's sort of an antivisual approach, unlike montages which are the exact opposite—totally visual. That's what I had to do with *Fred Claus* and *Wedding Crashers*, given the amount of improvisation in those films. Because of my approach to dialogue, I was well suited to working with so much improvising. Literally, you are taking improvisations that are very long or where no two takes are alike, and you find the best bits and try to turn them into coherent sentences. Sometimes that involves even taking *syllables* from the footage.

I noticed on the Wedding Crashers *DVD that some outtakes presented a much longer dialogue from which you utilized* only one line *for the final film.*

Yes. That is the extreme and maybe the best case for talking about my approach to cutting dialogue, where I would listen only to the dialogue being constructed. This is not to take away from the work of the actors who created great material, but in the process of editing the scene, I basically have to "watch with my ears." Later I look at the scene with my eyes to see all the pieces cut together, and then hopefully find how to cut away to something that will allow me to hide the splices. For instance, the scene where Vince Vaughn is sitting at a table with Henry Gibson—Vince did amazing improvisation there and Henry didn't say a word. So first I boiled down Vince's talk and then cut to Henry's best goofy expressions to hide those cuts.

Indeed, some improvisations in the outtakes were rambling and irrelevant to the story.

Really strange tangents, yes.

They seemed more of a personal harangue between the two actors.

And that is part of the challenge of editing improvised material. What balance can you find when an improvisation becomes so tangential that it loses the story thrust? After the initial point is made in the improvisation, the rest becomes gravy. So to figure out when you're tipping too far over—well, you can have an instinct for it. But sometimes other people can tell you better, like preview audiences.

This instinct issue is easier said than done, isn't it? Becoming an editor requires knowing rules and tools, but how does one hone instinct?

Well, if you want to be a writer, keep writing. I suppose it's the same thing with being an editor.

How does one know one has "made it" as an editor? Winning an award perhaps?

Awards are the icing, not the point. I feel like I've "made it" if I love what I'm doing and I can support my family doing it. And, I guess, achieving a certain amount of critical success doesn't hurt.

On the Prada *DVD commentary, the director David Frankel said an editor is an artist and you said you thought an editor was judge, jury, and executioner.*

I said that? (*Laughs.*)

Yes. What is the difference, then, between artist and judge-jury-executioner?

I don't think they are mutually exclusive, actually. Judge, jury, and executioner I believe was a reference I made to editing being an interpretive art and craft.

Specifically, Frankel referred to some scenes that were deleted, the "face on the cutting room floor" sort of thing. In Prada, *one entire scene with a human resources woman was thrown out.*

Yes, I did execute her! For the most part, though, an editor is not as involved up front in the script process. An editor is a whole new set of eyes for what will make the story work, and what works in a screenplay will not necessarily work in the film. With that in mind, a director may be invested in and love how he shot a scene. The writer may love the way he or she wrote the scene. The actors may feel a scene was their best performance in the film. And the DP [director of photography] may think that a shot is the most beautiful one in the whole movie. But when I as the editor get the material, if it's not moving the story forward or not telling it in the best possible way for whatever reason, then I have no qualms about throwing it out or about figuring out another way to make it work—if it can be made to work. That's why I don't like going to the set during shooting. There are other reasons too, like I might have a coughing fit just as the camera starts rolling or my cell phone'll go off or I'll trip over a cable and ruin the take! But more important, I prefer not to go because I don't want to be as invested as everyone else is in what they are doing there. That happened on *Prada* in the scene where Miranda and her entourage go to the James Holt presentation and they get stuck in traffic. David Frankel shot this wonderful crane shot of Miranda getting out of the car in a huff because she will not let traffic stop her, of course. Then she takes off and walks the rest of the way. Unfortunately, that whole scene—that "beat"—ultimately wasn't even necessary.

You threw out a whole crane shot?

Yes. They shot that in downtown Manhattan near where I was cutting. Just by accident, I took a walk at lunch time to clear my head and I saw a movie shooting in the distance, so I walked closer, to find out . . . it's my movie! Florian Ballhaus, the DP, and David Frankel, the director, saw me and said, "Oh, Mark! Look at this! We'll play this back for you! It's an amazing shot! A great shot!" They were so excited. And I saw this crane shot on the video playback and I was very impressed. Two days later, I got the shot in the cutting room and there I was, watching this slo-o-o-o-w crane shot (*laughs*), and it stopped the movie dead! It's like somebody pulled the emergency brake on the movie! And I tried to make this shot work. It was in my head that they loved the scene so much. I tried and I tried to find ways to cut in deeper. I tried at one point to jump cut it forward by breaking it into three pieces. Nothing worked. Nothing! I tried to put music under it to speed it up. Again nothing. So finally, I sat there and said, "Damn! It's out!" I realized that this beat was just not necessary in the first place. David, more than virtually anyone else I've worked with, encourages me to remove things from a film at my own discretion before he ever sees it. So with gusto, I pulled out the crane shot! Lesson learned: keep your distance. That worked out very well because right after that, I was on the set of *Fred Claus* all the time and managed to keep my perspective.

Didn't being on the set of Fred Claus *cloud your clarity?*

No. I mean, I didn't necessarily want to be on the set, but for that film, it was the only practical way to work. I had to be close to the set and David Dobkin would pop into the edit when he was between setups or at lunch to look at scenes. Normally, David does not like to edit during the shooting because he prefers to keep everything separate and compartmentalized so he can concentrate on one thing at a time. But for *Fred Claus,* we were forced to go into the edit while shooting to lock scenes for the visual effects folks so that we could stay on schedule.

That's a lot of pressure on you, isn't it?

It doesn't seem that way when your release date's a year away! But it comes up quick. In the end, every film I've worked on lately has had many visual effects. *Prada* had its share, *Marley and Me* had a bunch, like green screens in cars. It happens more than one thinks.

Where is the most pressure in the process of editing?

During dailies. It's always my goal to have as polished a film at the end of the editor's assembly as possible. This means keeping up with the shoot—you know, not falling behind—as well as allowing time for multiple passes on each scene later on to further nuance the material. Add to this sound-effects work, temp visual effects, what have you. And music. I usually bring music editor Dan DiPrima in to help out before showing a cut to the director—all of this needs to be done before the director walks in the door. But I also do this as a way to keep ahead of the game and move on to my favorite part of the process, which is the period with the director and the director's cut. The chaos is hopefully minimized at that point. The architecture's in place, the structure's in place, and it becomes collaboration. For me, it's playtime.

At that point, is it more refining the film based on your editorial decisions made before the director sees the assembly?

I don't want to give myself too much credit and say it's all gravy at that point. With *Marley and Me,* I was strutting around like a peacock because I got the film down to an hour-fifty during my assembly—I had taken it upon myself, with David Frankel's blessing, to lift about ten minutes of redundant material. My cut was very polished—I even had the main titles in place when he finally came in. But I found I took out what amounted to the *wrong ten minutes.* It's a humbling lesson. Give me the responsibility for editing the film and I'll do the best I can, but that doesn't mean

I'm necessarily going to make all the right decisions. That's why the collaborative process is so important. It always takes more than one person to make a film.

Does the new technology create new pressures in editing? Faster schedules? More excess footage to sift through?

Well, that's always been part of the editor's job description! Luckily I've not had to deal with situations where I scratch my head wondering why I get such footage.

Except for the crane shot in Prada.

Actually it seemed like a good idea at the time! (*Laughs.*) I applaud the director having the freedom to explore ideas. If shooting tons of footage helps a director do his best work, so be it. If there's too much to handle, bring on another editor! (*Laughs.*) Let's explore the options. It's all an exploration.

Then the new technology has actually facilitated that exploration for you.

Yes, I find it liberating because the trial and error involved in the exploration is infinite. You can try ideas all day and take more chances. I think about a film like *All That Jazz* and the amazing work Alan Heim did in cutting that film, or Dede Allen's work on *Bonnie and Clyde.* Of course, whatever the tools, creatively you can get to where you want to get. But it's an incredible accomplishment to have done those films with tape splices, maybe making miscuts, taping them over and over. Talk about throwing off rhythm with bad sound cuts! Those editors were trained to get past watching the picture jump in the gate all the time. Doing complicated montages, lap dissolves, and so on before computer technology existed is to me an incredible feat because it all had to be well thought-out ahead of time. Laid out in your brain and then physically laid out. Even finding the frames you needed took forever! An assistant would look for them, but if they were lost, you'd have to get reprints. Of course, even with film, trial and error was needed to get to the end point, but it was a long, long process, often days instead of minutes before one would see the results. I know if I were cutting on film, I would be a lot more careful about where I made my cuts. With an Avid, I cut, I make mistakes, I undo the mistakes. I take chances. If something seems absurd, I delete. With such immediate access at your fingertips to all the creative parts of the brain, you cannot be afraid to fail. You can hide your mistakes! (*Laughs.*)

No one need know, right?

No one need know! Now schedules are compressing in reaction to how fast editing can be done. It's all part and parcel of the phenomenon of how fast you can execute these choices. If you can edit a film faster, you can break new ground all the time. If it doesn't work, it doesn't work. Delete!

So working faster isn't necessarily an obstacle to creativity?

It isn't for me. There is something to the raw energy of working faster. That said, however, I think you can overedit a film. In the same sense that you never want to finish working on a film because you haven't considered all the options, you can also take a film too far and work it to death, edit the life out of it.

Is finding that balance between too little and too much editing an art or a craft?

I think art and craft are two sides of the same coin. Glass blowing is a craft, glass blowing is an art. You can create art with glass, but you have to learn the rudimentary craft to make it an art form. Or think of Razzles, it's a candy *and* a gum. Why can't it be both? (*Laughs.*) As an editor, I know I aspire to be artful in my work—I think we all do. Finding that balance between too little and too much is case by case. Going back to the stew idea, it's trial and error as you taste your way to making the perfect dish. Or playing jazz.

Not to mix metaphors, of course. (Laughs.) *So then is editing all about improvisation?*

In jazz, you honor the backbone of a song, but you explore new expressions and make it your own. Similarly, editing is an infinite playlist of possibilities with perfectly viable ways to play, no two of which are the same or the best or only way. I was tuned into this idea by director Cameron Crowe when I was cutting *Vanilla Sky* with Joe Hutshing. I was working on the scene where the Tom Cruise character kills his girlfriend, smothering her while making love. I cut that scene as scripted and did it pretty conventionally. When Cameron saw it, he said, "Okay . . . but not quite there." He kept pushing me a little further, a little further. "Play jazz with it," he said. Feel it, emote it, really get into it. So I started playing with the idea of putting in pieces from other places in the film, and—with

Joe's and Cameron's guidance—I created this huge psychodrama ping-pong match in the character's head, where everything was starting to spin out of control because—spoiler alert—Tom's character is having a dream. He's short-circuiting, so everything is buzzing in his head from other parts of his life. Cameron's words freed me to improvise and, most importantly, put myself in the head of Tom's character. Cameron helped me to discover that the key to effective editing is emotion—tapping into it and finding emotional truth in every scene, and that's the lesson that has gotten me through every day since.

2. Pushing the Envelope

ANGELO CORRAO

1986 *Dream Love* (coeditor), dir. Alan J. Pakula

1986 *Off Beat* (coeditor), dir. Michael Dinner

1987 *The Pick-up Artist* (coeditor), dir. James Toback

1988 *Let's Get Lost,* dir. Bruce Weber

1989 *Signs of Life,* dir. John David Coles

1990 *Through the Wire,* dir. Nina Rosenblum

1990 *Dr. Bethune,* dir. Phillip Borsos

1991 *Backyard Movie,* dir. Bruce Weber

1991 *Darrow,* TV, dir. John David Coles

1991 *True Colors* (additional editor), dir. Herbert Ross

1992 *A Child Lost Forever: The Jerry Sherwood Story,* TV, dir. Claudia Weill

1993 *A Dangerous Woman* (additional editor), dir. Stephen Gyllenhaal

1994 *Long Shadows,* TV, dir. Sheldon Larry

1994 *Against Her Will: The Carrie Buck Story,* TV, dir. John David Coles

1995 *Friends at Last,* TV, dir. John David Coles

1995 *New York News,* TV series

1995 *Legacy of Sin: The William Coit Story,* TV, dir. Steven Schachter

1996 *The Line King: The Al Hirschfeld Story*, dir. Susan W. Dryfoos

1997 *Subway Stories: Tales from the Underground*, TV:

- "The 5:24," dir. Bob Balaban

1997 *Crossing Fields*, dir. James Rosenow

1997 *Primary Colors* (additional editor), dir. Mike Nichols

1999 *To Walk with Lions*, dir. Carl Schultz

1999 *The Intruder*, dir. David Bailey

1999 *The Lady in Question*, TV, dir. Joyce Chopra

2001 *A Zen Tale* (short), dir. Magdalena Sole

2000 *Wonderland*, TV series

2001 *Chop Suey*, dir. Bruce Weber

2002 *The Beatle Fan* (short), dir. Peter McArdle

2003 *Nine Good Teeth*, dir. Alex Halpern

2003 *Psychoanalysis Changed My Life* (short), dir. Ellen Novack

2003 *Tabla Beat Science: Talamanam Sound Clash*, dir. Zane Vella and Alex Winter

2005 *Downtown Girls: The Hookers of Honolulu*, TV, dir. Brent Owens

2005 *Virgin Red* (short), dir. Edouard Getaz

2006 *Bleached* (short), dir. Nicholas Corrao

2007 *Damages*, TV series

- Episode 3: "And My Paralyzing Fear of Death," dir. John David Coles
- Episode 5: "She Spat on Me," dir. Mario Van Peebles
- Episode 9: "Do You Regret What We Did," dir. Thomas Carter
- Episode 12 (credit shared with Daniel Valverde and Aaron Kuhn): "There's No 'We' Anymore," dir. Mario Van Peebles

2008 *Patti Smith: Dream of Life*, dir. Steven Sebring

2009 *Alienadas* (short), dir. Andrew Bouchelon

2009 *Freud's Magic Powder* (short), dir. Edouard Getaz

2010 *Saving Lieb House* (short), dir. John Halpern and James Venturi

2010 *Moonwatcher*, dir. Hans Pfleiderer

AWARDS

1997 Cine Golden Eagle, Associate Producer and Editor, *The Line King: The Al Hirschfeld Story*

2002 Eddie Award (ACE) nomination, Best Edited Documentary Film, *Chop Suey*

Forty years after assisting legendary editor Dede Allen, Angelo Corrao provides an important historic link to editing some of the iconoclastic films of the 1960s and 1970s. Echoing many experiences of the veteran editors in the first volume of *First Cut*, Corrao speaks of the pure physical labor that editing entailed back then. He recalls spinning reels, spliced film running through a Moviola, and trims hanging like ribbons in a bin. His mentors, Carl Lerner on *Klute* and Sam O'Steen on *Silkwood*, "would sit quietly reading the scene over and over to refresh themselves and slowly ask for the rolls of film they needed. If they liked a take, they would make a China mark at the beginning and end of the piece and take it back to their bench. You would never hear a peep from the rest of us." While choosing the best shots has always been crucial to editors, Corrao recognizes that today's technology has made that decision making much easier.

Corrao's rich feature film experience prompted him to question traditional cinematic storytelling and inquire into the possibilities of "nonconventional" editing in documentaries. His conversation segues into the nature of editing documentaries, and its differences and similarities to the fiction film world that Livolsi described in the previous chapter. Documentary editors face unique challenges not only because they lack a script but because sometimes they lack even a director's *idea* of the film's structure. According to Corrao, documentary editors are themselves scriptwriters and filmmakers, who discover the film's backbone from the footage, and identify patterns, emotions, and hidden truths connecting seemingly disparate images and sounds. Documentary editors must also address issues of "reality," which is especially challenging given what Corrao points out as today's looser interpretations of reality that blur truth and fiction, yet nonetheless reveal a universal human condition. Creating documentaries requires questioning and experimenting—goals to which this veteran editor continually aspires.

I got into film editing in a strange way. I was a premed major at Queens College in New York City. I was put onto this path by various relatives, but in the back of my mind, I didn't know whether I was really suited for it. They said, "You're a sensitive, wonderful human being! You'd be great dealing with people's problems and their sicknesses." And I said, "But the sciences are not my forte!"

The sciences are pretty crucial for a doctor. (Laughs.)

Yes! Midway through my junior year, I became ill with tuberculosis and had to go to a sanatorium for six months. During that time, I had to rethink what I wanted to do in life. My family, being immigrants from Sicily, couldn't afford to pay for a private college education. And I realized that the only thing I really loved was motion pictures. When I got out of the sanatorium, I told my parents I wanted to pursue that, to their dismay. Queens College did not have a film program, not even one single film class, although at that time, 1964, the whole arts scene was changing and everybody was going to film school. It was the beginning of a new cinema generation, with Scorsese, Coppola, Lucas, and others. But Queens College had an up-and-coming theater department, so I majored in theater/speech, thinking that I would have to know about directing, acting, blocking, script analysis, and all that. My great love, of course, was film, and during the summers, I found jobs cleaning or rejuvenating films at storage houses. After I graduated college, I worked for a film production company as a facility manager, which involved every department including editing. I was a quiet and shy kid who didn't even have a driver's license, and they needed someone with a bit more aggressive personality. But where I really shined—and I had no idea I would—was when freelance editors would come into the facility to work on their projects, whether industrials, commercials, or small indie movies, and I would help them in the edit room and they said, "You're pretty good! You should rethink this." One of them told me about an apprenticeship at ABC Films, and I spent two years there and got my first job working as an apprentice editor on Elaine May's film *A New Leaf*, in 1969. That was my first feature.

Did you make your own films while you were majoring in theater?

Yeah, I had a Super 8mm camera and I was making my personal films and experimental Polaroid photography, with the idea that maybe I would be a director. The 8mm camera was becoming an inexpensive tool, not like the expensive 16mm cameras and film of previous decades. Unfortunately, my work hours were long and continuing to make shorts became impossible. But, a few years after starting in the editing room, I took two film courses at the School of Visual Arts in New York, one on editing and the other on directing actors for the camera. I soon realized the solitary and analytical nature of editing suited my shy, contemplative personality.

Editing would allow me to indulge all my interests, to examine all of a story's components, like a puzzle, and build a new whole. When I got my first job in film, the New York feature film industry was rather small. We generally worked in three or four buildings: 1619 Broadway, 1600 Broadway, Magno Sound, all located around Broadway and Forty-ninth Street in Midtown Manhattan. New York editors had created a miniworld that they had nurtured throughout the fifties and early sixties. You know, great editors like Carl Lerner and Dede Allen and others.

New York also had a resurgence of filmmaking at that time with on-location shooting.

Yes, with neorealism and the postwar noir aesthetic and location shooting, studios began to reconsider how they made their films. So whether it was *Roman Holiday* on location in Rome or *The Naked City* on location in New York, they decided what interiors they needed and the rest would be shot right on the streets. New York City afforded a vivid, lively background for stories and also had *the* major theatrical scene in the U.S. with great stage actors who could be hired to work in film and television. Because New York filmmakers formed a small community, we all knew each other. Across the street from where I was working on *A New Leaf,* Dede Allen was cutting *Alice's Restaurant*—she had just finished *Bonnie and Clyde.* I got a call to work on her next film *Little Big Man,* which I did. And then her best friend and mentor, Carl Lerner (who was down the hall), hired me to work as second assistant on *Klute.* Word got around this small community: "There's this quiet kid who shuts his mouth and does his work. Put him in the corner, give him work, and forget about it!"

As part of the New York editing scene, did you now understand more deeply the feelings you had as a kid about film?

Filmmaking was a different world from anything I knew about as a kid. As I said, we emigrated after World War Two from Sicily to New York City and we lived in a blue-collar neighborhood in Queens. My parents never allowed us bikes, and we never owned a car. The only thing they allowed us to do was go to movies. Carte blanche, every Saturday, whatever we wanted. Some ethnic theaters still existed in New York at that time, and the Italian cinemas would show prints in Italian that weren't even subtitled. One theater was Cinema Verdi, right across the street from the old Metropolitan Opera House in Manhattan. My mother would take me and my brother who was three years younger to see the films of Ingrid Bergman / Rossellini, Fellini, DeSica, and others: *The Bicycle Thief, Voyage* to Italy, *La Strada,* and so on. I didn't know what I was experiencing, but they were quite distinctive and affected me. They were stories from my mother country which left an impression on me. But I also sensed there was something there for me, a mode of visual expression that intrigued me. Besides the Italian films, I went to see American fare every Saturday too. That was the start. My brother and I had this license from our parents that movies were okay, and we really made the most of it!

Did the movies seem larger than life to you?

Early on as a small child, the largeness of the screen does affect you, but once you go every week, it almost doesn't matter because you are immersed in the story. But I soon began to sense the grandness of scale and outsized emotions, and to understand through the movies the vast, mythic, prosperous land of opportunity that was postwar America. We went to a little theater called the Plaza at 103rd Street and Roosevelt Avenue in Corona, Queens, with the magnificent double staircase, balconies, like an old-style movie palace in miniature. We could only go to the kiddie section and were thrown out at five o'clock when the grownup features started, but as we got older, we found ways of not getting kicked out. *From Here to Eternity,* Anthony Mann Westerns with James Stewart—these films exposed me to more adult psychological issues. For example, my father had been a fisherman, strong but sensitive, and those films showed the male figure struggling to redefine himself after the war. Then came the naturalistic, Method acting with Montgomery Clift, Marlon Brando, James Dean. This naturalistic or "realistic" style soon took over not just acting, but all aspects of filmmaking like editing, cinematography, and so on.

I imagine your theater major in college informed your perspective.

My theater studies did help me understand that not everything has to be totally naturalistic: just look again at some of those special moments in Brando's *A Streetcar Named Desire* or *On the Waterfront* or Dean's *East of Eden*—where internalized theatrical mannerisms spring through their naturalistic approach. Then I began to see experimental films that addressed naturalism, theatricality, and abstraction at another level, like Andy Warhol's *Chelsea Girls*—I remember seeing that film the first time it was presented, projected on a white sheet! I shifted into this adult fare with a growing love of film. But because of my Italian background and the impact of neorealism, and later the French New Wave, I noticed a real difference between American and European films. In European movies, filmmaking combined well-scripted, well-acted dramas but with a certain avant-gardism or abstraction, a way of expressing things less concretely, more ambiguously, more ephemerally, with a poetic, lyrical feel. I also sensed that while Hollywood films tended to be more plot-driven star vehicles, European films were character-driven, more observational in nature and pacing. I started reading more film criticism, especially Andrew Sarris—I read him religiously—and Pauline Kael. I approached reading about Hitchcock and Welles as I would Dante, Shakespeare, or Austen. That was a crucial part of my education. Also, continuing to learn about allusions and symbols helped me see things in less literal, more purely visual and expressive ways to examine the human condition.

Clearly much of your documentary work reflects this poetic and abstract approach, as we'll discuss later. Why did you think it was important to integrate that style into your work?

Many devices can help us understand the deeper meaning of things in life, including the nonverbal and nonliteral. Today we need to reconsider what's going on artistically, aesthetically in cinema. Generally speaking, financial considerations and profitability have overwhelmed the film medium and tend to discourage experimentation in storytelling other than in purely technological ways. This tendency toward conventionality or dumbing-down rather than using the medium in more expressive ways has certainly occurred in studio-backed films. Unfortunately, it has also crept into lower-budget independent films. Many young filmmakers use their small, indie films as their calling cards to the big leagues. Daring or unconventional filmmakers may have a short moment in the sun, but rather quickly, they will be judged by their immediate commercial success. Of course this happens in all art forms—music, painting, et cetera. But because filmmaking is more expensive that most of these other forms, it is more susceptible to financial considerations, and thus to "dumbing-down." I sort of straddle this line in my career—having worked on traditional, plot-heavy films, but also films that used more abstract, experimental approaches to the material and trying to figure out what something *means*. Maybe it's hard for someone to sit through something too abstract for two hours! (*Laughs.*) But why *not*, where appropriate, at least attempt to take chances and push the boundaries of film expression? For example, films portray time through editing: why not jump time, condense time, play with time, choose nonconventional things to show, and how and when to show them? Why can't we use all the filmmaking tools at our disposal and be a little more abstract, lyrical, poetic, expressive in exploring emotions or ideas in characters or in the narrative? Experiment! Of course, giving ourselves enough time to produce these more experimental or evocative scenes and build them into the story organically is crucial; otherwise they might seem superfluous, redundant, or too different. The main priority is to produce a coherent, effective, dramatic film.

But some of your early film work certainly grounded you in more conventional forms of storytelling.

Yes, and they were great films. I was so happy to land in the editing room working on big studio features, some of the best films being made in New York at that time. They formed a solid foundation for storytelling concepts. But between what I was working on and all the films I saw growing up, I knew there was a difference I wanted to explore about expressiveness in film.

Did you know they were great films when you worked on them?

Each time you started a film, you wondered, of course. But sometimes you knew. When we got the dailies on *Klute* and saw Jane Fonda's performance, we said, "Wow! This is a whole new ballgame." When I worked on *Saturday Night Fever,* we screened the dailies (rushes) at night, and they would ask to see the same reels over and over with the great soundtrack music: it felt like a party every night screening dailies. *Dog Day Afternoon,* that was a trickier film. Was it comedy? Was it drama? That was a real mystery to me in the sense of how that film would work. Although one might say that we as editors are the first audience, sometimes a more intricate film is harder to judge. Here, the balance was so beautifully delicate, and we were really only able to react to what we had done when we had our first preview. You could feel the tension in the room. The audience laughed at the comic moments and were riveted by the dramatic moments. Then I realized, what a balance! What a terrific picture!

Do you think the editing on Dog Day Afternoon *ultimately determined how that balance was achieved?*

Well, I wasn't the editor, I was the first assistant, but Dede Allen certainly knew that it would work, as did the director, Sidney Lumet. It was a solid script with an unconventional storyline with only two major locations, inside and outside a bank holdup and hostage scenario. So the lack of traditional action made pacing and creating involving moments for the audience a challenge, as did the difficult balancing of comedy and drama. Story moments and nuances in the acting had to be carefully worked out in the editing. Also the pacing, with fast and slow sections, was challenging, and a tendency to speed things up for no reason was avoided. Time flowed slowly as it would in the actual situation, and even had an abstract feeling of standing still. Editing involves working for months in isolation on minute moments. It can be hard to see the whole from that position until the first audience reactions. I wondered, "Is this one going to work? I hope this is good." And it was. The movie succeeded commercially and critically, and won the Oscar for Best Screenplay. I learned so much from those experiences. That's another reason why I continued working with Dede: she was cutting some of the best, most challenging films. When I spoke at Dede's memorial service in 2010, I said that she ran the best film school in the world!

You must have been motivated to become an editor just by working with her.

Yes, I was and I loved working on those important films, but I gave little thought to my career as an "editor." I never really pushed that. I only took small scenes and sequences to cut. I turned down Dede's offer to give me more because I thought that the films were much too important and being an assistant was enough for me. And of course, everyone wanted to work for Dede so people were lining up behind me, hoping I'd drop out! But Dede had already heard my protestations and said, "Listen, that's enough, you either shit or get off the pot, Angelo. You *need* to edit!" (*Laughs.*) She's known for getting to the point! Just as importantly, I got married and started having kids! It finally dawned on me that I needed a job that would pay a *little* bit more. (*Laughs.*) So it was through Dede that I got my first editing job on *Reds*, but it took me from about '69 to '81 to get there! *Reds* was a tremendous opportunity for me because the film was gigantic in scope and length, there were going to be many editors, and scenes were cut and recut all the time.

This exposure must have been key to how you thought about the ways a film could work—even if you did stay off in the corner.

Yes, because I was always testing my ability to analyze and understand a work at its fullest level, that is, how the dynamics in film medium, directing, acting, cinematography, and editing work together differently than those in theater. I was thinking about aesthetic principles in film editing and montage. Could something come between this scene and that scene—or that shot and the next shot—that might help one understand more subtle connections? I could ask: how can that performance be better?

Or why make some juxtapositions so obvious? Scale back. Let something come as a surprise. I was already playing all this in my brain. Not quite editorial games, but ways of thinking about art and its expression. I wanted to work on films that were artistically challenging.

Did working on Reds *finally give you that challenge?*
That film was interesting because, yes, it was plot-driven and character-driven, but it also had the nonconventional concept of incorporating present-day interviews with the "Witnesses" into the film.

Much like a documentary.
Yes, Warren Beatty, the director as well as the star, went around interviewing dozens of people he called the "Witnesses"—artists, politicos, painters, suffragettes, writers, and so on—who were part of the generation in the 1910s and 1920s when the Bolshevik revolution took place in Russia and the American journalist John Reed promoted communist ideals in his writings. These Witnesses were of a certain age and were beginning to die away, and Warren was hurrying to interview the last of the group on film. That whole concept interested me and these documentary interviews were incorporated into the film in a special structural way which intrigued me. Warren was presenting a dramatized biography, a fictionalized account of what had happened to John Reed, but these Witnesses would be a contrast to that by providing the veracity and background of their own personal experiences. Now Warren did another controversial thing. He *never* identified the Witnesses by name during the film (which is standard in documentaries). Only in the end credits were their names listed. Warren got criticized for that, but it didn't harm the drama and I saw the technique of weaving fiction and nonfiction elements as an intelligent concept— making a traditional Hollywood biography fresh and forcing a different dynamic interplay between parts and whole. It felt like a reference back to *Citizen Kane* or even *Rashomon,* by asking: Who remembers what about what really happened? Are our memories of the facts to be trusted or is there always a shifting perspective? What is history anyway? I admired that Warren had taken an adventurous leap like that, no matter what anybody thought. We had a whole department dealing with this "documentary" side of the film, which cataloged the footage by subject, person, male, female, jokes, facts, and so on. That was going on while we were also editing the scripted footage with Warren Beatty, Diane Keaton, Jack Nicholson, Maureen Stapleton, Gene Hackman, and so many others who were acting their hearts out. But that experience was my first real

editing responsibility in a big film with such complicated good material. I could finally say, "Okay, relax. You're going to be an editor. Let's see what comes of it."

After Reds, *did you start striking out more on your own?*

Yes, I slowly phased myself out of the assistant work that followed, including *Silkwood* with another great editor, Sam O'Steen, and then started getting small editing gigs. I was eventually a coeditor with Dede on the comedy *Off Beat.* I also worked as a coeditor on *The Pick-up Artist.* But my big break didn't happen until Dede was called by Bruce Weber, the fashion photographer and filmmaker, to recommend an editor to cut his documentary film about the trumpeter and singer Chet Baker, to be called *Let's Get Lost.* And Dede found it in her heart—as she always did for everybody—to recommend me. I had a great love of music of all types, but I had no background in it and I had never done a documentary except for my experiences on *Reds,* which opened me up to this dialectic between fiction and nonfiction. What does that frisson provide? What does it do for the film, for the audience? What are the traditional strengths of a documentary film? What are the components, and where and how might they be modulated or bent? I was intrigued.

Of course, you had seen documentaries in your regular movie-going experience, right?

Oh sure, I would go to see the major ones. In the early sixties, I started going to the Thalia and the New Yorker theaters in Manhattan, where they had great film retrospectives and revived all kinds of films that hadn't been seen in twenty or thirty years, including documentaries like *Nanook of the North, Man of Aran,* and more current ones, *Point of Order, Grey Gardens.* That was my education going to those venues to see these magnificent old films and soaking up film culture. So, I certainly didn't shy away from documentaries. In fact, I was drawn to them.

How did you prepare to assume responsibility for your first solo editing job?

It was tough. I'd never worked in 16mm before, except for a couple of little indie films helping out my friends in the early seventies. *Let's Get Lost* was a documentary, but it was going to be more of a biography, not a concert film. It would be a "musical" in the sense that we would be playing the music of the subject, Chet Baker, throughout the film and it would be a major element. I would have to use multiple audio tracks on a

Steenbeck editing machine to allow me to weave together many dialogue and music sound elements. Another challenge was that there was going to be a *lot* of footage—and some footage looked like B-roll and didn't feature Chet and *seemingly* had nothing to do with the subject of the film!

Did Weber plan it that way?

Yes. As a photographer, Bruce was trying to re-create a feeling of time, place, the fifties and sixties Jazz scene, especially visually. He kept shooting scenes, some quite lyrical or abstract, that would evoke these sensations, hoping that they would be useful for the film. Besides the visual, he was interested in evoking time and place with music and sound too. For Bruce, sound and image are linked on a very deep level. He has great taste in an extraordinary range of music. Thankfully, when I wasn't working with Dede, she encouraged me to work in sound departments to understand the picture-sound dynamic. So, having worked with Dede and Bruce, I think the work I do has also been infused with layers of sound and sound-image juxtaposition.

Did Weber present you with a script?

Not at all.

An outline?

No. (*Laughs.*) Just a lot of footage! My assistant, Martin Levenstein, and I went to Bruce's country house and sat down with him to watch the raw material. Then we listened to every album Chet Baker ever recorded—and he recorded a lot. We got to the point at the end of this two-and-a-half month period of listening and viewing where we knew we would have to return to New York and start editing. So I said to my assistant, "We haven't talked about structure. I'm going to have to ask Bruce." And my assistant said, "Yeah, you're gonna have to!" (*Laughs.*) So casually in a conversation, I said, "Oh, by the way, Bruce, do *you* have any ideas about the beginning of the film? Or the structure of the film? Or . . ." Bruce went silent for a second and said, "Well, no, I haven't really thought about it quite that way." But he added, "I can tell you what we shot first, then second, and so on. That's a good way to start editing and we'll go from there." So, that's the way I started. We could begin with vérité footage from Santa Monica Beach and a bunch of people talking about music and so on—without Chet's presence—then catch up with him at a recording studio, then go to Oklahoma where Baker's family was, then on and on until we reached Cannes, where Baker was performing a gig during the film festival, as a sort of reflecting-on-his-life moment to end the film. So I thought, "Well, let me use those as signposts to structure the film. At least then I won't feel lost or frightened to touch any roll of film on my shelf!" Then, as I began to structure the story, Bruce would also send us standard documentary elements like photographs and archival material of Baker's movies which we could use in traditional biographical sequences. Of course, many scenes or sequences did not stay in their original chronological shooting position. We would cut up long sequences into smaller ones and rearrange scenes for more dramatic impact—all this while still trying to keep a complex story more or less understandable. As the structure took shape, Bruce was able to give us more feedback and direction.

Did the material begin to feel like a typical documentary?

Yes. A concrete narrative began to emerge, but we didn't overwhelm the more lyrical sequences. With all this footage—and not all of it featured Chet prominently—we were creating a sort of lyrical, poetical journey, if you will. Some scenes—with or without Chet present—were meant to evoke the time, place, and feel of fifties and sixties West Coast jazz, but also a haunted and haunting timelessness. It was about re-creating more of a feeling than of factual detail. I used whatever images I could—whether they were intended or not—to express these feelings: swaying palm trees against the sky, or a young woman (who we see many times, a muse?) dancing, twirling on the beach, who conjures up Chet's first image in the film. We didn't want to break the vibe of that journey, but we had to give the audience various scenes or signposts that are normal to the documentary form to anchor them along the way. So yes, there were many "traditional" biographical sequences including vérité scenes. But the funny part was that for the first ten minutes of the film, we hadn't really mentioned or shown Chet properly as the subject of the film—he was just some shadowy figure in the back of a car. And I said, "This is intriguing, but it may be difficult for the audience. If this is going to be a successful commercial film, we may need to bring Baker up sooner." But Bruce was like, "Oh, I love the way this goes. It's wonderful!" I said, "Well, okay, I love it too, but when we have the first screening, we might get reactions." And while the reactions were terrific, there were a few comments like, "Do we really have to wait that long to see Chet Baker? We need something to hold on to earlier for the ride." So Bruce came up with a clever idea: he had done an audio recording about the first time he had seen Chet in a car, across from Tiffany's in New

York, while it was snowing. We juxtaposed that with a sequence of a car driving through Santa Monica—without Chet visible—with palm trees slowly swaying overhead—a poetic touch. And as the car travels along, we let Bruce's voice come in to say, "I remember the first time I saw Chet Baker . . ." Then when we see him again in the back of the car, we recognize him as the subject of the film. So we condensed the first ten minutes of the film to six or less, thereby adding a mysterious biographical introduction to our subject, embedded in an evocative, abstracted sequence. This withholding of information worked to set an un-ease and a tone for a strange film about a strange and elusive character. Soon after that intro, we had to jump into our first conventional scenes with Bruce talking about Chet, then seeing Chet's photographs and so on as you would in a traditional documentary. But by including a few concrete signposts, I found I didn't have to shut off the poetic impulses that were natural to the material and part of my aesthetic or adhere to the timing of information in the prescribed or chronological way. It sometimes may be good to break with convention. For example, if someone leaves the room in a scene, the "convention" is to cut to a wide shot so we can see them cross to where they are going. But why do we have to do it that way? Matching action doesn't always have to be our primary concern. It might break into a dramatic interior moment prematurely. Or let's say maybe a person just closed a door and I want to hold on it for one-and-a-half seconds longer than usual. Someone might say, "Now explain to me, why are we holding on that shot a little bit more than we expect? Nothing physically meaningful is visible." Well, I say, "Because it expresses something that can't be approximated or expressed any other way." Maybe we want to explore the emotions of one character watching another character leave, rather than the mundane physics of a character exiting and a door closing. And maybe by holding on the door a bit longer, drawing the moment out, unnaturally, we make explicit a hidden emotional dimension.

Isn't seamless matching an important editing consideration?

Yes. Of course I try to match the action, but not as a slave to convention. Let me put it this way. If I was cutting a big conventional narrative, I would have coverage of every angle in every scene, and I would also be burdened by huge commercial expectations, and so, I would run the risk of too smooth and safe a cut. This is not to say that cutting a traditional narrative film is any easier than a documentary. In narrative film shoots, there can be extensive coverage for *specific* moments, but less so in ragtag documentary shoots. This forces a kind of overcompensation which can open interesting creative possibilities. Also, when you start a nonfiction piece, there is no story or script to follow, and while the editorial process can be more difficult or challenging, it's sometimes richer with possibility. Finally, having less pressure to be extremely commercially successful allows freedom to explore those possibilities. So getting back to your question, I'm matching, not mechanically, but by finding something unifying in the visual imagery—some movement, some color, some contrast. Or matching shots based on music or sound effects instead of just the visual match. I use whatever feels truthful to me and I "write" the film as I'm going along. Some of these impulses, using images eclectically, were influenced by the experimental and New Wave films I saw as a kid. Some of it may be choppy and some fluid, but if you're limited in what you have to work with, you have to find a way to make things work, emotively or for story. And I wasn't afraid to ask, "Is that all there is?" I've tried to bring that creative freedom to every project I work on, regardless of fiction or nonfiction, big budget or small.

I'm wondering then about the line one crosses when taking aesthetic liberties in a documentary that should show the "truth" about a person or situation. Why not just hire an actor to play a person and take those liberties within a fictionalized context?

We can talk about specific tools we use for each genre and what we try to do with a specific story. But really, is there a big difference between narrative and documentary? I mean, in both, aren't we ultimately searching for a particular kind of truth about an event, a person or an issue?

Is there a truth in fiction?

There's an emotional truth about the characters and about the thematic points being made. Something always happens beyond just the comedy or the drama, where we immerse ourselves in the spirit of the emotions that the actors are portraying. So, yes, there is a truth component that we try to reach in both, and we just use different tools to get there. I will say that the accepted tools for documentary have loosened up recently because of reality TV, because *every*body now has a video camera. All that Twitter and YouTube stuff, clips of cats with booties on and all those tricks being played on the viewer. It's a lingua franca, so to speak. Because of reality TV, a whole new generation has become adept at using video equipment, but we end up with a lot of documentaries that aren't really . . . They're "fake" documentaries! But they are very creatively put together, like *This*

Is Spinal Tap or *Exit through the Gift Shop*. They straddle the line between truth and fiction, so we're seeing a much broader documentary landscape today. In previous decades, we were always afraid to play too much with supposed "objective" reality. Documentarians working in the cinéma vérité style, which is very pure and distilled, may use no voiceover or music. It was just a camera set in a particular spot and left to roll. It recorded an event or a place or a profession—the Social Security office, the insane asylum, the salesman—and removed all baggage of scripted-ness, trying to be as truthful and real as possible, allowing the innate drama to unfold. But ultimately, wherever the filmmaker put that camera *was* a selected position and what he did with that footage wasn't totally objective either. Today, these considerations are looser, but previously, we had to really think about them. As a first-time editor on a documentary like *Let's Get Lost*, I didn't know how far I could take it, so I would ask Bruce, but we had similar aesthetic tastes. I knew we had to be very careful because we at least had to keep in mind some professional commercial considerations.

What is an example of a rule or convention you feel you broke in that film?

At times it wasn't that we were doing something that had never been done—it had just not been done in that context. I took techniques and storytelling devices that were common in narrative films, and applied them to the documentary format and "pushed the envelope" in that way. For example, intercutting or cross-cutting of time and people talking to one another who are not in the same space. Chet talked about how wonderful it was that he was getting these awards from *Downbeat*, but we already heard his mother say earlier in her room that she loved her son and how wonderful the awards were, but she was ultimately so disappointed in him because of his drug problem. So when Chet's going on about his achieve-ments, I cut away to a silent close-up of his mother in her home, "listen-ing" while *his* voice continues on over her image. It was a way to get at a truth by looking at two sides of the same story. I didn't know whether I was allowed to do that, but I knew times were changing and I was going to help them change! (*Laughs.*) I also tried a few other things in that vein. In one sequence, I intercut Chet's exwife, shot in one location, and his former girlfriend, shot in another. While the wife bitches about how the girlfriend ruined Chet and got him into drugs, I intercut the girlfriend nonchalantly fanning herself and not responding—until it's her chance to let the exwife verbally have it between the eyes. Another involved a more traditional arguing between characters who contradict each other about how Chet's teeth got knocked out.

Did you feel you were creating something new with film?

I wouldn't call it new. I heard that other people did similar things, or tried. I knew it was unusual and I didn't think I'd seen it before in docs. Anybody I described it to told me I was making a mistake doing these kinds of things! But I said, "I'm going to do it anyway. Wherever this feeling is taking me, it's going to be fluid *and* shocking." I wasn't going to stop myself from feeling the material and use editing to make a mini-story out of that moment with the tools I had—the use of unconventional images, photographs, archival or vérité. And I said, "I'm going to leave it in until somebody else sees it and we can discuss it further."

In general, how do you know when you click with material?

You click in different ways at different points in the process. It helps to contrast a fiction film with a documentary to see this. In a fiction film, there's a script that's probably been worked on for years which you've read and analyzed, and the points to be made are clearly spelled out. The actors bring in their nuances and tensions, but generally speaking, the dramatic points are not going to change. So you are going to click at that early stage, though you hope to keep discovering new dimensions as you edit. In a documentary, there's no script and you write as you go along, you create the structural order and create the moments with no indications from a script. You may click a bit when you first sit with the director looking at the raw footage and sense its potential. But you may not really click until after you start editing and discover themes and story. Now, with Chet Baker, how could I not be immediately moved by his interviews or his music? When Bruce and I first started working, he played all different kinds of music for me—Ella Fitzgerald, Frank Sinatra, and others. As I listened, I became more confident I could do the film because Chet's music liberated my feelings about the subject and the material. This was not a concert film, but the music would take the film to another level. The film was beautifully shot in black and white, and I sensed the filmmaker's struggle to maintain his romantic notion about this guy—a theme that interested me. So here was a unique character who intrigued me with his almost effeminate, angelic voice, a serious musician who was also a drug addict. And there was already a lyrical, poetic nature to his singing and trumpet-playing style. The music loosened me up and the floodgates opened! I was still frightened because I didn't think I should be working on such a big film as my first solo project, but these signposts showed me that I had an affinity for the subject and understood the film's potential.

And you had a director who welcomed experimentation.

He certainly did. But "poetic," "lyrical," "abstract" can seem like dirty words to some, and strike fear in the hearts of men. What are normal concepts in the other arts are too rarely mentioned or barely whispered in filmmaking. It all seems very suspect and disheartening. So, welcoming experimentation to me is a great thing, whether it's in fiction or nonfiction work. I'd seen many documentaries, and after I got this job I went to see more. But I realized the subject of the film was different from anything I had seen—a lost, tragic figure, alive, yet a walking ghost. And Bruce loved him with such passion. I couldn't help feeling, "Whoa! Let me be part of this!" Through editing that film, I found ways to consolidate what I had learned and felt about filmmaking, stuffing all the devices and techniques I could into the film—the first film syndrome where you put everything you got into it. For me, it was almost like *Let's Get Lost* was as much about editing as it was about Chet Baker. For example, there were sequences of young people at night, barely visible because it's so dark, running through the fields and playing around (but no Chet), and when I put very evocative music underneath, it suddenly became almost Fellini-esque, expressing a lost innocence, a romantic ideal. Each time I viewed the material, it would conjure up other films, other filmmakers, and fresh new ideas. And for me, it became a question of how can I, through editing, express my feelings with all these pieces of film? How can I immerse you in or tell you the story through images and sound, in nonverbal ways— even in a documentary? When I could, I tried to choose images creatively, in a poetic or lyrical way that can't be translated into prose or shouldn't be—they speak to another "truth." I told myself at various junctions, "You can't be afraid." Of course later, I couldn't tell myself that anymore, I was too far into it! And I knew that people were likely to have different opinions about what I was doing, but truthfully, I didn't meet much resistance at the screenings. It was more often an issue of length, commercial considerations about the film's running time, rather than of concept, and the response was usually positive. I remember after one screening, Chet's girlfriend, Diane, called us hysterically saying that he was dead. It took us hours to get a response from Reuters to find out if it was true. We had been rushing to prepare the mix for the Venice Film Festival because we wanted to make sure everything was okay when Chet saw it, but unfortunately, it was too late. There were all kinds of theories about how he died—drugs, suicide. It seemed mysterious, but Bruce settled on the main version that he could understand and that most people said was the truth—that Baker accidentally fell off a balcony. We included that information in the film at the end to update the biographical aspect, but then the film became almost like a memorial to him. As for the film itself, we won the Critics prize at Venice and many other awards including an Academy Award nomination for Best Documentary Feature. Even though some may think we were perhaps a little overindulgent in the film, it still had a truthful spirit that mirrored who Chet Baker was, and the editing may have been adventurous—maybe even a little odd—but it suited him perfectly. After that film, my phone rang for years! People were saying, "I like what you did in that film. I want you to . . ." I didn't want to be typecast—was I supposed to do all films this way from now on? (*Laughs.*) Ultimately, I've tried to do a good job, be true to the material and be innovative where possible, and that's what's important.

What exactly does the request "I want you to do a film like Let's Get Lost" *mean?*

Because the film was shot beautifully with whites and blacks and grays, it has a special kind of moodiness, a haunting quality. That feeling was compounded by the music and the visual abstractions. I tried to maintain that through the editing—balancing the gritty with a poetic use of images not usually found in biographical documentaries. It created a lyrical visual and aural landscape that was as seductive as the factual biographical one. Pauline Kael wrote some terrific reviews about *Let's Get Lost*, and how the man, the era, and the West Coast cool jazz scene were perfectly captured. So when people say they want something like *Let's Get Lost*, they're looking for a certain fluidity of image and sound and image-sound juxtaposition and layering—an artistic ambition beyond the nuts and bolts. They don't want a conventionally cut film. That's not what's dancing in their heads. A lyrical quality goes beyond moving someone across a room in a series of shots or cutting from photograph to photograph. It's a sensation that accumulates over time, revealing more to what we're seeing than what is immediately obvious. Honesty and truth are still there, but it's trying for a more inner or emotional truth of the character that can't be expressed by sheer facts.

How is emotional cutting, so to speak, learned?

You've got to connect to the material at the deepest level: subjective/objective, factual/lyrical, image/sound, and so on, and be sensitive and

open to all the tools you have to work with. There are different kinds of
fluidity. It may involve layering sound, or when the sound stops, letting
unique images take over, or letting music or sound effects move you to
the next scene. Dede Allen was a master at overlapping sounds. I used
to watch her at the old-style synchronizer, marking where one track
would start and the other would end, overlapping dialogue, sound effects
or music—it was like watching a magnificent juggler throwing balls into
the air. But it's simply not all about matching, it's the visual, the aural,
and the sense of what you can do to express character and story. For
example, in one scene where Baker is on a rooftop playing with his
trumpet, I actually put two songs together—running concurrently. One
was an instrumental solo and another was like a memory song, but they
weren't even in the same key and certainly a musical person would never
put them together. But I did it as a sort of musical counterpoint, which
brought me into the "inner" world of the character, in his head, where
maybe different things are bumping into each other. This seemed like a
good way to introduce a conflicted character, whose mind we are about
to enter. Still, as much as *Let's Get Lost* was all about music, which I
loved, I felt sometimes it was maybe too much wall-to-wall, so certain
scenes just had silence. For example, we had some footage that was put
on the side because it was "damaged" by a light leak, and it fuzzed out
and haloed the image, almost like a Doris Day filter! We weren't planning to use it because the rest of the film was shot so beautifully that it
would look weird by comparison. But when I saw the footage again, I
said, "These images are intriguing. We gotta use them!" And I did—I
used them as a short transition scene of Chet at a mirror preparing
himself to go to a recording session, all silence, no sound: Dreamlike,
romantic, unlike the reality of the music business. The effect interested
me the most.

*Was that the case for the footage with the puppy dogs on the beach? Like
what did puppy dogs have to do with Chet Baker?*

That was a funny story. While Bruce was away for shoots as a still
photographer for weeks at a time, my assistant and I were overwhelmed
with all the footage and trying to make sense of the film. But every time
Bruce would come back, he would always ask me, "Did you cut the puppy
dog scene?" And I'd say, "The puppy dog scene?" I had so many cut
scenes that I wanted him to look at, but he'd keep asking, "Did you do
the puppy dog scene?" And I said, "No, I'm sorry, Bruce. I'll do it, I'll
get to it soon." So eventually when I knew he was coming back again, I

asked my assistant, Marty, "Can you *please* get the roll of the puppy dogs?" (*Laughs.*)

What was it about the puppy dogs?

Bruce is an animal lover! Dogs are like his children, and he just loved the footage of puppy dogs on a beach! So what could I possibly do with it? Meanwhile, we had an interview with a musician talking about Chet and this difference between the East and West Coasts, but we were told that the musician didn't want us to use his image, only his audio. So, I thought we could use footage of the West Coast—sun, beach, the whole atmosphere—with the voiceover dialogue describing West Coast jazz. Then I thought about the playing puppy dogs. Well, they were on a beach too, so it didn't take a lot of brains to figure what to do with the dogs playing in the sun—they became *the* scene! As I watched, I realized that in addition to weaving in these two important elements, by juxtaposing them, I had added a poetic element. The emotional truth of the puppies, lost or abandoned at the beach in the visuals, were now, in fact, a partner to the audio, and alluded to the lost Chet. So, the footage of the puppies found its perfect placement in the film and also reinforced character development. Of course, none of it was an overly literal representation of what was being said, which some people can find problematic. But when Bruce saw it, he almost fell off his chair with delight and never changed a frame. When you're forced to think, "What am I going to do with *this* footage!?" you never know what the poetic possibilities are.

You also used imagery and sound or silence to make interesting transitions from indoors to outdoors, while moving the story along.

Yes, there were many. They're a product of my years working with Dede, as well as Bruce's musical interests, and of course my own sensibilities. After the first biographical sequence with photos where the photographer William Claxton talks about "discovering" Chet, we land on a Santa Monica beach hotel rooftop. The music ends. Silence. Chet is alone on the roof. I cut together a shot of Chet on a hotel roof "listening to" or "remembering" an archival musical performance of him as a younger man in 1953 at the San Remo Festival. We cut away from the archival piece and back to the roof, where Chet finishes "remembering" the performance and there's silence again. He's doddering up there in the wind, but we linger on his ravaged face before watching him enter the hotel room. This then leads to a scene of Chet preparing for and heading into a studio recording session—that "damaged," fuzzy footage I mentioned earlier—where he's combing his hair, putting on a jacket, and fixing his trumpet case. At first, it's total silence. Then we begin to hear the voices of people in the recording studio whom we don't see until the next scene. Then the recording studio scene takes over. Again, we weren't going to use that hotel room material, but it worked perfectly.

What did that sequence accomplish?

The musical "remembrance" and the incoming musical recording session were contrasted and amplified by the silent moments in between. It got us into Chet's head not by his music but by the silences. It gave us a moment to stop the music and stop moving around, and just be silent and engaged with this person, with his inner life—even though he probably didn't want to share it. What *could* be going on? (*Laughs*.) I was conscious of pushing some editing techniques, but that didn't stop me from thinking of ways to use unusual material. Learning to think "outside the box" is an important lesson to share with your assistants. I open up my cutting room to give my assistants a lot of latitude to work on scenes and contribute, just like Dede did for me. I challenge them with what I know about film history, which maybe they don't. "Have you ever seen *I Am Cuba?* Have you seen the silent film *The Last Laugh?*" And they go, "Huh? What?" or "Oh, that was so *slooow*." I'm telling them to use their eyes and ears in different ways. Maybe I'm wrong—maybe the only good films are the plot-driven, compact Hollywood films? (*Laughs*.) But look at how the characters are portrayed, look at the landscape they're inhabiting. Do they always have to be presented in conventional, uninspired ways? Can't a room, object, knife be presented a bit off-kilter? Can't an image last on the screen a hair longer to indicate something is wrong? Catch someone by surprise. Those are the moments that will stick in someone's memory and inform their aesthetic ideas about motion pictures and art—well, about life itself! That's what I try to accomplish.

When you try an alternative—say, a shot should be x *seconds longer—are you consciously making the audience feel something specific?*

Yeah, I have a conscious rationale. Sometimes it is purely mechanical. Sometimes I may be referencing something Antonioni did. Sometimes I leave uncertainty at the end of a shot, a bit of nonverbal information the audience needs to bring into the next scene—a feeling or comment about the characters that is reinforced or contradicted. I'm leaving space for the audience to feel something that informs the rest of the film. It's no longer just the fact of the moment, but a new chance to reflect on the action before moving on.

In addition to Let's Get Lost, *you edited a film about another complex musician, Patti Smith, which also became a somewhat abstract, sensual, visceral filmic interpretation of her life and work. How did working on* Baker *prepare you for* Smith?

Well, I always want to respond honestly to a film and not say, "Here's another musician, we'll make *this* kind of film." But we all have certain editorial strengths and aesthetic ideas that we do carry from film to film. Of course, the Baker and Smith films were similar because both subjects were musicians—Chet in jazz and Patti in rock and punk, although she's also a poet and an activist. Another link between the two films was that the directors, Bruce Weber and Steven Sebring, were both professional still photographers and young filmmakers. Steven in fact had been gathering material for ten years before we began to cut the film. Both directors also accumulated much footage of beautiful images as well as vérité footage with or without sync sound. Because of that, two things automatically happened. First, the projects became so big that they finally concluded, well, maybe there's a feature film here! Second, their shooting style or aesthetic remained varied throughout—the images could be lyrical, abstract, natural, almost raw. Because each director happened to be a photographer, the material had a specific look to it that I as the editor could never change. We knew *Patti Smith: Dream of Life* would be a very abstract, lyrical film, almost like one large montage of feelings and sequences that reflected Patti's mindset and mirrored her aesthetics. *She* certainly didn't want a conventional documentary or concert film. No way! When we finally agreed to a full-length documentary, she said, "They want to see *more* of me?? Please, no!" But people did. So to make a more theatrical (commercial) documentary, Steven brought Patti more intimately into the film by shooting new vérité sequences. They did not want talking heads so they planned to shoot her in her little room, ruminating out loud about some of the people who mattered in her life. She also invited certain people like playwright-actor-musician Sam Shepard to her room to have a jam session, or visited with Flea of the Red Hot Chili Peppers on a beach and so on. Soon we realized that these visits would become not only the structural spine for the film, but also anchor the various stylized or abstracted sequences. So wherever else we went with Patti—to visit her parents, to a concert, a foreign country, a cemetery, a protest march, on the road with Bob Dylan—we would always come back to her room and she would tell more stories and continue her biographical reminiscences. That way, we also came to grips with what else we needed to shoot. The documentary form enabled us to write as we went along to figure out story, themes, and structure.

Smith also read several of her poems in the film. Was that a constraint for you as editor because you were obligated to fit images to words, not the other way around?

The images were not always shot with specific poem readings in mind and that can be tricky. Of course, one thing people said was, "Well, you're not supposed to be that literal when illustrating poems." At the same time, when you're being abstract, the mind and the eye can have difficulty absorbing and dealing with voiceover dialogue and its meaning, and contrasting images. You can actually get a headache! (*Laughs.*) It becomes a question of balance. It also helped that when I started working on the Smith film, a kind of template was already in place. I was brought on board because Steven and the producer, Margie Smilow, had seen *Let's Get Lost* and realized that film had many lyrical similarities to the sequences and montages they were assembling for their test reel. So basically, they had a template for the *feeling* of the film. Steven liked difficult visual and audio layering, and I could either shy away from or go with it, depending on the material. That was also the gamble I had on *Let's Get Lost,* but because Baker was a cool jazz musician, it was easier to lay that "softer" music underneath dialogue or montage sequences for both feeling and content—his mellifluous vocal or haunting trumpet could be used anywhere. Whereas Patti's music was hard rock vocals which was more difficult to layer with other audio or visual material. I had to constantly ask, "Is this too much? Can one sequence be next to another because of it? If one sequence is loud, should the next one be soft?" It's contrast and sequencing. Just as they used to do in LPs, like with Sinatra recordings—the balance between fast and slow tracks was a miracle of recording artistry. It's paying attention to how feelings have modulations and climaxes.

These two films contrast greatly with a film like The Line King, *which celebrates decades of Al Hirschfeld's caricatures of Broadway and film stars. There, you were more straightforward, presenting each decade of Hirschfeld's life as a chapter of both his artwork and what was happening in show business. Hardly any abstractions!*

Right, and Hirschfeld as the subject didn't warrant that. He was gentlemanly, with a twinkle in his eye, a "lighter" subject. It also wasn't a style the director, Susan Dryfoos, seemed interested in. Hirschfeld was a very concrete, terrific raconteur of the theater. He didn't need bells and whistles to evoke abstraction, artifice, or nostalgia. I thought that his stories of the theater and his artwork, which illustrated the performer's art, said it all. I used his drawings, photographs, and music from different decades to illustrate his life, the passage of time, and what was happening in the theater and film in each successive decade. I didn't have to use any "tricks" or layerings to evoke things because the drawings, musicals, and voiceovers themselves already had built-in nostalgia and expressiveness. Perhaps the only sound layering we did occurred with the montages we created, all set to music, for each decade, and in the opening credits sequence, which was a montage of celebrities and their reactions to being caricatured by Hirschfeld. The film took ten years to make and I was only on it for six months! But I wanted to capture the thrill of the theater and the energy of performance that this artist caught in every one of his fantastic drawings. The film went on to receive an Academy Award nomination as Best Documentary Feature. By the way, my theater background at Queens College really helped on that film!

What about the subject of the charming film Nine Good Teeth? *She wasn't a celebrity—she was the director's grandmother—but telling her life story seemed straightforward. Or was it?*

Again, as with *The Line King,* we wanted to match our approach to the subject. "Nana" was the family raconteur. So we needed an approach that captured her playful persona, which served her well for one hundred and eight years!

So much for the fortune teller who told her at the start of the film that she wouldn't live past the age of ninety-six.

Yeah, when Nana was ninety-five, she told Alex Halpern, the director—and her grandson—what the fortune teller had predicted. He said, "Well, Nana, if the fortune teller said ninety-six, I better start cracking!" Alex had this wonderful wacky family and his Nana told these fantastic stories with which she regaled her grandchildren. The film was originally called *Three Centuries of Nana* because she was born in 1899 in Brooklyn and died in 2008, but we ended up using Nana's phrase for the title, which referred to the only teeth she had left in her mouth! Interestingly, Alex, as a film student at New York

University twelve years earlier, had seen *Let's Get Lost* and it had affected him deeply.

Yet another person influenced by that film . . .

As I said, people can be touched by many moments in films that they see at a particular sensitive age and carry those moments with them forever. Even if they are not the greatest films, they can impact us in unforgettable ways and even help us coalesce our identity and aesthetic sensibility. So Alex told an editor friend of mine, "I don't want to do this film on my own. If I could only find the editor of *Let's Get Lost.*" And my friend said, "I know him and he's working just a couple blocks away! And he was born in Sicily, just like your grandmother's family!" Then Alex asked, "Do you think he would work on a small film like this?" My friend responded, "I don't think so!" By the time I met Alex, things had changed in the documentary world, so some of the things I had been pushing didn't seem so outlandish anymore, but Alex still wanted a bit of a poetic feel to capture his grandmother's reminiscences. He and I worked on the film for about a year, weaving in all the elements of Nana's story- telling, her personal feelings about love, sex, or death, the personal family history of extramarital affairs, murders—lots of stuff! (*Laughs.*) The first scenes of *Nine Good Teeth* start in archival—actually home movies of the shores of Sicily and the volcano Stromboli and then the local cemetery, because Sicilians are preoccupied with death, as the film explains. The film is going to be about dying anyway—after all, the fortune teller told Nana she only had one more year to live! Some of the home movies had flares and flashes and we didn't know how we were going to use them, if at all. But when Alex later shot muted color footage of his own, we thought, "Let's desaturate it, take out the color, and it will match the weird black- and-white footage that has flares and seems 'damaged.' This will give us a *feeling* of a long ago time and place. We're not explaining facts right here. We're setting up a mood too." I thought it might be terrific to start the film with Sicilian voices hawking their wares, ethnic musical drones, and this strange footage of volcanoes and cemeteries.

Almost otherworldly.

It really was. Then we moved into a more traditional style. At times, when we couldn't get enough footage, we did some re-creation, such as in the "murder scene." This is a murder story that Nana didn't want to tell but always brought up! It seems a man named Carmelo was interested in her mother, which was scandalous in their small Sicilian community in Brooklyn. He didn't take the hint that he shouldn't chase a married woman. When a woman relative tried to protect Nana's mother from Carmelo, he spit on her, so a family member, offended by that, shot the guy as an honor killing. Then there was retribution from the murdered guy's family who sliced the face of Nana's father—scarred for life. Of course, Nana didn't want to tell this story on camera because it involved sex and scandal, and she always interrupted herself to say, "We don't have to go into that, do we?" but she'd come right back with, "Oh, and I remember . . ." Then, just as she hit on something Alex was interested in, she'd stop the story again! Alex asked his own mother on camera, "What's this about Carmelo that Nana doesn't want to talk about?" And his mother would say, "Forget about it. She won't go that far." He also asked his cousin Frankie on camera, who said, "Who knows? She never talks about it." It was such funny material that we didn't want to throw it out, so we constructed a sequence that was more narrative in technique. First, because we only had talking heads, we did a little re-creation, like a shadowy figure on the street or going upstairs, cut in with shots of people saying, "No, we never talked about Carmelo. NO! We never talked about it in our family." We also used photographs from the time, but because no one knew if Carmelo was in any of them, we cropped them and lit them to create a shadowy film noir effect! Why wasn't anyone telling this story? What really happened? The way we built the sequence became so tense that it reached a crescendo with Nana yelling out, "Leave me alone. I'm not gonna tell you!" (*Laughs.*) And then we cut away from this dinner argument to a more benign scene of her singing as if we were giving her time to rethink this stubbornness. Eventually, Nana gave in—it wasn't that she didn't want to tell the story, she just never learned all the facts herself! So we had developed an intriguing, mininoir narrative out of a simple request: "Grandma, let's talk about that story!"

Do you actually script out the progression of events in a film like that?

In this instance we had to script that because we were going to do some re-creations, so we had to carefully build the sequence dramatically. In fiction and nonfiction editing, we sometimes use a color-coded card system to plot the progression of scenes in the structure. It's putting different colored file cards on a wall or board that represent different kinds of scenes. Say, every time you go to Nana's house, the card is yellow. If it's archival, it's green. And so you begin to see color patterns on the wall not only of edits shot to shot but also scene to scene, and you get a sense of the rhythm of the film's continuity. In *Patti Smith,* for example, we actually saw some types of scenes, or colors, missing that needed to be filled for story development and better pacing. That system also helps you see the scenes in terms of their placement in a three-act structure, and the story or character arcs within each act. So while you're thinking about individual edits, you can also step back and think about the bigger picture, the editing rhythms of scene to scene or of the whole film.

The ending of Nine Good Teeth *was a shocker. Throughout the film, Nana prepared for her inevitable death. She had even picked out the dress she wanted to be buried in. Then at the end, you hold on a lengthy, heartrending shot of her stretched out in that dress on her deathbed.*
    (*Laughs.*)

And then she sits up!
    Yes! Even though she was old and physical things were difficult for her to do, she still had that spark of humor and life in her. So when Alex got the idea for that deathbed scene, she went for it. At first, *I* wasn't so sure about the scene. But it seemed logical since this was a family that took movies and pictures of *everything,* so why not take a picture of Nana on her deathbed . . . supposedly?

You even set it up by showing poignant images of Nana walking in a cemetery or riding her chair up the staircase . . .
    . . . as if ascending into the heaven she doesn't believe in! (*Laughs.*) And on the soundtrack, I used a famous Italian song from my childhood about living life to the fullest—which is so emotional for me that I cry each time I hear it.

But I began to sense something wasn't what it appeared to be. You were holding too *long on the shot of Nana stretched out on the bed—as if waiting for a punchline.*
    Yes, holding back, holding back, making things uncomfortable and then—okay! She's alive! And she's in on the trick! It gets laughs every time. People really enjoyed the joke and appreciated her spunk.

But up until she sat up, did the audience believe she had died during the filming?
    I think a lot of people were confused by it at first because this *was* a film about death. We presented that subject at the beginning, we returned

to it at the end, and it was mentioned throughout. Nana had already celebrated her hundredth birthday by the end of the film—everybody thought: how many years could she possibly have left? Nobody could imagine we were going to play a trick on that subject. But we did, as fate often does!

So that leads me back to the question of how much is manipulated in a documentary.

This is a controversial topic and I can only speak for myself. As I said earlier, we're in a time now where there is much more leeway in what's considered a documentary. In the "old days," you didn't mix your metaphors, so to speak, because supposed objective purity was the thing. Everything else was looked down on as manipulation and unworthy of reportage or journalism. But as the decades have worn on, the genre rules have loosened. With films like *Spinal Tap,* or *I'm Still Here* with Joaquin Phoenix, and *Exit through the Gift Shop,* definitions of what is "real" have blurred. The filmmaker may be a prankster and maybe doesn't even exist! Maybe the filmmaker actually becomes the subject of the film or the guy who doesn't exist becomes the filmmaker! Convolution, but beautifully done. It's as if the documentary almost becomes a document of how the filmmaker can construct a house of cards to lead you to see life in new ways by fooling you or confounding genre expectations. With reality TV, the truth becomes convoluted and unclear as well. People crying on *American Idol*? Bachelors or bachelorettes professing undying love? To a point, an audience can be outraged or shocked when they feel they've been manipulated, but the entertainment factor is also right there under the surface. If there's a little manipulation to squeeze that juice of outrageousness and fun out of it, they're okay. If there's no feeling toward the characters or material and it *all* seems fake, then there will be no pleasure in it. Maybe there's even anger.

Maybe, like Nana, the truth comes in the form of a "wink" at us, saying we need to look past the obvious?

Yes, ultimately, there is a truth, often a less obvious truth below the surface. That is the kind of film that ends up making a difference to me. It grips us in a way that we will never forget: we are witness to the thinking, feelings, and soul of someone who engages us, and through that encounter we see *ourselves* differently, more clearly. Yes, you can draw all kinds of lines between subjective and objective and between what's acceptable and not, especially in very strict formats of news journalism, and it is an important enough issue that we should always think about what journalistic truth is. But there are times in some works when certain techniques can make you feel or understand or express the essence of something, as much as or even more than a barrage of facts or literal truth.

What would you say to filmmakers who come into the documentary world with the chance to experiment with the genre?

Be open. Experiment. Whenever I give a lecture somewhere, I always ask, "How many of you want to be editors?" And those few will often come up to me afterwards to ask a question or two about something a little beyond the norm, and I realize, okay, they're doing their homework. They have the passion and probably the talent to succeed and continue to educate themselves in film culture and all the other arts, but also history, science, philosophy, psychology—everything. They should be open to everything and push into new ways of thinking. I know I always drag myself away from the editing room so that I can learn from other disciplines. And that allows me to push the envelope of what an editor can contribute to a film. I've had tremendous film influences growing up— Fellini, Antonioni, Godard, Hitchcock, Welles, Dreyer, Ozu, Visconti, Bresson. They've helped me examine the human condition and understand how artists can present it to both entertain and to inform—to challenge our perception of the world and of ourselves. They were unafraid to express themselves at the highest level of the film medium, to try what nobody had done before with light, dark, silence, and sound, and for me, they created moments I can never forget.

3. Cutting from the Gut

JULIE MONROE

1991 *JFK* (associate editor), dir. Oliver Stone

1993 *Indecent Proposal* (additional editor), dir. Adrian Lyne

1997 *Lolita*, dir. Adrian Lyne

1999 *At First Sight*, dir. Irwin Winkler

2000 *Hanging Up*, dir. Diane Keaton

2000 *The Patriot* (additional editor), dir. Roland Emmerich

2001 *Life as a House*, dir. Irwin Winkler

2003 *Gigli*, dir. Martin Brest

2004 *De-Lovely*, dir. Irwin Winkler

2005 *The Big White*, dir. Mark Mylod

2006 *World Trade Center*, dir. Oliver Stone

2008 *W.*, dir. Oliver Stone

2010 *Wall Street: Money Never Sleeps*, dir. Oliver Stone

2011 *What's Your Number*, dir. Mark Mylod

2011 *Shameless*, TV, episodes 9 and 12, dir. Mark Mylod

2011 *Once upon a Time*, TV pilot, dir. Mark Mylod

AWARDS

2005 Eddie Award (ACE) nomination, Best Edited Feature Film—
Comedy or Musical, *De-Lovely*

As a young volunteer in the American Film Institute program, Julie Monroe first apprenticed on Oliver Stone's *Salvador*, a fortuitous event that has fixed Julie in "the Stone camp" for years. She quickly learned the valuable emotional response of "cutting from the gut," or breaking rules, that has guided her ever since. Monroe's work with other directors as well has broadened her understanding of different directorial styles and approaches to filmmaking. She also points out the vital nature of collaboration with other editors and the contributions that such a team eventually makes to key sequences within a film that are often not scripted. In addition to collaborating with "picture" editors, Monroe discusses her experiences of working closely with both sound and music editors, specialists in their fields who are integral not only to finessing the audio components of a film in postproduction, but also to making important determinations in the early stages of cutting. Opportunities to absorb the physical ambience of a set with a sound editor or to work closely with a composer and music editor can give "picture" editors a newfound sense of dimension to the scenes they cut—sometimes physically moving them out of the editing room in order to more deeply understand the subtleties of the film itself when they return to it. Monroe mentions how nuanced "soundscapes" with minute details, such as the rustling of an actor's shirt sleeve, can significantly impact an audience's subliminal viewing. In the hands of all postproduction editors, sound, music, and dialogue in conjunction with the visual become characters of their own, telling the story as vividly as the human actors do.

Monroe's conversation here includes her remarks on the film *W.*, which were published in a spring 2009 *Cineaste* article (vol. 34, no. 2) entitled "Cutting Remarks on *W.*: An Interview with Julie Monroe, Joe Hutshing, and Wylie Stateman." Permission from Mr. Gary Crowdus at *Cineaste* to reprint Monroe's statements here is gratefully acknowledged.

I always knew I wanted to be involved in film in some way. My father was a camera assistant and I was always around that world. He worked mostly in commercials, and so right out of high school, I got a job in a commercial production house as an office PA [production assistant]. They had an on-site editing room, which intrigued me. Shortly thereafter, I went into a volunteer program at the American Film Institute, where I worked in the cutting room for free. With almost no editing background, I interned on a couple of films as both a picture and sound assistant. A fellow volunteer, Lisa Leeman, was contacted by then New York editor Claire Simpson, who was about to start a low-budget film shooting mostly in Mexico and finishing in L.A. Claire knew very few people in Los Angeles and hired Lisa who, in turn, recommended me. I hit it off with Claire, who hired me very young to be an apprentice in the *Salvador* cutting room.

That must have been an amazing experience to start off on a big film with an important director like Oliver Stone.

Yes. It was an incredibly difficult film and a very small crew, so I learned a lot very quickly and stuck with Claire through *Salvador, Platoon,* and *Wall Street.* David Brenner, with whom I have worked many times over the years, also came on as an assistant on *Salvador* and *Platoon,* and later joined Claire as editor on *Wall Street,* as did Joe Hutshing, whom I've since worked with many times as well. I continued as an assistant on *Wall Street,* followed by *Born on the Fourth of July* and *The Doors,* and became an associate editor on *JFK.* I stayed in the Oliver Stone camp for more than ten years. After *JFK,* I took a hiatus from Oliver's films for a while and worked with other directors, and then returned for three films— *World Trade Center, W.,* and *Wall Street: Money Never Sleeps.* It's been about twenty years now with Oliver on and off.

What did you learn about editing while observing these experts?

What impressed me the most was Claire Simpson's bravery. She really cuts from the gut. Convention and continuity don't necessarily matter. It's all about performance and emotion and energy. I saw her breaking so many of the rules that I thought applied to editing. Things that maybe one learns in film school weren't as important as cutting from the gut. Claire would lock herself in the room and become completely absorbed in the story, characters, and performances. She was never afraid to try things. And Oliver is like an incredible open vessel to all ideas and continues to be to this day. On *Salvador* and on every film I have edited with him to date, he would come into the cutting room and, as opposed to sitting and going through the minutiae of the process, he would just watch and react. He'll know when something feels wrong or a performance feels disingenu- ine, but won't watch alternate takes and work it through with you neces- sarily. He would say, "It's not right," knowing that the material existed to make it right. Eventually, all the right pieces would find their way into the cut. We'll spend a lot of time with Oliver in dailies getting his initial reaction to the material. While he's still in the middle of shooting, he may start out with, "These are my selected takes, my favorite performance or blocking preferences," but after that, he absorbs and reacts to the film as a whole and doesn't go through the step-by-step process of a cut per se. So cutting the film becomes structurally open. I've worked with other directors who prefer to sit next to you and compare each take, and enjoy looking for specific nuances with the editor. That's a great way to work as well, but it's not Oliver's style.

It's almost as if Stone becomes an audience member and reacts to the creativity you give to his footage.

Completely. Obviously because he's both writer and director, he has an idea in mind of what he expects to see. But unless there is a problem with how something is constructed, he tends to just sit and absorb the material. It's wonderful especially because his projects are so complicated story-wise, we get to see if what we are doing makes sense. Personally, I can't even imagine how a writer-director can separate himself from the process, but Oliver does.

Given the complexity of his films, with multiple storylines, switching past/present, and numerous characters, how do you feel when you receive a huge amount of material to sort through?

Oliver's films have actually changed much over the years. The story in *JFK* was always meant to be told through flashbacks and through a combination of real and re-created footage. It was such a mass of footages and styles, actual news footage, the Zapruter film, some reenacted versions of events using a variety of film formats, actual consumer formats that were accurate to the time (8mm, 16mm). The shooting of Oswald was covered with the same type of camera that captured the event on the day he was assassinated. We could tell the story visually in so many ways that at times we were completely lost in what we were doing and trying to figure out how to put all of the material together, how to combine dialogue, structure, and visuals in the way they best told the story. It was sometimes hit-and-miss. There was also so much actual documentary footage about Kennedy as well as the imagery that Bob Richardson, the director of photography, brilliantly shot in a documentary style, in addition to less historical and more traditionally-shot pieces. I have to say that overall, we felt we had a jumble for a very long time until we honed down the footage and determined what were the strongest visuals to tell a complicated story. With each witness to the shooting, each alleged conspirator, we had different ways to present the material visually. I think it was finally realizing that there was *no* set pattern of rules to what we chose that gave us the freedom to go for whatever felt the most powerful. That, combined with having several editors working at the same time, made the jumble become the film's style. At the time, I don't think anyone had made a film that looked quite like what Oliver created in *JFK*. As far as my role in the whole project, however, I was very much following the lead of the other editors. *JFK* was really Pietro Scalia's and Joe Hutshing's film, and I worked on certain sections or did changes on sequences that had already been constructed. For some reason, I got a lot of the Joe Pesci and John Candy scenes, and some of the family stuff was in my room more than the other editors' room. Hank Corwin, who was initially hired just to cut the opening montage, ended up joining the team and became a huge contributor to the visual feel of the film. His style was much freer and more instinctive than any of the rest of us, myself in particular. All three editors' styles trickled down to what I ended up doing and it became a huge learning process for me. I also learned so much about structure on *JFK*. Because it was a very dense script, we restructured and montaged quite a bit of the story in order to truncate the footage. I think the trial contained many more flashbacks than in the original script. The witnesses that Jim Garrison (Kevin Costner) interviewed were originally all separate scenes. We found threads within their testimony and, eventually, some of those scenes became montaged, really propelling the second act of the film.

That experience must have been indispensable for later work.

Yes, this work style in particular gave me a lot of information to draw on, especially when I had my first big responsibility as editor, on the film *Lolita,* directed by Adrian Lyne. I had worked as an additional editor on *Indecent Proposal* for Adrian with Joe Hutshing, and for some reason still unknown to me (*laughs*), Adrian let me cut his passion project, *Lolita.* David Brenner joined me after the wrap, but I was on my own and terrified through production. It was a very, very long and complicated script, and ultimately we had to weed down a lot of stories, scenes, and even characters because otherwise it could have easily been a three- or four-hour movie. As brilliant as the script was, we did so much combining of situations and stories and moving pieces around that sometimes aspects of the original script were nowhere to be found in the final film! (*Laughs.*) As green as I was on *JFK*, I would never have realized that editors had such license, but *JFK* gave me confidence on *Lolita* to sit down with Adrian and help him do what he does best: figure out how to get "all the best bits" and tell an amazing, emotional story with incredible nuance and humanity. He's so smart about his characters and what his actors bring to a film. He taught me so much about letting myself, as an editor, get into the actors'—and therefore the characters'—heads. The actors sometimes bring incredible insights that you would have never imagined on the day of the shoot. Adrian loves and encourages that spontaneity. There was a scene in *Indecent Proposal* where Woody Harrelson was joking around trying to make Robert Redford and Demi Moore laugh. None of the dialogue was usable story-wise, but their laughter was so genuine and so infectious that we used it as a kind of pantomime during a musical montage. Adrian pointed out that it is nearly impossible to fake absolutely genuine laughter. I have never stopped hunting for those moments in any film I work on. It sounds so simple, but it was a revelation for me, especially for editing comedies. Another director I've worked with a lot, Mark Mylod, really appreciates and understands this as well. Mark has the best instinct for comedy of anyone I have ever met. It's a big coup for me if I can find something that genuinely makes him laugh that has absolutely nothing to do with the film itself. I love finding those moments. What *you* do in the editing room with what the director has provided you has infinite possibilities. It never stops being exciting once you find the best bits of the story and the best bits of the characters to tell that story.

Some of Stone's films seem to have less frenetic editing and more traditional structure these days.

Interestingly, for his later films, *World Trade Center, W.,* and *Wall Street: Money Never Sleeps,* Oliver shot less footage and the stories were more specific and straightforward. *Wall Street: Money Never Sleeps,* to me, feels stylistically like one of the great films of the seventies. Oliver will probably be the first to admit that at this particular time of his life, and as an audience member, he likes to see that kind of film. Which is good for me, because it's hard for me to wrap my head around the frenetic style of some of his films like *Natural Born Killers* and *U-Turn.* It was probably good that I wasn't editing his films during that time in his career. (*Laughs.*) I like the more narrative sense. I like what Oliver's become as a story-driven, performance-driven artist. Not that *Natural Born Killers* and *U-Turn* weren't brilliant, and the material very much lent itself to frenetic cutting. It's just not something that comes naturally to me. I'm getting better, though! I'm in the middle of doing a couple of episodes of the Showtime series *Shameless,* which Mark Mylod is directing. That show, and Mark's style in this particular project, has been an amazingly freeing foray into energetic, jump-cutty, no-rules storytelling. I love it!

Returning to what you said about truncating the script of Lolita, *what exactly did you do to the filmed version of the script in the editing room?*

Adrian would be the first to admit that he knowingly shoots more scenes than will end up in the final film, just because it's hard to know which scene will lend the best to telling the story. A lot of the Clare Quilty character, played by Frank Langella, was omitted in the final film. He became more shadowy in the center of the film and his murder, which was bookended in the beginning and end of the original script, only appeared at the end. Adrian shot beautiful scenes with amazing iconic images, yet sometimes only a single shot was used from an entire scene. Any montage became an opportunity to add a beautiful shot that was part of a lifted scene. A tennis match from an omitted scene became three shots in a montage. My favorite example was using only one shot from a scene in which Lolita sits in a car at a gas station. I can't even remember the focus of the original scene or why we took it out of the movie, but we inserted just one moment of Lolita putting on lipstick in the middle of a montage. It was not even part of an actual take! Adrian had actress Dominique Swain put on her own lipstick rather than have a makeup artist apply it so it would look realistic, and the camera caught her doing her makeup in the side-view mirror. In another example, an entire scene in the film originally ran several minutes between Humbert and Lolita. The scene was amazing, but was ultimately lifted from the film and reduced to one slow-motion shot of Lolita tossing an apple in the air! In fact, it's not in the film itself, but appears *after* the credits—it's an absolutely gorgeous shot. In my opinion, Adrian is like few others in creating such beautiful images. Every insert he shoots has its own reason and personality and emotion. The film had such a wealth of riches, but so much ended up on the cutting-room floor! That being said, I think it's an incredible film and I am so proud to have been a part of it. At the beginning of a film, as you know, you always have continuity, which is a list of every scene in numerical order and a description of that scene. One of my proudest moments was seeing the original continuity of *Lolita* and the final continuity of *Lolita*—where now scene 75 might be where scene 32 was before—and I knew that the story was still well told. That's when the process of editing becomes unbelievably exciting because you can really change things for the better. I'm not an editor who can look at a script and say, "Gosh, this scene will never work, we're going to have to find a different place for that scene." David

Brenner, who edited *Lolita* with me, can do that very well. He can quickly see when something needs to be moved structurally. I'm pretty good at reacting to material and knowing how to construct a scene, but I can't see the bigger picture before seeing the footage. When it's all together, then I can see different ways to tell the story, but I've got to let it all come together on its own first.

You've mentioned the printed word and the visual. What about sound? Do you make final decisions about soundtrack or is that the realm of the sound editor?

Because everything is digital now and films rely so much on screenings and audience reactions, picture editors do a lot of sound *and* music work. When I work with supervising sound editor Wylie Stateman on Oliver's films, we collaborate on the sound of the film from the get-go. Wylie has a long history and background with Oliver. He'll come to the set of every movie just to get a feel for the reality of what is going on there and record authentic sounds of the location. For *World Trade Center,* I walked with Wylie on the structure of the fake Ground Zero, which was in Culver City, to get the feel of what that was like. By physically being on each set, Wylie comes up with incredible ideas for the sound that we can then incorporate within our cuts early in the process. His collaboration is absolutely there from the outset and progresses afterwards, so by the time we're at the temp dub, we're already final-mixing, in a sense. It also helps Oliver get an idea of what the final sound will be. Every time you screen the movie, it helps to have some of the sound design that will ultimately be part of it.

Do you visit the set on every film?

Actually, not often. But sometimes, particularly when Oliver gets an idea at a given moment, he'll want to talk it through with his editors. He's not someone who will pick up the phone and have a conversation. He likes to do things face to face. He'll summon me to the set and whenever that happens, I'll assume I've done something horrendously wrong! (*Laughs.*)

Sounds like being called to the principal's office!

It feels like that! I think it's best to keep things as unbiased as possible, which is hard when you're on set. Frankly, I've never been comfortable on a film set anyway. I love watching dailies with directors and with the cast and crew, though. It's one of my favorite parts of the process and a really valuable part. Sometimes if schedules are tight or budgets don't allow the editor to be on location, that can't happen—which is a shame. But for the most part, I'm back in the editing room during the shooting.

Can you give instances from different films that illustrate how sound enhanced your visual choices?

Well, going back to two of Oliver's films that we've already mentioned, *W.* was more straightforward in sound, being such a heavy dialogue film, than, say, *World Trade Center,* where the sound was continually coming out of the silence underneath Ground Zero, with fireballs shooting out or pieces of debris dropping and so on. Everything placed underground had a very specific feel. I mean, you could accidentally delete the sound of a piece of debris falling from the track and *feel* that it was missing. Sound became kind of a character in that film. The unique qualities of the sounds became so much a part of what those scenes were. It was all part of that horrifying world for the two Port Authority police officers (played by Nicolas Cage and Michael Peña) who were trapped underground after the Towers collapsed. By contrast, *W.* was more straightforward, yet Wylie created some great nuances with sound there. For example, Josh Brolin is a very physical actor who did subtle things like clicking his teeth when eating or licking his fingers. Some sound editors would clean out the sounds behind these nuances and make pristine tracks, but Wylie instinctively left them alone because these physical quirks were part of the actor's characterization. Josh Brolin did this one action where he shifted his sleeve, probably at least a half dozen times in the film *W.* I asked Josh, "What's up with this? It looks like you're not comfortable in your own clothing. Did you mean that?" He wouldn't tell me if it was intentional or not, he just laughed, and I could only assume it was very well thought out. It was something I mentioned in passing to Wylie, and sure enough, when we were on the mixing stage, I heard a sense of that sound in Foley! Wylie enhanced Josh's action of shifting his clothing in Foley so that if it was, in fact, something Josh was trying to portray about W., Wylie very subtly helped that.

In a number of scenes, the sound and visual editing enhanced an other-worldly feel to what was happening. For example, when W. is jogging and collapses on the road, you hear typical outdoor sounds of birds and his running steps. But you also suddenly hear thunder on a sunny day. Why did that sound help transition into the next interior scene with W. and Reverend Hudd (Stacy Keach)?

The intention of that scene was very subtle. The jogging, as originally cut, had specific backgrounds—the sound of birds, leaves rustling in trees—and these sounds also actually continued into the next scene with the Reverend. This was a kind of sound ghosting, as if to say W. would remember from one scene to the next when he had hit rock-bottom in his life. There was no visual indication of a storm, but you hear a bit of distant thunder. Without being heavy-handed at all, the sound lent an ominous quality creeping in and out of those scenes and underscoring W.'s situation.

Editorial choices can be subtle forms of commentary as well. What was your approach to making a film about George W. Bush, who was still in office when the film was released?

We always knew that we wanted to take an observer's look at the situation and not be heavy-handed. Let the circumstances speak for themselves, which hopefully they did. This was clear in Stanley Weiser's script, which didn't feel like it was forcing an opinion on anybody, and Oliver took a real fly-on-the-wall approach. We were always very aware of not being too caricature-y. The goal was to film a small slice of the presidency. There was so much material we didn't go into, such as the 9/11 specifics, Hurricane Katrina, and so on. If Oliver had made this movie ten years from now or had made it five years earlier, it would be a much different film. But Oliver picked certain episodes that he wanted to show; for example, we always wanted to have W.'s religious background, the Christian aspects of his life, and how that affected his presidency. Which leads me to the music end of that film.

Yes, the score was very poignant. How did music convey the religious mood of the film?

Our composer, Paul Cantelon, who is the son of a faith healer, did a simple, beautiful sort of religious, churchy-sounding score. We had demos from him very early on. Most of the time in editing, you use temp music either from the composer you intend to work with, based on scores that have already been recorded, or from other composers whose material fits. This helps you to create the rhythm of the picture. Paul, however, was on location with us in Shreveport, with a little Casio keyboard, and he came up with themes and endless pieces of music for us to experiment with. He was just a music machine, giving us anything we talked about! Thus, we incorporated his music into the film from the outset. By the time the music editor, Sally Boldt, came in, we had already set an idea for themes and repeated sounds and instruments, musically mapping out the way we wanted it in the film. Some pieces in *W.*, by the way, are Paul's original synth version from the Casio in Shreveport. He would eventually orchestrate most of the material, and even though he went to Prague and recorded these beautiful orchestral pieces, there was a simplicity about some of Paul's themes played on the synthesizer that Oliver fell in love with and didn't want to change. And Oliver knew that instinctively from the get-go and warned both Paul and Sally all the time, "Don't make this too big! Don't make this too movielike!" Because simplicity sometimes just works better. There is a poignant scene where George Bush, Senior, is berating young W. for having gotten a girl pregnant and for all of his failures in business and politics, and W. is just saying that he only wants to play baseball. The very end of that scene is a simple synth guitar piece that I believe was Paul's original recording. I know on the mixing stage, we compared the old with the new arrangements, and the old won out. That same piece is repeated when Senior accepts W. once he's finally won the gubernatorial race and gives him a pair of cuff links. The piece is only used twice in the film, but it's the original. This way of composing was also the way Craig Armstrong worked with us on *World Trade Center* and later on *Wall Street: Money Never Sleeps*. On *World Trade Center*, in particular, he came up with several amazing themes before we even began shooting and those themes are basically the final score of the film. I think the main piano piece that he wrote for the film became for Oliver what Barber's *Adagio for Strings* was in *Platoon*. Repetition of a powerful theme like that can strike such an emotional chord.

What about the popular songs you incorporated into W.? *What relationships do they create between the visual and the musical?*

Well, "The Battle Hymn of the Republic" was used for the big conference room scene when the Cabinet is discussing the possibility of the Iraq War. By the time Joe Hutshing came on *W.* when we returned to Los Angeles, several musical themes had already been established, but Joe gave an impressive fresh ear and really honed in on what worked best for particular scenes. In the conference room scene, where the president's Cabinet was pressuring Colin Powell into accepting the Iraq War, Joe let the dialogue dictate that scene, but at the end, as "The Battle Hymn of the Republic" came in under the dialogue, the power of the piece kept pushing and pushing and pushing Colin until he acquiesced. He is, after all, a military man who follows his commander-in-chief and he goes along with the war idea. This was very much Joe's design of the scene from the start. It was an unusual thing for Oliver, actually letting the music lead and push the dialogue to a climactic and critical moment. But usually, music, if it is used, should enhance what the dialogue is saying, without distracting and without force. I think of the gorgeous music of *Lolita,* composed by Ennio Morricone, that underscored the affair between a much older man and a thirteen-year-old girl. The music was very emotional and treated the film very much like a love story, which was how Adrian looked at the material and how Jeremy Irons and the other actors played their roles. It was an incredibly romantic score. But that's how Humbert saw Lolita. It never distracted or commented, just reinforced.

You also judiciously used songs in W. *that were tongue-in-cheek, would you say? "Yellow Rose of Texas" seems obvious since Bush is from Texas, but why "Robin Hood" to underscore two scenes?*

We found various versions of "Yellow Rose of Texas" to use as kind of a Kubrickian theme throughout. Oliver had this in mind from the start and several of Paul's themes have "Yellow Rose" at their center. But I wish I had chosen "Robin Hood"! (*Laughs.*) Actually, Stanley Weiser came to Oliver with several CDs of music he liked. Before we started shooting, we sat with Oliver one afternoon listening to tons of material, and he absolutely loved "Robin Hood" because it suggested this delusion of grandeur theme for W. As soon as we got the dailies back for the Craw-ford Road scene at W.'s ranch in Texas, which is where we first used that song in the movie, it was pretty obvious it belonged there. It underscored the scene with W. and his band of merry Cabinet members plodding on behind him, and ultimately they miss the turn in the road!

A little irony there.

Yes, the simplicity of the man and his delusions of grandeur.

Moving from Bush for a moment but staying with music, you also cut the musical De-Lovely, *for which you were nominated for an Eddie. Did you have to shift mindsets to cut a musical or did you just "cut from the gut"?*

I happen to love musicals and I knew Cole Porter's music so well. Irwin Winkler made this film about Porter's life very much like a good old-fashioned Hollywood musical, and there was something so innately acces-sible and familiar to me as I was cutting it. As a kid, I loved musicals like *Oliver!* and *My Fair Lady.* I think that rhythm gets into your head. Hon-estly, a lot of what was comfortable about *De-Lovely* came from being a fan of the *That's Entertainment* films, which I think were made in the seventies—they were a kind of short-attention-span version of movie musicals! But effective nonetheless. (*Laughs.*) Honestly, I didn't prepare myself at all for *De-Lovely*. I came on the film after they had finished shooting it in London and it felt natural once I began to work on it. The multiple-camera aspect of shooting the musical numbers also helped. A lot of the time, two or three cameras were on the stage shows, and the point was to maintain the energy of each musical number and create the feel of watching a stage show, even though it was on film. We also had to convey a sense of fantasy or dreaminess that was set up in the first number, "Anything Goes," with all the significant people from Porter's past coming back to see him again.

Yes, that scene and similar ones replaying throughout the two-hour film were supposed to represent only ten seconds of Porter's life, flashing in front of his eyes before he dies.

Exactly. Sustaining that thread and keeping it alive and real, as long as Porter (played by Kevin Kline) was alive and real in the film, was important. It became a matter of choosing when we wanted to return to the theater with Porter as an old man talking with Death (Jonathan Pryce) and then flashing back to scenes of his life. Everything we needed for the story was emotionally present in Porter's music. At the beginning of the film, when Porter plays "In the Still of the Night," I took that very simple piano version of the song, a version that Kevin himself played, and used it as score. And to this day, I apologize to Stephen Endelman, who wanted to score the full movie and couldn't because of that piano piece! (*Laughs.*) Irwin liked using the simple piano. That song is the opening notes of the film, it's the recurring love theme between Porter and his wife Linda, it's repeated when Porter falls off the horse that would cripple him for life, and it's sung by Porter and Linda as a sort of coda at the end of the film. I felt that running piano track gave a cohesiveness to the whole film, a thread that tied the film together. Then there are the scenes when Kevin would burst into song, where it was a matter of making each scene feel real and fun, almost like having an actual dialogue scene but set to music instead. Singing "Be a Clown" on the MGM backlot with Louis B. Mayer was a great homage to the MGM musical. But Porter singing "So in Love" to his dying wife was, to me, as moving as any dialogue scene I've ever cut.

Looking at dialogue scenes from another angle—without music—what guides your choices about using action/reaction shots?

Since we just mentioned Kevin Kline, I think right away of another Irwin Winkler film I edited with Kevin called *Life as a House*. That film was all about performance, and Kevin, who's a brilliant actor, gave such a genuine performance and kept a tough subject from becoming maudlin—a man dying of cancer who wants to build a house while reconnecting with his family before it's too late. I wanted to find pieces, moments, that felt accessible to everybody about father-son and husband-wife relationships, even if they're not in that same dramatic context for everyone. The idea that Kevin and his wife (Kristin Scott Thomas) could be pulled apart in their marriage yet still be drawn to each other—well, the actors were so terrific that it wasn't difficult to find moments you could use to drive home. But Irwin gave me a lot of freedom to put the film together in a way that I felt could convey this message of family. As I said before, I like performance-driven films, so my favorite thing is to find the actors' nuances and "up" them a level, possibly in ways that the actors themselves might not have pictured. I get so many compliments on that film. It touched a lot of people. I think it may be Irwin's best work as a director. He nailed the relationships and the emotions.

How do you "up" the level editorially?

By finding moments between the actors. For example, some of the scenes between Hayden Christiansen, who played Kevin's son, and Kevin himself were so real and a little unexpected. For me, it's a question of zeroing in on moments that don't seem "acted," but are real emotions. Irwin allowed a lot of improvising and physicality in the scenes between father and son. Hayden was amazing and so raw: he suddenly punches a wall, for example, when he and Kevin have their first blowout after the father learns that his son had been taking his painkillers. Because Irwin let them go wild during that scene, I just put the script down and simply watched what I had in front of me. Additionally, the use of reaction shots, particularly on Hayden, played a big role. I love when a reaction shot that was meant for something completely different can be used in another way as a pure emotional link between action and reaction. The result can be much more powerful than what was originally written. Going back to *W.*, which was less improvised, the lunch scene with W. and Vice President Dick Cheney (Richard Dreyfuss) is one example that very much played on many of Josh's reactions to what Richard was saying rather than on the speaker. It's never a formula. You watch dailies and find an amazing reaction shot that hits you in a certain way, and you note that to yourself and try to use it. On that scene, I believe there was a B camera covering a wide shot or an overhead shot, but the first coverage of the scene was all on Josh. Later, the camera turned around and did all of Richard's coverage. To be honest, probably two takes were prominently used because Josh nailed the scene right away. I think a lot of Josh's work in the film came from his first takes. Sometimes I fight feeling that I'm being a lazy editor working with only one or two takes, but ultimately you have to realize: no, this *is* the performance, this *is* the through-line, I need to use those reaction shots because they're saying so much. Whatever Richard threw at him, Josh's reactions were so genuine in those early takes that they became the primary part of the scene.

Speaking of a shot that may say so much, I have to ask you about the barbecue scene . . .
   Are you going to say the corn shot? (*Laughs.*)

As a matter of fact, yes. The hostess of the barbecue is leading W. over to meet Laura for the first time, and, as the hostess is speaking to him, you cut to her foot stepping on a corn cob. Why?
   We had a great second-unit DP, Danny Hiele, who shot an unbelievable amount of footage of "gluttony" for that scene—people eating potato salad, the rich Texas barbecue—which included a female extra stepping on a corn cob. In the film, that is not even the hostess stepping on the corn! But it looks that way because I made the hostess step on the corn cob by cutting the shot of the extra's foot into the dialogue scene. I just loved that foot shot when I saw it and, to be honest, I don't know why I did it! I've heard many ideas about what the corn shot must "mean." For some, it represents the gluttony of the rich. Someone thought it was an ethanol reference for clean corn-burning fuel! So many people commented on the corn at one screening that we pulled out the shot because it was becoming too big a deal. But at the next screening, everyone was asking where the corn shot was! Oliver doesn't care what it means; it made him laugh, so we kept it in.

Such quick shots can also capture the essence of a character, like the belt-buckle close-ups in W.
   Yes, for the preacher, a close-up of the gleaming buckle is his flashing glamour. For W., who wears presidential and gubernatorial belt buckles throughout the film, it's a little touch of Texas, who he is. That's all very much Oliver's style and we incorporated it. He did that a lot in *Nixon*, with images that identify the characters. By the way,

I didn't edit that film, but the orchids in the Sam Waterston scene come to mind.

Likewise your use of transitions, such as dissolves or fades, to characterize a moment within the story. How do you choose to embellish a scene with such devices?

Transitions are all connections, visual ways we can join cuts in a film. In one case, after W. collapses on the road while jogging, a close-up of his eye dissolves into the eye of the Jesus mosaic in the room with the preacher. In another scene, W. turns out the light in his bedroom and the light next switches on in the conference room. It's a way to truncate time, connecting points along the story line to tell the story most efficiently. Not every scene has to have a beginning-middle-end, and such transitions make the same connections in different scenes and link them story-wise. In *World Trade Center*, the transitions were unusual. Given the nature of that film, there were long spans of time and dialogue down in "the hole"—what we called the underground beneath the collapsed Towers—this occurred something like thirteen times in the original script. In the final film, there were maybe only half a dozen visits to the "hole." We ended up combining those thirteen scenes when we found ways to link the "hole" to the outside world, to the families, and to the rescue operations. Thank goodness for Seamus McGarvey, who was smart enough to shoot the "hole" scenes in a way that they could be combined. The scenes became fewer and were better connected with what happened above ground. I think the "black transitions" came out of that. As we saw the dailies, we knew, okay, we want to end the outside-world scene here, so we would then literally go to black and come back in with a line of dialogue from the "hole" which was in darkness, with only intense close-ups of Nicolas Cage or Michael Peña. The effect was of a completely confused feeling of time—have we been here for hours? days? weeks? This is what it must have felt like for the families and the trapped men. The transitions not only moved the action and combined the scenes, but became good storytelling. It ultimately became the need to make that connection between the two trapped men and their families above ground, and let each "world" dictate when we would move back and forth between those worlds. It's a lot to ask an audience to remain in the dark, barely able to see these two men for such long periods of time. It was hard for *us!* The whole process of that film was emotionally grueling. It was also hard for David Brenner and myself to see all the actual news footage along with the footage we were getting as dailies. We could never become completely desensitized to it, but ultimately at some point our brain had to realize we were just telling the story of these two men and the heroes of the tragedy, not the event itself. Everyone was a little nervous about the idea of making a film about the World Trade Center tragedy. We weren't sure if people actually wanted to live in that world all over again through a film.

How were those concerns allayed, if they were?

Oliver was incredibly respectful to the families of the victims and we screened portions of the films for the victims' families regularly, which was extremely hard. I flew back and forth to New York to participate in those screenings. Meeting the families was tough, but their strength was inspiring. We also used real police and firefighters who were there on the day, which was quite emotional. In the film, we used a lot of the actual radio broadcasts from the EMS workers and the fire and police departments talking to each other over walkie-talkies. What wasn't real recording was re-created by the men who were there. Throughout the film, we tried very hard to be sure we did not use the voice of anyone who had died in the tragedy. The survivors from the different departments could actually recognize the voices of their comrades in the broadcasts. When we did the ADR sessions, we used the real people who were there to re-create the radio broadcasts. It was brutal to see these big, tough guys in tears because they were reliving the experience. Or during a screening, to sit there with a mother and her two daughters who had lost their son and brother—while they were crying at the screening, they were so proud and brave, feeling so patriotic and emotional. Scott Strauss, the EMS worker who risked his own life to pull out the two men from the "hole," was a creative consultant for the film; he was played by Stephen Dorff. Scott was at every ADR session to get everything as close to that reality as possible. The film was an amazing experience of reality imitating art and art imitating life, and seeing up close the real lives affected by this tragedy.

But was it necessary as an art form to include the most graphic news footage, such as the bodies of victims falling from the Towers?

That was a very sensitive decision to make, and we tried to do it with sound alone rather than focus on the images. Wylie was incredibly tactful on that point in his sound design. So many people who were witnesses to 9/11 when the planes hit the Towers said that their strongest memory of that day was the sounds of bodies falling and then looking up to see more coming down. It became, tragically, an iconic image of that day, and affected people so strongly that I don't think we could have left it out of the film. It was a hard decision for Oliver and the producers to make and we went back and forth on it many times. The truth is, for days and weeks, the world watched over and over, on their TV sets in their own living rooms, the images of the falling Towers and the falling bodies. I think it ultimately would have felt like we were intentionally avoiding it if it wasn't in the film. For several weeks before even starting the film, David Brenner and I pulled news footage that we could use to cut the sequences that were on TV as playback. It really affected us. It does to this day.

The DVD of World Trade Center *actually featured some deleted scenes that would have, by contrast, slowed down or even jarred with the film's tension. I'm thinking of an odd scene with Nicolas Cage's character wearing a flashy apron and barbecuing for his family at home, before he was trapped underground.*

Yes, that was meant to be a fun scene, a flashback that Nic Cage's character is thinking about when he is trapped, but in fact we had already established his family and their close relationship in the film. It ultimately proved unnecessary to include the barbecue scene. You can feel that lack of fit when you screen it as a whole. We had a lot of "why am I here at this barbecue!?" reactions when it was in the cut. Oliver's ruthless with himself with that sort of thing. He will never hang on to something if it's not working to progress the story. Another scene we deleted was when Nic Cage does the roll call of the Transit Authority officers before they go on duty, and he has them showing their guns when suddenly someone's cell phone goes off. It did show the procedure they went through every day and added some light moments. It was also intended to establish important, very strong characters. But we already got that sense from another scene when they were on the bus heading downtown to the World Trade Center, so the procedural scene began to feel unnecessary by contrast. It seemed a good idea to learn about the characters gradually and treat the day like any ordinary day, with nobody suspecting the terrible event about to happen. So it made sense to shoot the scene, but then it became very clear that it was not progressing the story and the scene was deleted.

You do create a sense of "ordinary day" through the very moving opening montage of New York, which seems to wake up like a character itself in the morning. Along with city shots, you include the actions of Nicolas Cage getting out of bed, going into traffic, and so on, to introduce the story. Yet the montage was latent with foreboding.

Yes. New York waking up was exactly what Oliver wanted to accomplish with that opening montage. The second unit team went out and captured early morning images of New York that make you feel what the city is all about—the fish market, the meat market, the ferry at dawn. It started at the earliest point in the morning when Nic Cage woke up for work, to Wall Street waking up, to the whole city waking up. It was a definite intentional progression in time. There was also a shot, for example, of a simple fire escape with an American flag that said so much visually, especially as we showed that same image in a montage of the next day, with the flag covered in ash from the collapsed Towers. Similarly, we showed a ferryboat crossing the East River early in the morning as it normally did, and then later on it was just sitting in the harbor, recalling the character of Christopher Amoroso, who went to work by ferry and died in the tragedy. The montages, then, not only established the setting and progression of time, but also eventually created a sense of loss for these particular men in very subtle ways.

Being attuned to cutting from the gut and seeking out subtleties of performance, do you find that the digital revolution in editing in any way adversely affects an editor's ability to discover those meaningful moments?
     The digital process actually makes revisiting footage a lot easier. The hard thing is to have the time to do it. What scares me a little in that regard is not the digital aspect, but the schedules. We did an incredibly rapid-fire schedule on *W.* to get the film out before the election in 2008—it was like a forty-five-day shoot. We were literally on the mixing stage about thirteen weeks after wrapping principal photography. There were great aspects to that schedule—we just moved forward, sharked our way through the project, and never looked back—and never got bored with our material. But we also didn't have audience reactions because we didn't have time to show the film to many audiences. Ultimately, I'm afraid that because of economics and because of how much one can do with digital editing these days, schedules will get shorter and shorter. Which is too bad because I like the screening process, I like the reacting process, and I'd like to spend a little more time on a film than we did on *W.!*

Do you miss the touch of film at all, given that much of your work has been on Avid?
     A bit. To be honest, I love seeing the film projected the first time, even when you do a DI [digital intermediate]. The image is digital. It still feels a little like you are in your editing room looking at a monitor. You can do so much to manipulate the image, but you are still looking at the film shot by shot. Oliver once remarked that he missed the lab process because

you had to comment on the film as a whole, the lab would make changes for a day or two, and then you'd see the whole thing fresh again. It's still pretty astonishing when you go to a lab the first time and it's now film and not a high-density clean image. It takes on a sort of photo-chemical look that digital doesn't quite emulate. I love that. But I think, overall, in both color timing and in editing itself, digital makes you much braver and allows you to try things you could never do on film. You could say, "This is a really strange idea, but I'm going to try it anyway just because I *can*." I wouldn't trade that for anything. I do think with film, you had to be very decisive and choose your moments because it took too much time to try many different things—although editors did it, of course, when there was no other choice! But now, it's nothing to try out an unusual cut or strange action/reaction. You can try four or five pieces of music, or do something bizarre with color timing or changing speed. Actually, I don't miss film at all! (*Laughs.*)

So no going backwards for you.
   No! It would be really difficult.

Can you think of one word that epitomizes editing?
   (*Pauses.*) Patience. What you have to have when you're in the cutting room.

Is that your advice for an up-and-coming editor?
   Yes, have patience, and just go into cutting rooms, volunteer to get lunches for people. Watch, listen, and learn. See as many movies as possible. And that's not a patience thing. That's just really important.

4. **Sensing Psychology**

JONATHAN OPPENHEIM

1984 *Streetwise* (associate editor), dir. Martin Bell

1990 *Paris Is Burning*, dir. Jennie Livingston

1993 *Hookers, Hustlers, Pimps, and Their Johns*, TV, dir. Beeban Kidron

1994 *Lives in Hazard*, TV, dir. Susan Todd and Andrew Young

1995 *What Can We Do about Violence? A Bill Moyers Special*, TV

1997 *Arguing the World*, dir. Joseph Dorman

1998 *Frontline: The High Price of Health Care*, TV, dir. Rachel Dretzin

2001 *Children Underground* (also coproduced), dir. Edet Belzberg

2002 *Caught in the Crossfire*, TV, dir. Brad Lichtenstein and David Van Taylor

2002 *Sister Helen* (coeditor), dir. Rebecca Cammisa and Rob Fruchtman

2004 *Out of the Shadow* (coeditor), dir. Susan Smiley

2004 *Love Iranian-American Style*, dir. Tanaz Eshaghian

2005 *Prison Lullabies* (coeditor), dir. Odile Isralson and Lina Matta

2006 *Cowboys, Indians, and Lawyers*, TV, dir. Julia Dengel and Jonathan Oppenheim

2008 *Youssou Ndour: I Bring What I Love* (coeditor), dir. Elizabeth Chai Vasarhelyi

2009 *Strongman* (coeditor), dir. Zachary Levy

2010 *Phyllis and Harold* (also coproduced), dir. Cindy Kleine

2010 *The Oath* (also coproduced), dir. Laura Poitras

2011 *Our School* (supervising editor), dir. Mona Nicoara and Miruna Coca-Cozma

Jonathan Oppenheim was hoping to be a painter, despite growing up with a close connection to film. His mother was Oscar-winning actress Judy Holliday. His father, David Oppenheim, was a renowned classical clarinetist and later head of Columbia Records Classical Division, who then moved into documentary film producing for Omnibus and CBS Reports, and finally became dean of New York University's Tisch School of the Arts, where he presided for twenty years, during which time the school became one of the preeminent film schools in America. Oppenheim eventually discovered his own voice in documentary film editing, once he had understood the remarkable process of eliciting form and meaning from fragments of footage. In embracing this amalgam of words, sounds, and images, Oppenheim also found a channel for probing the psychology of the characters in documentary films. As an editor, he transforms them into dimensional human beings who share their stories, however troubled they may be. Oppenheim's in-depth discussion of *Arguing the World* demonstrates the peaks and valleys of the editing process, the continuous experimentation necessary to understand what works for an audience, and the often painful decisions of letting go of seemingly good ideas. In speaking of *The Oath*, a film that captured his post-9/11 anxieties, Oppenheim discusses an editor's responsibility to remain objective when faced with the task of presenting an enemy as a real human being.

Oppenheim's conversation builds on previous points raised by Corrao on how documentary editors are filmmakers in their own right. To this, he adds a unique perspective of how documentary filmmaking relies intensely on human psychology, allowing audiences to relate to the characters they meet—even those who may threaten an audience's sense of security. In such circumstances, the documentary editor becomes an anchor in a sea of truth that is inevitably mixed with uncertainty.

Coming from a film family, did you always want to work in film?

Actually, I was very committed to painting and had been doing it since I was a teenager. But at a certain point, I guess in my early to mid-twenties, I was looking for a way to make a living, and a friend of the family, Dena Levitt, who was a film editor, said, "Editing is a great way to make a living! Why don't you come into the cutting room and see if you like it?" So that was it. I went in and helped her for two or three days. She was working on a montage of a picnic, I remember. That night I had a dream about the equipment and the film going through it. When I woke up, I said to myself, "Something about this feels right." I got a job as an apprentice editor on a documentary a few months later.

Did you purposely bypass Hollywood movies for documentaries?

I did work for several years as an assistant on both narrative features and documentaries so I had a taste of each, but I still didn't know what I was going to do. Then, when I worked with Nancy Baker on *Streetwise* as an associate editor, I had an epiphany: I understood that documentary editing could be an art form, which hadn't hit me before. I watched the footage, and what *I* perceived was a hundred hours worth of fragments. Over the next few months, I watched Nancy create a six- to eight-hour assembly and gradually reduce it to ninety-five minutes, rearranging scene cards on a wall to help find the form of the story and creating a structure. Those fragments I'd watched took on a powerful meaning. It was amazing to see it all unfold, and I knew that this was what I really wanted to do. Nancy became my role model, especially during my first full-scale immersion in editing, which was *Paris Is Burning.*

Did editing have parallels to painting?

Yes, in very particular ways that relate to my process. For instance, if you change one thing in a painting, it affects the rest of the painting. You may have to rework the entire painting because you are constantly working on the whole. With editing, when you've refined things to a certain point, tiny shifts can have powerful effects, so you always have to be aware of what those shifts are doing to the whole film. You can markedly strengthen or weaken a film. So I think a lot in terms of "the whole." It's a very useful approach to film editing. I also have an emotional-sensual response to the film material, which relates to my experience of painting. It's a similar visceral excitement, but when I was painting and in a purely visual realm, I felt completely isolated. I was in a wordless universe, and I had to have the radio on, with words coming in to me as I painted. When I'm editing, I live in a world of words *and* sounds *and* the visual. You're working with telling a story in time. It's not so isolating. You can be alone in an editing room and not feel isolated the way you do when you're painting.

So you are connecting with people, even if they are only in the film.

Yes, essentially they are talking to you and you are talking back to them. You are molding what they're going to say and how they're going to come across. You're engaging in a kind of dialogue. That is how I approach working with—let's say, for lack of a better word—*characters* in a documentary. I'll take them in in the way I would take in a flesh-and-blood person in front of me. And I see things in those characters that are compelling to me. I make a connection with them and want to bring out who they are.

Can you talk about a character you brought out to full potential?

Well, I think of *Out of the Shadow,* which I became involved with after the director, Susan Smiley, had been editing it for several years and was frustrated in her attempts to bring to life a story about her mother who was paranoid schizophrenic. It was a very hard story for her to tell, filled with pain.

What wasn't working about her version of the film?

At that time, the film wasn't so much about her mother as about Susan's difficulties shepherding her mother through the state mental health system. When I screened the raw footage, I felt a tremendous strength in the material was not being tapped; there just wasn't enough of her mother in the film. The mother had to really be *in* this film. You had to allow her to talk and be herself. It was hard for Susan to see this because it was her mother, after all, and a woman with devastating problems. But experiencing her mother's state of mind was of vital importance. Every moment with the mother was a revelation about her distress with the world—and her impact on Susan. For me, her mother's personality was the key to the film. I tried to work with the scenes involving her mother and make them the bed of the story, always returning to her and letting the audience enter her mind. The other key to the film was writing Susan's voiceover, which involved her coming to grips with her own trauma in a very heroic way. But my point here is that I felt I had the sense of a dialogue with the mother. I was trying to bring her out and let her tell her own story.

When you "dialogue," do you construct a communication between your-self and the characters?

Yes.

Do you say something like, "Well, Character A, if I ask you a question, I'd expect you to answer in a certain way, so I will find a way for you to tell me that answer"?

Well, not so literal as that. It's more like I have a strong sense of this person's psychology, and my burning desire is to elicit that psychology in what feels like a connection between us in a vital way. That's what I mean by dialogue.

In other words, the characters are showing you both good and bad aspects of their personalities and you are responding to those aspects.
Yes, responding in a way that's both receptive and active.

Did you discover the lack of the mother's presence in Out of the Shadow *because you were more objective toward the material than the director was?*
Let's say I was outside the material. When I screen footage, I am very sensitive to my responses to it and sometimes I feel very worked up by it. It wasn't so much that I initially saw the mother was missing in the film. Rather, when I screened the material that Susan had *not* put into the film, I had a powerful response to her mother and felt she shouldn't be presented as "simply" paranoid schizophrenic. She should be presented for how she was manifesting at different points in time, and an audience should experience her the way I was experiencing her. I began to have a very strong sense of how I could work with this material and with Susan. So I think it was a combination of being outside the material, yes, but having a strong, strong response to the mother's humanness despite her freaky, scary parts.

As the film reveals, she was very scary in how she treated her two daughters.
Yes, she's scary. But at the end, when she's a little less scary and in a better place, you can feel it. So you must go through that valley of fear with her and come out feeling able to take a breath with her at the end.

Do you maintain your initial intense responses to the material as you continue to work with it? Or do you get bored after a while or find unexpected things?
I do see new things. I make connections that I didn't expect and everything evolves. But certain essential, visceral sparks remain. You could get tired of working on a film and still have a strong connection to what initially excited you. But you can definitely run out of gas and you need to find a way to fill up! (*Laughs.*)

What causes you to run out of gas?
It depends on the project. Sometimes projects become mired in personality differences or differences in vision that are poisonous to the

process. Other times, it's because you have been working on certain problems in a film for so long that you can't see how to resolve them and it tires you out. That doesn't mean they are not solvable, but you have to find a way to get a leg up. It helps to bring others in and see the film through their eyes. Sometimes all it takes is a specific comment that mirrors my own reactions, which might be just below the surface. Suddenly I will understand something about the film that I hadn't understood in a year, some missing element, and my understanding of the film is revitalized. I'll give an example from *The Oath*, which tells the story of two brothers-in-law who were associated with Al Qaeda and had worked as Osama bin Laden's driver and bodyguard. One man, Abu Jandal, ended up becoming a taxi driver in Yemen, while the other, Salim Hamdan, was in a military tribunal in Guantanamo Bay. After about nine months of editing and many screenings in which people responded well but with a mysterious discomfort they couldn't quite articulate, we screened for someone who expressed a point of view I didn't consider particularly helpful. But something in my understanding was stimulated by this screening experience. It's like, in listening to his negative feedback, I was able to grasp the problem we were having even though he didn't reference it. In this instance, I realized that people had felt unconsciously anxious because they sensed we were being used by a terrorist (the taxi driver) to tell his story. Thus, I saw that it was necessary to find ways to interpose the presence of the filmmaker in the story, to push back and, in effect, contain the audience's experience so they could engage with the film. So, among other things, we introduced the voice of the director, Laura Poitras, into the film, questioning Abu Jandal in the interviews. This helped create a big difference in audience response. But—back to the question about running out of gas—the ways you fill your tank are extremely variable. Often you have a relationship with a director in which you can revivify each other.

You mentioned some relationships can be poisonous to the process. Have you had that experience?
    Oh sure.

What's happening there? Clash of personalities?
    I've realized by now that if someone respects and accepts my process, I can work with that person even if we have differences. If I feel they have a vision and also accept my vision, we can work together. But if they shut me out of their process, and by the same token if I don't feel

they have a vision, then it's a disaster. In each of my negative experiences, I had a sense going in that there might be a problem with the filmmaker's approach or personality—they're kind of indistinguishable, really. But in each case, I had a reason for taking the job and, unfortunately, I was right in my concern each time. So I think it's critical that if you have enough of a career where you can make choices about what you work on, be very careful. I haven't always made the right choices, but I am very cautious.

Because so much of your energy is invested as well.

Well, you're basically getting married to somebody when you work on a film. (*Laughs.*) It's a process in which you and the director are growing together, even if you, as the editor, might sometimes have more experience. And you know, being married to the right person is just fine. But sometimes, maybe you just take them on a lunch date and that's it! (*Laughs.*)

Do you find that because some filmmakers don't have a strong vision for the film at the outset, they will gather a ton of material and just hand it over to you to figure it out?

By and large, with feature documentaries, filmmakers often do shoot for a long time, and sometimes their ideas are not very evolved, but there is a tremendous sense of purpose in spite of that. Something is driving them to shoot and they are following their instincts and immersing themselves in a world. In addition, because of the nature of shooting documentary or even conducting the interviews for a documentary, you don't really know what you're getting until you begin screening the material. In Europe, it seems, they tend to work very differently. I remember, for *Paris Is Burning*, we worked with a British commissioning editor and he was like, "You've got to be kidding! All this footage? This endless schedule?" There, they spend like three months from idea to mix, with a script and a very tight, controlled schedule. The American way is to shoot and keep shooting; this was true even before the digital revolution.

What is the rationale for that excess? To cover every angle in case you need it?

Often it's looking for a story, knowing that you will need to form it and work it out in the editing room. So you need to cover more bases than you even knew you had—better to err on the side of caution and shoot more. From my standpoint, of course, this makes for a more arduous screening process, but later on, I am often happy about the wealth of choices.

Perhaps that partly comes from knowing that unexpected things can happen while shooting a documentary . . . like people die, as in Phyllis and Harold.

Yes, Cindy Kleine, the director, wanted to tell a story about her parents' marriage and what she learned about her mother's affair during that marriage. She had been shooting that film for years, but then her father Harold died in the process, and then her mother Phyllis died. But that reflects the natural evolution of a documentary. It's not like a movie star dying unexpectedly in the middle of a feature shoot!

Which might even shelve the film entirely. But certainly the documentary story had to shift gears in those cases.

But not its original intention, usually. Different aspects are affected depending on the circumstances. With *Phyllis and Harold,* both parents had died by the time I began editing, so that was already a given in the story I was telling. Their deaths were a crucial part of the meaning of the film from the outset. In *Streetwise,* one character, Duane, killed himself while we were editing, and the director Martin Bell shot his funeral, which became part of the film. In *Paris Is Burning,* Venus, one of the transvestites in the film, died towards the end of the editing process. We also filmed material around her death. Those deaths were terribly painful, both very young people. Their deaths underscored for me the extreme vulnerability that the members of those worlds, Seattle street kids and Harlem drag queens, were subject to.

As sad as those turns of fate can be, they also dimensionalize the characters as real people and help cap the story of their lives.

Yes, and as an editor, you need to be open to anything and everything that will give characters dimension. There are many ways to achieve this, but you must always concern yourself with the portrayal's emotional and dramatic logic. You are maintaining credibility and trust with the audience, just as you need to in a fiction film. In fiction, it's a combination of the screenwriter's and director's sensibility and what the director is doing with the actors. In documentaries, the *editing* is the script. And the editor is in control of many of those elements of credibility and trust with the audience.

Yet certain filmic devices typically associated with documentaries might also distance an audience from engaging in the story . . . namely, "talking heads."

Well, I feel everything rests on how you approach the "talking head." I think a talking head should be treated like a scene. You should feel this person is giving you the same energy you might get if you were watching them in their life. For example, *Arguing the World* is all talking heads! And my sense was that ultimately it didn't matter. The interview doesn't have to pull you out of the story. When people are in the moment, in the grip of what they are telling you, then you *are* pulled in. But if they are not in the moment, then it's deadly—then it's a true "talking head." So you have to be very sensitive to the way the "head" is talking! (*Laughs.*) It's all about making the subject come alive. It doesn't matter whether it's someone sitting still and flapping their lips at the camera, or whether they're talking while moving around cooking a meal and being stressed. It's all grist for generating feelings—or it should be. In a film with the deadly kind of talking heads, you're not just being pulled out of the experience, you're being *kept out.*

Joseph Dorman, who directed Arguing the World, *interviewed a number of American communists to include in the film, but then you threw out all those interviews. Why?*

(*Laughs.*) We had to. We were groping so intensively with the material and were so without a clue for how we could make it work!

Let's hear the details.

Well, the film is about four New York intellectuals—Irving Howe, Nathan Glazer, Daniel Bell, and Irving Kristol—and it follows them over sixty years. It was the most uniquely challenging and demanding film I have ever worked on. It was enormously difficult to figure out how to be true to each of their four life stories, to the history of those sixty years, and to capturing the flow of dramatic movement in the film. I was really happy when I first saw the material and felt these were incredibly funny, articulate men. The first material I worked on was the "easy" stuff, their early memories. The advantage of working on a sequence based on childhood recollection was that I didn't need much background knowledge for their early years. But once I finished editing this sequence, my lack of knowledge of what these four men were *really* talking about became a pressing concern for me. Though I had a skeletal knowledge of the subject matter, working with most of the remaining interview material required my knowledge to be both sweeping and specific. I kept asking: how do we tell the *rest* of the story? How do we make it dramatic? How do we make it alive? And we were in a pit for months! This happens with documentaries sometimes—you can really go to some very dark places! (*Laughs.*)

And get paid while you're down there, right?

You get paid! I mean, the poor director might not be getting paid or needs to take on other work, but the editor usually gets paid.

How does one come up with new approaches to the material while in a dark pit?

You revisit the film daily and you struggle with it. The demands of every film are different. In this case, I knew that to construct a credible narrative, I had to grasp the nuances of these four men's stories—plus six decades of world and political intellectual history! Joe began to feed me a constant diet of books and articles, writings by the four men, histories of the American Left, transcripts of HUAC [House Un-American Activities Committee] sessions, autobiographies of American communists, and much, much more. It took me six months of reading just to get up to speed and I had to continue reading for the duration of the project. Joe and I had also developed parallel idiosyncratic ideas about the use of traditional narration in the film. Joe's notion was the idea of "minidocumentaries," two- to four-minute sequences throughout the film, each encapsulating a historical period—the Popular Front, the McCarthy period, the late sixties. These minidocumentaries would provide the necessary historical backdrop for each section of the film and free us to concentrate on the four men's stories and let their arguments rip, so to speak.

Narration is another potentially deadly documentary device, isn't it?

Yes, and I wanted to dispense with the narration completely, except within the minidocumentaries. It's been my experience that narration can flatten a film, particularly if a filmmaker uses it to avoid the challenge of telling a story organically. If the minidocumentaries worked properly, narration in the body of the film would not be necessary. An outside voice wouldn't have to step on the liveliness of this sixty-year story being told through these men's arguments. I made a ten-hour assembly organized by theme—we had twenty themes—and spent the next months attempting to refine it. We began to feel excited about the process and about the many possibilities the film could have.

I gather the excitement didn't last long.

A nagging sense was growing that we didn't really understand how to tell such a huge story—or even what was most important in it. Perhaps there were too many possibilities. In addition, Joe and I began to disagree all the time politically. We had heated discussions about communism, McCarthyism, and the sixties. We were anxious that the other's political point of view would contaminate the film. Out of this intense seesawing of our own arguments came a disturbing notion: the communist point of view constantly referenced in the interviews with the four men was not adequately represented in the film by actual communists! Given that the communists were the opposition, how could there be any lively and true back-and-forth without adding them into the mix? So with my encouragement, Joe proceeded to shoot interviews with several American communists.

Which should have helped balance the arguments.

So we thought. We spent a lot of time trying to integrate the communists into the film. One or two were lively enough, engaging, even inspiring. They should have enlivened the film and fleshed out the issues in the thirties, forties, and fifties. We worked and reworked the communist interviews, trying different versions and combinations. It seemed inconceivable to us that their presence wouldn't help the film. But somehow, no matter what we did, the sequences never gelled. Gradually, the communist interviews fell away from the film one by one. This was a terrible feeling: we had gotten no return on a huge investment of time and labor. We did, however, come to a painful understanding of one important reality: the film worked best when we closely adhered to the point of view of the four intellectuals. What proved most interesting over and over were their debates with each other and their evolving *attitudes* about the opposition. Including the actual voices of the opposition only seemed to flatten the film. With this focus in mind, we completed a three-and-a-half-hour long version of the film after a year of editing, laced with minidocumentaries and no narration. We were ready to screen it. We had modest hopes that we were on the right track, but we didn't dare hope for much. The result, however, was crushing. The film was so formless and boring, it took our breath away! Too stunned to turn the lights up when the film was over, Joe and I sat there expressing our feelings of fear in the dark. What had we been doing all this time and how could it have been so wrong? By the time we turned on the lights, we understood the truth: we had to add narration. We had been trying to tell the entire story only through what came out of people's mouths, putting a huge burden on the four men's interviews, and it was sinking the film.

You must have had a major mindset shift to accept narration when you were so opposed to it. How did you work through that process?

We located sections of the film where we felt narration might be needed and removed the extensive interview material that had served the function of narration. Joe would then draft a narration line which we would discuss and try out. Each piece of narration usually went through ten drafts, and often many more, because it had to convey complex information as tersely as possible. Each draft of each line would be recorded to try it against the footage. Typically, to muffle room noise while recording, one of us would crouch under my down jacket while reading into a microphone! This happened hundreds of times. As draft after draft was put in and improved, the film began to flow. Now the *minidocumentaries* felt like interruptions and were removed. Any last remnant of a communist interview also bit the dust. The film began to work as a story, but now a new problem emerged.

As you said earlier, when you change one part of the film, it affects the whole.

Yes. Now the film *moved*, but it was virtually an unbroken mass of older, male voices! We needed other kinds of sounds to break up the low throaty rumble. We addressed the problem in three ways. First, we began to place background sound effects under the archival footage in the film. The second line of attack was to find a narrator who had neither a typical neutral narrator's voice nor one too close in character to the older men in the film. We needed a voice that would exist in some natural relation to the four men, but not be of their generation—a youthful voice with a New York feel to it. After listening to scores of audition tapes, we heard Alan Rosenberg read a short story and felt he was exactly right. The third and most pivotal solution was opening up the film with music. We pinpointed many spots that could take music and worked with composer Adam Guettel, who had a deep and insightful take on the film and whose music was crucial in bringing it to another level. He created lovely evocative music which we used very pragmatically to break the sound of the voices.

It's as if you have an all-blue painting and you take a trowel and put slashes of yellow in it—that's how I was responding to the film physically with the music. While not an easy film, you can take it in more easily with the breathing of the music.

Another allusion to your painting experience. Can you think of other parallels for what editing this film felt like?

Well, yes. Editing this film was like playing a game of three-dimensional chess. We always had to consider several elements at any given moment: four men's stories, sixty years of history, the dramatic momentum, the pace, the visual component—all occurring simultaneously. We had to be true to each element and could not drop one because it didn't seem to work. Doing so might cause us to misrepresent a person's point of view or historical circumstance. We had to constantly search for a successful way to combine what worked emotionally with what was true in these men's stories, what was true at the historical moment, and what was true to the film's momentum. This level of stricture is unique in my editing experience. Other film projects might have long stretches where the major concern is only what feels right at a given moment and one's sole reference point is the film's structure. But that's more like two-dimensional chess!

While this was likely a one-of-a-kind experience, it must have posed valuable lessons for you as editor.

Yes, it did. One lesson was that our attempt to work without narration for as long as we did helped push us to tell the story through what was strong in the interviews and create a back-and-forth with the four protagonists. Those misbegotten minidocumentaries were also a valuable exercise in condensing complex historical material which helped when we created the narration. Dropping the communist interviews helped us to perceive the film's true nature—that we must relentlessly focus on the four men. Even the constant friction of our political differences helped us reach a standoff and we were impelled to embrace evenhandedness as our guiding principle. So I suppose the real lesson for me in all of this was that bad ideas can be fertilizer—they can lay a fertile ground for crucial realizations.

The four intellectuals were very open about their thoughts and feelings. Can you give an example where you had to dig more deeply into the psychology of multiple characters who were not as open?

The most extreme example of the need to unearth the psychology of the subjects is *Children Underground.* Here, I was presented with a group of Romanian kids living a very, very primitive life on the street and in the subways, where just finding an empty bottle to put water in is a major daily task and they are constantly taking drugs which affect their minds. They have violent drug-induced altercations on a regular basis. The one given in the material was that by the end of the film, some kids would be going home to their parents, if only to visit. Therefore, to establish their individuality in any way and create interest in them as people was the major task of the film—to make that life on the street, and the children's interaction with it, something that an audience could identify with on some level. Some kids were more expressive than others, but some were quite close-mouthed and others almost deranged. There was a huge need to excavate their personalities and find out how they could come alive in this dark world so that, by the end, you could go home with them and be interested in their fate. One challenge was that the content of many scenes was bizarre and unfamiliar—like there might be a noisy street battle over trading a drug for some fish to eat. There was the danger that you could be distracted by these events and miss getting character information. So we constantly used smatterings of voiceovers—a child, a social worker—and sometimes got a tremendous amount of information just from the look on someone's face. Fully revealing scenes for many of these kids only came at the end when they went home, so everything else about their individuality and psychology had to be teased out in small ways. When I first saw a bit of the footage, very graphic and untranslated, I didn't think I would be able to work on the film, that I would find it too depressing. I was actually skeptical about whether it could even work as a film. But once I had watched a few of the translated interview pieces, I saw the potential to draw real characters and this gave me a very positive feeling about moving forward with the editing.

How do you know which pieces of film are necessary to a story and which are not? That is, you may start out with an eight-hour assembly and boil it down to a hundred and ten minutes. What goes and what stays?

Well, with *Paris Is Burning,* we had a twenty-hour assembly—or collection, I should say. Then we had three hours, then an hour-forty rough cut, then we were down to sixty-five minutes by the last two weeks of editing.

And the actual running time was seventy-eight minutes.

Yes. Director Jennie Livingston said, "Look, it can't be so short, it needs to be at least seventy-five minutes. And there are scenes we really want in." And I said, "But it's really working now!"

In other words, leave it alone! (Laughs.)

But Jennie said, "What about this scene? And this scene?" There was a scene of Brooke and Carmen, transsexual and transvestite, frolicking on the beach, and another scene of Pepper LaBeiga speaking out against getting a sex change—both great scenes. Now when I had been an assistant editor and learning editing largely by osmosis, I had gleaned that if something is really close to finished and tightly structured, you can sometimes find spots to put in extra material. It's counterintuitive but true. So I was able to find places for those two scenes. That added three-and-a-half minutes of the ten-plus minutes we needed. Then I said, "Why don't we have a seven-minute end credit sequence to push the running time over seventy-five minutes?" *(Laughs.)* Which we ended up doing! We added many of our favorite moments that hadn't made it into the film and our structure was left intact.

You had recognized the limit of what would fit in or what had to be taken out of the film.

Well, you do know what has to go after a while. I mean, have you ever looked at a reassembled version of *Lawrence of Arabia*—which I love, by the way. Seeing that film with the extra minutes added back in, you just *know* where those minutes are because the film seems to die there. You can feel it. And in editing a film, you reach a point where the emotions flow well enough that you become very sensitive to what may actually be interfering or to material that is subtly repetitive. So, in *Lawrence of Arabia,* I can feel the dead spots. But, in a seeming twist, you can also *reintroduce* moments that were formerly cut out because the structure is such that it can accommodate good material. It's especially critical with long-form documentary that you have enough time to edit so that you *can* bring back ideas you had early on discarded because they didn't seem to work then. That would not be possible without a solid structure in place. In fact, it can actually become essential to reintroduce material. Certain scenes might have been part of your initial vision, but you sifted them out early on because the proper context for them didn't exist. Only later do they eventually find their way back in.

Such as?

Again, in *The Oath,* the protagonist Abu Jandal had worked for Osama bin Laden. He is a very articulate and smart man, but also elusive and tricky. He has become a taxi driver and, in a few scenes, he's driving and lying to his passengers about the camera they see attached to the window. He says it's broken. This is, of course, the very camera that is filming the scene. So I cut a sequence of him lying to this passenger and to that passenger. But once I saw that sequence, I said, forget it, this is not good. It was an interesting idea that would show he was deceptive, but it wasn't working with the material we had put together at that point. After a series of screenings, as I mentioned before, people seemed to like the film, but there was something missing for them which they couldn't define—something was wrong.

Yes, this was where you said you had made a pivotal discovery. Can you elaborate?

People were missing the presence of the *filmmaker* pushing back against this guy. All along, we'd tried to let him tell his own story, but people felt uncomfortable because they didn't approve of him as a person and didn't want him to tell his story to them. They had felt subtly insecure in their viewing experience. So at a certain point in the film, I reinserted the scene of him lying about the camera and added some questions that director Laura Poitras asked him in their interviews. That completely changed the viewing experience of the film. The audience felt reassured that the filmmakers were not having the wool pulled over their eyes as dupes of some Al Qaeda demagogue. While this idea was very much on our minds early on, it could not be part of the construction of the story at the beginning. But once we had enough of a structure in place, the need for that scene became clear and imperative.

So the character—and what he represented for post-9/11 audiences—was so uncomfortable for them that you needed to insert a reminder that the filmmaker, and not this character, was telling this story.

Essentially. What made people unconsciously uncomfortable was the sense that we were being his mouthpiece. So we were affirming for them that *we* were in control of the process. We understood that he was a liar and that he needed to be questioned and not just presented as someone telling his story. We were pushing back against him and allowing the audience enough security to have an emotional experience about him, acting as a container for the audience's feelings. In telling a story about someone so unusual and suspect, the filmmaker's presence in the film became an anchor—something we had overlooked initially because our focus had been to provide a structure for the film. Now the taxi/camera scene became a zone where the audience could feel the character wasn't dominating the viewing experience. Rather, the director had a conscious-ness of the character's qualities and was, in a sense, pursuing him. We also removed all the cutaways during his interviews, which were subliminally suggesting to the audience that we were helping him tell his story. We chose to go with plain jump cuts.

Would you consider that manipulating the audience—even for a good reason?

In any film, there's not a moment, not even a molecule of *not* manipu-lating an audience. And *I'm* the audience. Basically, I'm manipulating myself! *(Laughs.)* But you don't even have to use the word *manipulating*. It's working to create a vision of the material. I'm trying to fulfill or express a vision, and there's just no objectivity there. You can be true to something insofar as *your* understanding of the truth is being fulfilled. You can be true to something by your own lights, and that is pretty much the most you can do. You can also be false to something, which is a sin in documentary.

When would that happen?

When someone lies about a fact to make the story better or creates facts that didn't happen. I know somebody who does this.

That person should work in fiction film, then. (Laughs.)

That person should. To be true to our vision of the film, we attempt to ground it in reality, in true moments. But it's a fallacy to even think about objectivity.

However, the way you color a perspective can sway a film in different directions. Propaganda films take it to an extreme.

You're always coloring something in film. There's no way around it. How would you not color something? But it's all about intention. I'm *not* making propaganda films. The *intention* with which you approach the documentary filmmaking process is critical. If someone intends to make a propaganda film, you are still using the inevitable tools of coloring or manipulation—whatever you want to call it—but you have a different intention.

So your intention in making documentaries is to probe your subjects for what they reveal about themselves in a way that is safe for the audience.

My intention is to make art, and in documentary, one of the major building blocks of the artistic process is human psychology. That is what I respond to most intensely. However, the question of safety for the audience changes from film to film. In some films, it is not an issue. In *The Oath*, it was necessary. In *Children Underground*, it was important for the audience to feel unsafe, although grounded in individual psychology.

What were your feelings about taking on the editing of The Oath, *a controversial film which you must have thought would inflame American audience sensitivities around 9/11?*

For me, editing is a form of self-expression. Through it, I am able to convey aspects of my feeling about life. I try hard to work on projects that allow for this, both through their subject matter and their lack of a preset agenda. When I began to work with the material that became *The Oath*, I felt it was a real opportunity for me to experience some measure of healing around my own 9/11 trauma. As a New Yorker and an American, I had spent years feeling terribly upset by the blow delivered by bin Laden and the subsequent blows delivered by President Bush. *The Oath* contained material that addressed both the nature of the threat from radical Islam and the threat to our Constitution from an overzealous executive branch—in this, it seemed unique. The story contained both Abu Jandal, bin Laden's former bodyguard who was the taxi driver, and his brother-in-law, Salim Hamdan, facing military trial at Guantanamo. I felt that the director had created a really great vehicle for understanding our whole terrorism situation in depth. An unforeseen and important challenge then emerged because Abu Jandal exhibited so many sides to his personality. Often, in working with a character, I will encounter what feels like two sides. For instance, an idealist who has a self-serving streak, or a devoted parent with a bad temper. This is frequently the limit of what people show in front of a camera. With Abu Jandal, I witnessed a parade of eight or ten personalities: nuanced intellectual, haranguing ideologue, loyal friend and retainer, treacherous self-promoter. He was charming, fierce, gentle, garrulous, and dead-eyed—not to mention a brilliant liar and a reliable source of Al Qaeda lore. So this was the first big obstacle I encountered. I couldn't conceive of a credible narrative about an individual who exhibited this many personalities. What sort of context could hold it together and not make it feel like a bizarre series of fragments? In the end, all we could do was edit scenes that reflected all these sides, string them together, and live with this assembly, watching it repeatedly and refining it. This slowly evolved into making the revelation of these sides the heart of the film's story, so that it became a surprise, a pleasure, *and* a danger to encounter each facet of his personality. This, in turn, served a very important point of the film, which was to present our enemy as a multifaceted human being. To help understand exactly what we are dealing with and not just regenerate images promoted by the government and the mainstream media since 9/11. Those images of the Muslim world, by the way, are a good example of propaganda.

Do you find this psychology in fiction films also?
    It should be there, yes. Oddly, it often goes missing.

Does Lawrence of Arabia *fit that bill for you?*
    I think *Lawrence of Arabia* definitely was an exploration of the psychology of a real person, someone who was ripe for it. You just want to know what drove Lawrence of Arabia.

How would you turn his story into a documentary and achieve the same psychology?
    In documentary, you have a real challenge when you work with subjects who are no longer living. One of the hardest jobs is to make someone alive again in a documentary. Fiction films do that better because someone can actually embody the person. Get a good actor who can embody that person's character and being. In a documentary, you have to jump through hoops to do that.

You could have reenactors.
    Yes, but why bother? Why not just make a fiction film? What's interesting is to work with people's real lives, to be affected by living people who have been filmed and find your vision of their story. I'm all for fiction films! *(Laughs.)* I'm all for them probing the psychology of individuals if

somebody has a real feeling for what humans are. Many fiction films don't do that. They are formulaic and not very interesting. However, I think I would much rather see *Lawrence of Arabia* the fiction film than *Lawrence of Arabia* the documentary. Joe Dorman, the director who made *Arguing the World,* is now making a film about Sholem Aleichem, the Yiddish writer, which is coming along beautifully because it's working on the level of poetry. It's a visual and auditory poem. But there is a tremendous disadvantage in not having a live subject, so you're forced into making filmic poetry, and some people don't know how to do that. I personally endeavor not to work on films about people who are no longer alive. I like 'em living! *(Laughs.)*

Wouldn't you have more imaginative play with fictional characters?

As an editor? For me, the writing function of a documentary editor is so compelling—making the story out of the footage. I have edited fiction and I just don't find it anywhere near as fulfilling and as gripping as editing documentary. Maybe if I wrote the screenplay of a fiction film and *then* edited it! But from my experience on features, you feel the pressure of money weighing on you daily. It's enormously stressful. And the editor is often low man on the totem pole. But in documentary, the editing room is a critical place and the editor is the screenwriter. That's too good to pass up!

Do you think there's also a specific psychology to becoming an editor? Or is editing something a person just falls into doing?

I fell into it! I don't think people are enough aware of editing to make a decision about doing it, especially when they're children! *(Laughs.)* I always liked movies growing up, watched *Million Dollar Movie* on TV, where they'd run the same movie over and over, and I'd see films like *The Alamo* or *Ben-Hur* six or more times. I don't know whether that had any effect on me, but my goal wasn't to go into movies.

Ironic, isn't it.

Yes, it is. And I think editing is still a very anonymous situation. Now, I hate the anonymity of an editor. I resent it. But once, after a screening of *Phyllis and Harold,* Cindy Kleine's husband, Andre Gregory, the theater director—you know, *My Dinner with Andre*—was blown away by it. He said to me, "I can't believe what you did. You're like the cathedral builders!" *(Laughs.)* Anonymous artists. However, I feel the critical and scholarly study of a given documentary is not valid unless it addresses the editor's role in the creation of that film. It is important to understand how vital and integral editing is and how specific and wide-ranging the editor's contribution is. It is also contemplative, like writing. People who are contemplative and interested in how events unfold over time, as in a story, might find themselves becoming editors. I think of it as hands-on contemplation. But, of course, you can't become an editor the way you used to, which was to spend five years as an assistant and gain wisdom by osmosis. Now you learn the Avid, learn Final Cut, master the guts of the computer, and then jump into editing films. It's straight up the mountain now and you learn everything on the job. But when I started editing, I had a pool of voices in my head, the voices of people concerned about how to tell a story or how to solve problems with a character. Nowadays people might not find that anymore, but they still have to confront the same problems of story and character. They're jumping in and learning in a very different way. It's not a worse way, just different. Actually, I feel I've had the best of both worlds. Though I began my career when film was cut on flatbeds and I could learn by osmosis, most of my professional editing experience has been on computers, which I prefer. Unfortunately, it is now more isolated than when I started out. When I switched from painting, I was so used to being alone that when I went into a film editing room with two other people, it was like a party! People laughed at me when I said that because they considered the editing room a very lonely place. Now, one is often working alone, but even so, I don't generally feel isolated.

It seems you are in excellent company when you work with good characters.

It helps a lot. But you do need to talk to a real human once in a while!

Would you ever make your own film?

I did try to make a film a few years ago which didn't pan out. But my experience with production and shooting on that film and some of the documentaries I've edited gave me something very valuable. I understood what the other side was up against and it allowed me to have a gentler relationship with everyone's struggles and what they weren't able to capture on tape. It also made me understand—even though I might again try making a film—my own process, which is contemplative as opposed to intensely physically engaged. I deeply enjoy the process of contemplating the implications in the footage. And contemplation for me also involves an openness to impulses from the unconscious. You are working very much in tandem with your unconscious and you have to allow for accidents to bubble up.

How does your unconscious collaborate with your conscious mind?

The unconscious is always operating because you have responses to everything at all times that are not part of your thinking brain. And those unconscious responses inform a vision, which is essential to an editor. Once you finish screening raw footage, the most important task is to read that footage with a visceral imagining of its possibilities—what that film could be. At that point, you are thrown into a situation where you are trying to work with, perhaps in a very crude way, various elements that often take the form of scenes. That is when your receptivity to what bubbles up from your unconscious creates a symbiotic relationship with your intention and your conscious vision. There's a kind of unity between your vision and what rises from the unconscious, since the unconscious gave birth to your vision anyway. Working in this way, you can learn to be receptive and accept ideas—or you can reject them. Something may not feel right because it's not part of what you're envisioning. But it's vital to allow the overflow from the unconscious to fill your work. Also, when you have been doing this for a number of years, there is a second-nature aspect to it so that you're not thinking anymore as much about small details, such as whether two shots go together. You just *know*. And you can quickly reject ten choices, ten possibilities, whereas before you might have had to look at each one closely. Part of it all is having enough confidence in your unconscious process to ride it and let it give back to you some of what you are putting in.

Do you think an inability to understand these deep connections contributes to the types of poisonous working relationships you mentioned before?

Every artist goes through a similar process and if you're working with someone who respects your process, you will work out any problems between you. Someone who is not interested in your process will never understand what you are doing and you shouldn't work with that person— it's as simple as that! The most important thing for an editor to possess is the ability to have a vision for a film, to imagine, after screening the footage, what it could be—and hopefully to have that vision in some relationship with the director's vision. But sometimes it isn't. Then it's a question of whether you have enough faith in each other's process to negotiate a good working collaboration.

Did you have visions for your paintings too?

I did. I was painting from life, but I had a powerful sense of the object that I was painting and a way of seeing it. It was truly nonverbal and silent. Film gave me an opportunity to expand what I could express and to work on more levels. For me, the multifacetedness of film is exhibited in many ways. It's commonly said that a scene should do just one thing, but I always feel that each scene should accomplish at least two things, if not three or four.

For example?

In *Caught in the Crossfire,* there is a short scene with a Palestinian priest who is undergoing a crisis because his parents want to return to Palestine, where their hometown is under attack, and he is trying to convince them not to. You can see him almost dying on the couch because he is so upset. But by the end, he becomes passive-aggressive: "Okay, go ahead, go ahead, and call me from there." You are getting a very deep look at his personality; he's devastated because he's losing his parents, yet he shows this almost childish passive-aggressive side. And mostly, you see his face while you hear the voice of his wife trying to mediate between them. The scene works on several levels. It delivers an understanding of different aspects of his character—his morose charm, his love for his parents, and his passive-aggressiveness which you wouldn't have seen otherwise. There is a tremendous internal push-pull felt just by seeing his reactions. The scene also shines a light on a world situation from somebody's living room. And it's a very strong plot point which is resolved at the end of the film. If the material is rich and there is a need for it, there is no reason why a scene shouldn't do quadruple duty.

Would that be a kind of portrait you could capture on canvas?

The complex mix of visual and aural elements unfolding in time is unique to film. That particular experience simply cannot be replicated in any other medium.

5. **Capturing the Feeling**

LUCIA ZUCCHETTI

1995 *Soprano (Synchro Year 3)* (short), dir. Dani Williamson

1996 *Just a Little Crush* (short), dir. Louise Wadley

1996 *Small Deaths* (short), dir. Lynne Ramsay

1996 *Kill the Day* (short), dir. Lynne Ramsay

1998 *Anthrakitis* (short), dir. Sara Sugarman

1997 *Gasman* (short), dir. Lynne Ramsay

1999 *Ratcatcher,* dir. Lynne Ramsay

2000 *The Low Down,* dir. Jamie Thraves

2002 *Spyhole* (short), dir. Jodhi May

2002 *Long Time Dead,* dir. Marcus Adams

2002 *Morvern Callar,* dir. Lynne Ramsay

2002 *Ten Minutes Older: The Cello,* "Addicted to the Stars," dir. Michael Radford

2003 *Intermission,* dir. John Crowley

2003 *The Deal,* TV, dir. Stephen Frears

2004 *The Merchant of Venice,* dir. Michael Radford

2005 *Mrs. Henderson Presents,* dir. Stephen Frears

2006 *The Queen,* dir. Stephen Frears

2007 *Boy A,* dir. John Crowley

2009 *Cheri,* dir. Stephen Frears

2010 *Tilda*, TV pilot, dir. Bill Condon

2011 *Game Change*, dir. Jay Roach

AWARDS

2007 Eddie Award (ACE) nomination, Best Edited Feature Film—Dramatic, *The Queen*

2007 BAFTA Film Award nomination, Best Editing, *The Queen*

2007 European Film Awards nomination, Prix d'Excellence (Editing), *The Queen*

2008 BAFTA TV Award, Best Editing Fiction-Entertainment, *Boy A*

A common thread linking most editors' experiences is a sense of musicality, and Lucia Zucchetti emphasizes this point frequently in discussing what editors think about or feel when cutting. Whether music is part of a sequence—or purposely *not* used when expected—Zucchetti considers how music allows audiences to incorporate their personal feelings into what they are seeing. She cites several examples from the award-winning film *The Queen*, in which both the use and nonuse of music play a pivotal role in underscoring the poignant events surrounding the death of Princess Diana. Zucchetti also discusses more of the "atypical" in that narrative film through intercutting archival footage with principal photography. This unscripted combination created the vital component of tension that lifted mere "action" into a memorable tribute and a subtle commentary.

Zucchetti's fascination with the "atypical" recalls Corrao's inquiring-mind approach and Oppenheim's need to experiment in the editing room. Like Monroe as well, Zucchetti has edited for directors with contrasting styles, from a "free-form" quasi-documentary style creating dreamlike fiction films to more structured, glossy, traditional narratives. Zucchetti's comparisons and contrasts of these styles offer insights into unique ways of cutting to capture the pivotal feelings within the stories. "Great" editing, for Zucchetti, is the personal achievement of articulating the director's vision while creating a resonating "experience" for the audience—principles which many editors have echoed, particularly in the fiction-film domain. Collaborations with creative individuals in a film's productions can often trigger subjective and time-consuming debates, yet Zucchetti considers these perfect opportunities to pool the best resources available and grow the deepest essence from the film. The genteel intensity with which Zucchetti holds the greatest respect for her collaborators, her characters, and her audiences is clearly not up for debate.

How did you get involved in film editing?

All throughout my growing up in Italy, I was involved in the arts and performance world. As a child, I made up theater, created costumes, and loved to stage plays and choreographies. I also studied piano for a few years. When I think back now, that was probably the beginning of me expressing my passion for storytelling and the performing arts, something that grew in me and that I nurtured in my teenage years by going to drama school. Soon enough, however, I learned it was much harder to perform in front of a real audience—it seemed so much easier in front of family and friends! What I really enjoyed and what suited my personality was working on the ideas and preparation of everything, the behind-the-scenes.

Did you attend schools that fostered your interest in the arts?

Yes, eventually I did. In Italy, when you reach ninth grade, you can choose the orientation of your high school. For example, you could go to a more academic grammar school, study science, or go to an arts-oriented school. I chose the arts and I was lucky to go to a very progressive experimental school in Milan called Itsos, at Via Pace 10. This school's program was born out of the sixties' student movement and ideology—it was a place created as an alternative to very traditional, boring, stuffy Italian high schools. The school nurtured the growth of the individual rather than—as was most common in Italian schools—the acquisition of "data." In fact, it was the only place in Italy at the time where a teenager could study film as well as photography, graphic design, and cognitive psychology. Here, I became involved in making my very first film. This incredible experience as a teenager and a wonderfully supportive family gave me the strength to pursue my passion for film when I completed high school. Italy, again, did not have much to offer in terms of film and higher education. Most schools focused on academics rather than vocation. Since I had a sister studying in the U.K., I decided to explore what England had to offer. So I ended up in London and was offered a place to study at what used to be the Polytechnic of Central London (now University of Westminster), where I took a bachelor's in film, video, and photographic arts. During the three years I spent here, I "stumbled" upon editing and was inspired by brilliant teachers such as Joost Hunningher and wonderful industry professionals who were visiting tutors—screenwriter and director Tony Grisoni among them. Like many students, I don't think I knew what editing really was and what it entailed until I had a chance to do it myself. It is a very abstract art!

What did you finally come to understand about the editing process?

This course emphasized the importance of the collaborative process while making a film. We were encouraged to step into various head-of-department roles, and I remember not many people were putting their name forward to edit. I guess the glamour of directing or being on the set just wasn't associated with editing. So maybe out of good will—or accidentally—I was one of the first to "sacrifice" myself, and I volunteered to cut one student's film. I was surprised to discover that I not only loved the quiet, controlled, and self-reflective work that goes on in the cutting room—despite its "unglamorous" side—but that I had a knack for it as well. The job suited my creative skills *and* my introspective personality. I began to build a miniportfolio of student films that I edited, which allowed me to apply to the National Film and Television School in Beaconsfield, right outside London. I had always regarded this school as *the place* to study film in Europe, which had seemed so beyond my reach only a few years before. The best industry professionals visited, and students were lucky to shoot and edit film with the proper equipment, facilities, and support. These were the days when higher education in the U.K. was government-funded and one could get scholarships. Sadly, it's not like that anymore. Film education has become a real business.

Did you essentially major in editing?

I studied editing full-time for three years. It was a vocational postgraduate course of study, but you didn't have to have a degree to get in; you just applied to specialize in one area. If you were considered suitable for the course with the right qualities and experience, you would be offered a place. I edited many short films while I was there, but most importantly, I built relationships with fellow students that eventually took me out into the real world of making movies. The first feature I ever did, *Ratcatcher*, was directed by Lynne Ramsay, who was also a cinematography student there at the same time I was, as were other crucial collaborators on the project: DP Alwin Kuchler and Production Designer Jane Morton.

What was the knack for editing that you said you discovered?

It was many things. First, having a good instinct for choosing an image that is most relevant to the story or which image captures an emotion—and knowing how to preserve and heighten that emotion within the context of other images. I like to think all this connects to musicality and maybe to an innate quality of the heart—meaning one's ability to tap into one's own and other people's emotional spheres. I do regard myself as a highly emotional person—I take after my father *(laughs)*—and I did study piano when I was a child. In fact, one of my biggest regrets is not having pursued music more. You know, when you study music as a child, sometimes your desire to practice becomes a little dissolved by other things when you become a teenager. *(Sighs.)* But I do believe that my musical inclination and my innate sense of rhythm support my work as an editor enormously. All this, as I mentioned before, has to be combined with the right personality—an introspective personality—that can comfortably close the door and stay in a room pretty much by oneself to look at and feel the material. Then, working closely with one other person—the director—and becoming his or her eyes and ears. Finally, having an egoless approach to a project— that is *critical* for an editor. So I'd say the knack is a strange combination of artistic and diplomatic skills as well as self-confidence. Yet for all that, you have an absence of *you!* Editing is not about you, but about the director's vision and making the best film possible with what you are given. In my early days, however, I thought editing relied mostly on good musical instinct. All other intricacies became apparent later on.

Discovering the editing personality—and knowing you had one—must have felt personally rewarding.

Yes, it did. What makes one a good editor? I've discussed this question with other editors too and, of course, it is open to debate. Is one born with the qualities I just mentioned or does one learn them? Probably a bit of both. Though musicality, I believe, is something one is born with.

What about editing is musical, even if music is not part of a scene?

Much in a film is analogous to music. I would say while the cuts themselves can be compared to beats, the composition, movement, and light contained within an image have different degrees of energy that can be compared to notes and tone. So it's as if I feel a kind of music in my head when I put images together, like a sensation of beats and rhythms created by the visuals as well as by the cuts connecting the visuals. Sometimes it really feels like I am creating a melody when I edit. Of course, it is a very internal experience, so others might feel it differently. But when you discover that someone else, like the director or the audience, taps into it the same way you do, it can be the most rewarding feeling. In *Ratcatcher*, there is a sequence where the young boy James visits the vacant new housing scheme. The musicality of that sequence arose not only from the combination of shots and the length of each shot, but also from the internal energy and movement within the shots. I remember spending a *lot* of time on that sequence because Lynne Ramsay and DP Alwin Kuchler had shot so much footage. For the exterior part of this scene, they had gone into a real building site that they received permission to turn into a set, partly "dressed" it to make it look more like what was needed, and shot it in a very documentary style by letting the camera run while the kid jumped on scaffolding and played with building materials. I then had to cut this footage with interior shots, which, if I remember correctly, were shot on a set. We had a mountain of footage for that sequence and I recall we worked on it endlessly, but the sequence works beautifully, much like a quiet piece of classical music.

You basically created a montage of that boy's experience, without sound, speaking or musical score. With so many visuals to choose from, how did you know what to eliminate or keep? Is it a linear thinking process?

Again, I would probably attribute it to instinct. But I'd say building experience in the cutting room makes it easier to find one's way through the footage and choose what needs to stay, *why* it needs to stay, and in what order. Is it a linear process? Probably not, and I will get back to that in a moment. My recollection of editing *Ratcatcher* is that it was very hard work. All films are, of course, but this was my first feature, and I was cutting it on film (rather than digitally). I had beautiful visuals—in fact, too many beautiful pictures for some scenes. It is hard to be brutal with stunning images and to drop them because they do not help the film. What helped me be brave was remembering that whatever I decide to include in a sequence while cutting is actually not permanent, but only a step toward finding the perfect cut. When I realized that, I felt free to follow my instinct and find the best edits. There is nothing like the pressure to get it right the first time round, and it can happen, but in my experience, that most likely happens when you feel no pressure or when your director is not checking every single cut while you are making them! That is why I said that editing is not a linear process: when you place the sequence into the context of the larger film, you will almost certainly make new discoveries like the scene's real purpose or emphasis in the film, or how long a scene should be in the bigger scheme of things, or new bits of information that had not been so evident at script stage. These discoveries come out of the performances and/or the images themselves. As a result, these discoveries drive the director and editor to return to each scene to edit it to perfection—or at least certainly try.

As you describe it, the discovery process seems to be a process of clarification.

It is. You experience sudden feelings of increasing clarity for how everything should come together. It's no wonder that the very first cut coming out of the editing room is called the "first assembly." Of course, the editor tries to cut it as well as possible, but at this early stage during the shoot, an editor still won't know what images will precede or follow a scene being assembled, nor how other scenes yet to be shot will affect the scene that is now sitting in the editor's hands. There is the script continuity on paper, sure, but that does not identify the impact that the direction, visuals, and actors' interpretation may have on that continuity until the editor actually sees the footage. As the pieces slowly come together, it is easier to understand what will sharpen that original sequence—and then you tweak. Interestingly, you may find you got it absolutely right the first time around. How beautiful is the magic of editing! *(Laughs.)* But more often than not, editing a feature is an incredible—and incredibly long and complicated—journey of discovery.

The Queen *had a number of montages that either built tension or made subtle commentary. In the case of building tension, I think of the poignant montage soon after the film began of the fatal car crash involving Princess Diana. It mixed both archival material and re-creation with actors. What did you wish to capture by mixing those two forms instead of relying on one or the other?*

That sequence was the result of a lot of trials and tests and much debate. When I read the script, I remember that screenwriter Peter Morgan had ended the scene of the paparazzi chasing Dodi and Diana and the fatal accident in the Paris tunnel with a fade to black. No accident is shown, no sound is heard—everyone knows the outcome. I was so relieved to see that the script was only *suggesting* the event and not showing it in all its terrible detail. After all, the film was not about that. I felt at the time that nothing could represent the accident better than a fade to black, which would allow the audience to tap into their own memories of the event. Anyway, while on set, as sometimes happens, director Stephen Frears and DP Affonso Beato decided to shoot an image that was not originally planned, a shot that abstractly captured the moment of collision. I appreciated the attempt, it was abstract, it was subtle, but I never thought it would work. This became one subject of great discussion in editing that sequence. Everyone became involved—producers, director, writer, and in this case, the DP who strongly believed that what he shot was the right way to end the scene. Whenever he said that, Stephen would say to him, "Talk to Lucia!" He would joke about it because he knew how I felt. Of course, Stephen was the final arbitrator, but he is so open to his collaborators' suggestions that we did try the last shot in several ways. I'm happy to say I feel it finally became the best possible sequence we could have had.

The sequence ended up including archival footage, correct?

Yes, archive was the other major variable that affected the scene—and the film overall. It also amplified and lengthened the debates in the editing process. Once that archive "box" is open, endless possibilities spring out! Given that we were dealing with an event of historic proportions, the quantity of available material was vast. It was easy to spend a lot of time on it, sometimes losing the focus of what we were trying to achieve. We were extremely lucky to have a brilliant brain researching the material for us, Adam Curtis, who is a writer and documentarian. His excellent films such as *The Power of Nightmares* and *Century of the Self* were made solely out of archive and have a very specific voice and, because of it, have engendered much controversy. Again, Stephen, being so generous in giving space to his collaborators, brought Adam in for *The Queen* to present his ideas to us. We had actually worked together for the first time on *The Deal*, which Peter Morgan wrote as a kind of a prequel to *The Queen*, and then later on *Mrs. Henderson Presents* when we felt that the world wars—the context of the story—needed to be felt more vividly through archive. *The Deal* became our testing ground for the work that was needed to balance live action and archive footage in the smartest way possible. With his access to incredible archive footage, Adam can spot subtext in the imagery and understand juxtapositions as well as any editor would. We had regular sessions where Stephen would leave us to experiment with and debate the footage that would eventually support the scene and background to the story, and add complexity and wit. Adam's vision is brilliant but very specific, so I felt it important to ensure that what he brought to the film could be integrated—with regard to both substance and style—into Stephen's vision of the film.

What did that fortunate blend of archive and live action eventually produce?

Well, given that the use of archive was never intended to be there—in fact, it was probably not intended in many other parts of the film—we realized that if used just *so,* the archive would add an unbelievable texture, complexity, and emotion to our main story. As it was originally, the chase scene in Paris played too much like an action movie and did not feel right. I have to admit, we even got to the point of wondering why we were spending so much time on it! I think one of our producers finally encouraged us to experiment with archive for the chase, even though that was not the original plan. Adam had brought us so much incredible material of Diana that she was actually becoming a new character in the film—a ghostly presence, if you will. So we decided, why not push it further? The producer reinforced this by suggesting that we think about the idea that before one dies, it is said a person glimpses his or her whole life. That became the basis of our work on that sequence and every other scene in which Diana's past life reentered the story. We could not play the car chase from Diana's POV, of course, but the images we ultimately selected of her life to intercut into the car chase were charged with emotion and symbolism. The impact of the scene suddenly became heightened to the maximum. It was clever, it had heart, and everyone seemed to love it. At that point, I finally knew what would be the *last* shot of that chase sequence. Not the car crash. Not an abstract image of a collision. In the archive, I saw an image of Diana putting her hand up to cover the lens of a paparazzi's camera. *That* was the end. To me, it even topped the fade to black. We had reached the end of the moments of her life as she entered the tunnel, and her gesture closing off the camera lens was her way of saying, "Please leave me alone now." That completely fit the tone of the film.

Very touching indeed. The use of archival material had clearly elevated the montage to a new meaning. It no longer was a straightforward car chase scene, which could have been simply executed through re-creation.

Yes, and that really had been our starting point, as I said. I think in the original shooting script, that's the way that sequence was meant to be. We had a *lot* of footage for this chase, and the very first cut only used the principal photography, but the feeling of an action sequence did not fit. We knew we had to do something different, and fortunately, archive became the solution. It required so much of our time because, once archive becomes a variable in the film, too much of it can distract, dilute, and even destroy the story. It becomes a very fine balancing act.

Did you also feel that you wanted to comment editorially—perhaps it was in the script anyway—on the problem relationship Diana had with the royal family, who for the most part treated her rather coolly?

Well, everyone, as part of a team, has personal feelings about such issues, but sometimes it's almost better to keep those feelings private. *(Laughs.)* You're working in a team and, number one, you're trying to serve the director's vision. Of course, good directors will surround themselves with people who have the right sensibility for what they are trying to do. In other words, there is most likely a great respect for each other's opinion—even in the midst of a disagreement! Your train of thought as an editor will lead you to construct a film in a certain way even while listening to a director's notes—it is probably impossible to separate the two things. But once everyone sees what you are pulling together, the interpretation of the scene—whatever it turns out to be—will be appreciated, and that is fantastic! Of course, sometimes the sequence is appreciated for reasons other than the editor's intentions. It is only human for people to project their subjective experiences onto a film.

I mention the subtle commentary because I recall the striking image toward the end of the film, after the queen resisted paying tribute to Diana but finally yielded to public demand for an appearance by the royal family. At one key point, to conclude a scene after her funeral, you inserted an archival shot of Diana in a white-and-black outfit, slowly looking at the camera with—

A kind of smirk. Yes. And a little tinkly sound that goes with it. A sound that adds wit and punctuation.

A picture worth a thousand words on what Diana thought about the royals. (Laughs.)

That is pure Adam Curtis! I loved his idea and I believed very much it should stay in the cut, even if it was not planned that way.

Do you feel, then, that you are the final arbitrator among all these talented people?

I think the editor does end up being a bit of an arbitrator. The bigger the project, the more money and "intervening forces" are involved. As a result, the creative process can blur into the realm of the political— meaning, how does one diplomatically deal with all these external forces? And, I may add, all while trying to keep the clarity of what *you* think is the best film in the end and how you can convey that to your director. Of course, a good director will always give you the opportunity to speak out—and then decide whether he or she really wants to listen to you! *(Laughs.)* Being an editor is actually a privileged position—and I don't think many people outside of the business know this.

But do you feel that because directors have so much to do on a film and can lose a sense of objectivity, editors need to provide that clearheaded view?

It certainly is one reason why editors are valuable *(laughs)*. But the filmmaking process gets to a point where even the editor starts "using" other people's eyes to keep clarity and objectivity. The film is tested with different people, and editors learn to decode and interpret and put together different people's responses. Going from that to deciding what needs to be done becomes a real skill too. In my experience, what is often pointed out as a problem area in a film might not need editorial intervention at all. The problem might in fact lie elsewhere in the film. So learning to make the right "diagnosis" should be an editor's skill. But as I said, there easily may be multiple "forces" or points of view to deal with. Perhaps the story might benefit from dropping something, but so much work and money have gone into it that before the editor can suggest losing entire scenes and even entire characters, he or she has to really try and make it work as intended. I believe that is a duty we have. That goes back to having respect for all the work that has gone into the material before the editing process started. So I learned from a director like Stephen Frears. Directors who write their own material might have a completely different attitude toward the dailies during the editing—that is, they are happy to start "rewriting" the moment they walk into the cutting room. But directors who work with scripts written by other people are generally much more cautious and respectful, and so should an editor be unless he or she has been told otherwise. Of course, the editing process reveals amazing things whereby the final cut will almost never match the shooting script. As it is often said, the writing of a movie starts on the page and finishes in the cutting room. But one has to go through a slow and organic process before getting to that point and it involves very careful labor. I try not to watch the film over and over and over again while cutting, so as not to lose clarity too quickly. For example, as I put together a sequence, I keep cutting and don't look back until I'm absolutely ready. I think that discipline came from my having started out editing on film rather than on computers. The days when I went to film school—the early nineties—were really the moment of transition between analog and digital. But at film school, we were still shooting and cutting on film and that's how I learned, cutting on a flatbed. My first feature film, *Ratcatcher*, was shot on 35mm and I edited it on 35mm film. Those were the days.

Do you miss them?

Well, I can be romantic about it *(laughs)*, but no, I would never go back. If you asked me to cut a film on film right now, I'd be like, oh my God! But I do believe that starting that way was crucial for me.

Like who wants to use a typewriter anymore, right?

Exactly. But learning to cut on film gave me a discipline that has helped my editing full stop. When you were cutting on film, you would have to really, *really* watch your material before you cut anything. By contrast, when you cut on computers, you can always go back to your uncut rushes, regardless of whatever cuts you've already made, and you can start all over again. Of course, that is wonderful, and it makes fixing things easier, but my feeling remains that watching the rushes and *honestly* tapping into your feelings when you first watch them before starting to cut is one of the most valuable things an editor can do. Cutting on film used to impose that practice.

Was it because the process was slower and you had more time to think about your choices?

Yes. But also once you did a cut and decided to go back to see your slate, you would have to literally recompose and resplice the film together in its original form. So physically, you needed to think a *lot* more *before* you did your first cut and start chop-chopping up your piece of film.

Does that imply that those without the advantage of working on film—as is the case with many young filmmakers today—have less so-called discipline to look at film as deeply as you did?

I'm sure one can self-impose the discipline of watching and thinking before starting to cut, but I feel that computers—and the pressure imposed by production to deliver quickly—can push us all to jump in and cut with too much speed. Computers work fast but the human brain does not work any faster than it used to when we were cutting on film. What goes on in the editor's mind determines the speed of his or her good work. And, as old-fashioned as it might sound, there's nothing like the "break" editors used to have when respooling a reel of film just watched on a Steenbeck that would allow them to think of a solution to a problem. Whatever way one decides to work, what is fundamental is digesting your dailies and making sure you have captured and identified the best parts of what has been shot, what you think you want to include in your cut. If you rush through that process, chances are you will miss out on so much. I used to find the term *first assembly*—the very first attempt to put all your material together as per script—almost offensive. A lot of work goes into it! But I have come to believe it makes perfect sense. There is so much to try and incorporate, so many nuances that an editor cannot instantly bring out of the material in the time given to do it. I now believe the term first assembly protects editors from other people thinking that is the best they can do! With more work and more time, the first assembly will evolve to first cut and beyond.

Does that quick-choice mentality reveal itself in the final film, perhaps as a "thoughtless," so to speak, product? Or is it that gems will still be found eventually, but not necessarily in a slow-and-steady way?

I'd say given enough time overall, editors with both skill and the right material will come up with a good product—as they should! Technology has affected the process in general. Maybe with student films, it might be possible to see someone being pushed along by computers to cut something together too quickly without really thinking about what's there and poring over the material for the best of it. Still, there is a beauty about having such accessibility to filmmaking software on computers these days. For the first time *ever*, I myself have been contemplating having a cutting room in my own home!

Computers have also made it much easier for editors to work with music tracks as they cut, whether it's temp music or the actual score. What is your take on temp music, especially as you feel editing is already so musical?

I like to work without music. I like to see temp music coming into the film eventually, but I have a very strong feeling that music can make you *think* something is finished too early and that an edit is more final than it is. So I try and leave the music to the latter stages of the cut because it just seems to pollute my thinking of the overall way the edit works.

What about music gives a scene that sense of completion?

Music can offer the right emotion or tone for the piece—almost the way a hat caps off a beautiful outfit! *(Laughs.)* If you take off the hat, the outfit seems incomplete. I know it's a funny analogy, but putting music on when you're not finished with editing the scene is almost like putting on the hat before you have finished putting on your outfit.

Not that music is an accessory like a hat, though, is it?

Oh no, absolutely not. Music should be an intrinsic part of every film when used in the right amount and in the right places. Unfortunately, it is too often used as an "accessory," much like wallpaper. It is often not integral to a scene but used to lead an emotion, or worse, "cover" something that does not work so well. The music "carries" the good feeling and so one is more forgiving of the picture. The two elements should work together, but using music too early in the editing process almost locks you in, locks in the rhythm and length of a scene. It can distract you from seeing the picture and what can be better about it. As an editor, I need to focus on the picture first, see what feeling I can get out of it, and then think about the music. Obviously, when the time comes to introduce music, then you begin a chicken-or-egg conversation. You start adjusting one to the other and vice versa. Often, a composer will come back to you and say, "You know that shot, do you think you can make it longer? Do you think you have more there because I would love to hold that note for a beat longer?" That collaboration is beautiful when you get to that point, but I prefer to find the shape of the cut first. The opening scene of *Morvern Callar* is a great example of a sequence where music was expected, but we decided not to use it. The film opens with our main character lying on the floor of her apartment next to a Christmas tree and her boyfriend is lying nearby face down—we gradually reveal that he is actually dead. While working on that scene, we discovered nothing else equaled the power of the buzzing of the Christmas lights and the "void" created by the silence around it. It seemed to match beautifully the disturbing feeling we wanted to capture.

The Queen again has two contrasting scenes in which music, and then the lack of music and sound, have different impacts. In the scene when Tony Blair calls Diana the "the people's princess," music plays under his speech. By contrast, the highly emotional scene in which Charles views Diana's body is done in complete silence—no music, no sounds, not even the voice of the priest saying prayers behind the window of a closed door, although we see his mouth moving. These two scenes contradict a perhaps old-fashioned idea that music should underscore emotion (Charles's scene) and not distract from a speech (Blair's scene)—but you've done the opposite.

I'm sure there were debates about that—there always are! *(laughs)*—and I don't remember exactly the debate we had at that time, but definitely

Alexandre Desplat, who composed the music for *The Queen,* is an extremely clever and wonderful musician, and may even have been the one to suggest how music could be used in those scenes. I give him credit for not pushing music in necessarily the most obvious of places in *The Queen.* I am very much for *not* wanting to do what is expected! *(Laughs.)* I think the bottom line is: the atypical makes audiences think about what they're watching. Because music can ride or dictate the emotion, *not* having the music gives an audience more space to feel subjectively what the visuals are representing. It allows the space for an audience to respond to the material in a more personal way.

Obviously, music never really pops in and out of real life to underscore what happens to us (laughs). *So in Charles's scene, the utter silence intensifies the shock and loneliness that he must have felt upon seeing Diana's body.*
    Yes, a specific scene like that, which presents real events and people that we have read about in the news, permits the space to join what you're seeing with what you know and have experienced to think more deeply about it, from your personal perspective. I think this is a great example of how silence opens the space for emotions to float, to let personal feelings enter the film where they wouldn't before.

You have worked with two directors who have distinct filmmaking styles—Lynne Ramsay and Stephen Frears. These directorial styles must pose certain challenges, given that the films themselves create different moods or tones in how the stories are shot. Can you compare and contrast their styles?
    Yes, Lynne and Stephen are extremely different and I would say because of that, the work in the cutting room tends to be different. Since Lynne writes her own material, the cutting-room experience can be more intense because basically she starts rewriting the film as we edit. And because it's her own writing, she can be absolutely brutal. So the debates in the cutting room about what could be done and rewritten postshoot can actually involve a lot of the work. How Lynne shoots film almost makes them like documentaries, more free-form, and so the shaping that happens in the cutting room requires more time and thinking. Stephen, on the other hand, is really cautious about rewriting in the cutting room without involving the writer. He is extremely respectful of the writer's original intention and will consult him or her if the need arises to rethink a scene altogether. In both cases, being next to the

director-writer and advising on what could or couldn't work is a great responsibility.

As another distinction between directors, Frears's films depict a straight-forward reality, while Ramsay's films present almost a dreamlike quality. Is that in keeping with her free-form approach to filmmaking?

Probably yes. She started out as a photographer and works very much with sound and picture more like an artist than a traditional filmmaker. With Lynne, I discovered the importance of tapping into the *feeling* of something, and how the editing can make or break that. When you cut a sequence together, you want to know what the feeling of that moment needs to be. You look for those moments in your dailies, and if you find them, you put them together to preserve them as much as you can. The biggest compliments we received after *Morvern* was when people came up to us after seeing the film for the first time and said, "You know, that party scene, it felt like a real party! It really felt like my experience of being high at a party. It really felt like I was there and I've experienced that." In *Boy A*, which was wonderfully directed by John Crowley, there is a scene at a club with a character on a drug high, and similarly a lot of people appreciated that scene and the way it was cut. Again, I think it's because it somehow captured the feeling of the event it was representing. The main character Jack (Andrew Garfield) goes out on a date, accidentally takes an Ecstasy pill, and unwillingly experiences his first trip. When the drug kicks in, he begins dancing alone. John had worked extensively with the actor on the way he would dance and the scene was planned to be one long uncut shot. This shot worked out beautifully and we did use it, but then decided it felt right to use jump cuts, soft focus, even slight speed changes. My approach to that sequence was: what is the feeling somebody has when he's high? What we ended up with felt right.

So you visually approximated the experience of being high by using jump cuts.

Now doesn't that sound like the most obvious thing? *(Laughs.)*

But could you create the same feeling of being high by using dissolves?

Probably, yes. But in my interpretation of the experience, your mind feels jittery and your memory of it feels very fragmented. So jump cuts, and the combination of shots with slow motion and soft focus and funny movement, all put together to a certain rhythm, capture the feeling of that specific moment. Such editing may be easier to talk about within the context of a party scene or a scene where your states of mind are altered, and so you have more freedom to experiment with how shots can be joined. But I would say that sense of capturing the feeling applies to many scenes in a film.

Such as a "mundane" dinner-table scene or a dialogue between two people on a street.

Depending on what the story is, the form is dictated by the content. It may be harder to talk about the feeling in a scene that is not so obviously "out there," but if you really think about it, even a dinner-party sequence has "feeling" in it. Boredom? Seduction? I do believe you can tap into those feelings and cut a sequence in a way that will resonate with the audience.

What helps you to capture the feelings of a scene before you start cutting it?

Watching the uncut footage with care and taking good notes of my first response to it. And by it, I mean that the combination of performance and composition of the image is your starting point. Of course, as I said before, your director will have his or her own ideas about it and give you notes. And a lot of the time, you'll be in agreement—but not necessarily! *(Laughs.)* Then the debates and negotiations start! Technology has completely revolutionized the way editors and directors can work with each other. There is no longer the need to be in the same physical space as there once was. Footage and cuts can be placed in the "ether" and shared this way. I think this is in theory wonderful, but in my experience, it is really, really hard to do. There's nothing like some good face-to-face communication, and unless the director and editor really know each other and have a history of working together, it is very hard to build a good solid working relationship without being in the same physical space.

Does working separately from each other also have an impact on how editors continue to be perceived? As you suggested before, editors used to be "anonymous" and then became more acknowledged over time as being vital for making or breaking a film. Yet even today editors may remain "invisible." I'm thinking of the DVD featurettes called "The Making of Chéri" and "The Making of The Queen," in which director, producer, writer, actors—even costume designer—all gathered to speak of production, but never mentioned the editor. In the Chéri DVD, in fact, a producer said, "He"—meaning Stephen Frears—"cut the film very quickly. And

we went into the cutting room, and we knew we had it." No mention of a "she" who cut the film.
  (Laughs.)

Is editing still that overlooked in some cases?

It's an interesting issue. When an editor finally gets a nomination, it's like "Oh, somebody's recognizing my work!" Yet many times on awards shows, the editor's award is not even mentioned or just rushed through. Editing as an end result is often intangible. By contrast, I think, there is a tangibility of the work of a director of photography, of a costume person, of the production designer. Surprisingly, not many people really know, unless you're in the business, that a film is not shot the way it is ultimately seen. Often, what you finally see on the screen has actually been shot maybe twenty times, and then the editor has to choose portions of shots and make them work together to best tell a story. You do hear people talking of the director cutting a film, and you always know that it's not the director—or not *just* the director—and it is a little sad when an editor is not acknowledged. Yet, again, there is something about the editor's personality that suits being in the shadows, behind the scenes, instead of on the floor of a film with a massive crew that sometimes equals the movement of an army. A lot of creativity goes on there, but it is slowed down by the enormous machinery of a big crew. I often get frustrated when I go to set and experience all the waiting that has to be done for this or that thing to happen. In the cutting room, you are dictating your own pace of work and this pacing comes with enormous creative responsibility. Once you have the material, it's all up to you to make it happen. I don't know, perhaps if editors had bigger egos, they would be directors! *(Laughs.)* However, it's always nice when some light is shed on the art of editing and the editors behind the scenes. It is definitely important to all who have interest in film and want to learn about it.

I know you spent time reviewing your films in advance of answering my questions, and I also know that's hard for most editors to do—they don't like looking at their own films once they have finished them. How was that experience for you?

I thought I should look at my films again because recently, my father-in-law fancied watching *Mrs. Henderson Presents,* and I just caught a little bit of it and thought, oh my God, I don't remember it! Uh-oh, maybe I should refresh my memory. *(Laughs.)* So I went to the local video store and came out with six DVDs of the films I cut. Even walking out with these six films in my hands and looking at them in a pile just felt great. Then I watched them in the space of a few days, and it's a little scary because you, of course, say to yourself, "Am I going to see things that I would do differently today?" And yes, I did, but I will not tell you where! *(Laughs.)* I have much more clarity now because so much time has passed since I cut them. I think the best part of watching these films again was to realize that, just as in childbirth, all the pain that goes with the "delivery" has been forgotten, and I can just enjoy and take pride in the result.

6. Speaking Cinema

JOE BINI

1997 *Little Dieter Needs to Fly*, dir. Werner Herzog

1999 *My Best Fiend*, dir. Werner Herzog

2000 *Wings of Hope*, TV, dir. Werner Herzog

2001 *Invincible*, dir. Werner Herzog

2001 *Exploding Oedipus*, dir. Marc Lafia

2003 *DNA*, British TV series, 2 episodes

2003 *Off the Charts: The Song-Poem Story*, dir. Jamie Meltzer

2003 *Wheel of Time*, dir. Werner Herzog

2004 *The White Diamond*, dir. Werner Herzog

2004 *The Heist*, British TV Series

2005 *Grizzly Man*, dir. Werner Herzog

2005 *The Wild Blue Yonder*, dir. Werner Herzog

2005 *In the Edges: The "Grizzly Man" Session*, dir. Erik Nelson

2006 *Rescue Dawn*, dir. Werner Herzog

2007 *Encounters at the End of the World*, dir. Werner Herzog

2008 *Roman Polanski: Wanted and Desired*, dir. Marina Zenovich

2009 *The Bad Lieutenant: Port of Call—New Orleans*, dir. Werner Herzog

2009 *My Son, My Son, What Have Ye Done*, dir. Werner Herzog

2010 *All That Glitters*, dir. Tomas Kudrna

2010 *Cave of Forgotten Dreams*, dir. Werner Herzog

2011 *We Need to Talk about Kevin*, dir. Lynne Ramsay

2011 *Into the Abyss*, dir. Werner Herzog

AWARDS

2006 Eddie Award (ACE) nomination, Best Edited Documentary
Film, *Grizzly Man*

2008 Sundance Film Festival Award, Documentary Film Editing
Award, *Roman Polanski: Wanted and Desired*

2009 Emmy Award nomination, Outstanding Picture Editing for
Nonfiction Programming, *Roman Polanski: Wanted and Desired*

2009 Emmy Award, Outstanding Writing for Nonfiction
Programming, *Roman Polanski: Wanted and Desired*

2011 Eddie Award (ACE) nomination, Best Edited Documentary
Film, *Cave of Forgotten Dreams* (shared with Maya Hawke)

Because of the intense collaboration that molds the editorial process,
many editors develop relationships with particular directors that span
decades and are as tight as a family's. In such collaborations, editors and
directors learn shorthand language with which they complete each other's
thoughts and understand in a flash the nuances of a film that realize a
director's vision. Joe Bini has had a long relationship with Werner
Herzog, starting with *Little Dieter Learns to Fly* in 1997. He cites examples from several of the often controversial and visually striking films
that comprise the Herzog collection, including a consideration of the
"Dieter" story as both a documentary (*Little Dieter Learns to Fly*) and a
fictionalized film (*Rescue Dawn*). In particular, Bini's discussion of the
award-winning *Grizzly Man* exemplifies the tricky decisions that need to
be made in retelling the life of one who is no longer alive to give his
story. Bini also acknowledges the disappointments and occasional outrage
that come from realizing that documentaries and their editors are not
always as appreciated as they should be. Bini hopes to eventually return
to the aspiration of his college days: to be the consummate filmmaker.
For the 2009 film *Roman Polanski: Wanted and Desired*, he was not
only nominated for an Emmy for his editing, but won an Emmy for
writing. Clearly, Bini's work with documentaries, in which the script is

constructed in the cutting room, have reinforced his abilities as musician, writer, and director, ensuring a smooth transition into new levels of cinematic creativity and independence.

Bini's insights into what documentary editing is all about—playing jazz, creating an oil painting versus a charcoal sketch, and especially speaking a language—complement the perceptions of this field already posed by colleagues Corrao and Oppenheim. He likewise addresses the sensitive issue of "fabricating reality" in a documentary in a way that respects the truth while also creating a work of art that transcends consciousness, thereby painting a new reality that is perhaps even more truthful than originally imagined.

Were you involved with documentaries at the outset of your film career?

I actually started as a musician and a songwriter. I realize now that songwriting is a lot of what I'm doing in film, a sort of structural thing. But music was my interest until I was in my twenties, and then I was interested in the idea of music in film. I went to New York University with the goal of being a filmmaker. I grew up in the San Francisco Bay Area, so coming to New York in the eighties was a fantastic time. There were all those repertory cinemas with double features. That's the way to see films—in a dark room, on a big screen, and you get completely lost in them. In the three years I was at NYU, I must have seen a thousand films. Luis Buñuel, Federico Fellini—

Werner Herzog?

Not so much Herzog, although I did like his films certainly. I saw *Fitzcarraldo*, but I hadn't seen that many of them. Never saw his documentaries. I never had any documentary interest at all because I had a very limited idea about what documentary was. You could have focused on it in school, but it wasn't my interest. I was writing and acting and directing—I wanted to be a director. Made some short films at NYU and my first job out of college was an editorial job. I worked as an editor for a news agency for a guy who was actually an agent for newscasters. They basically trained people to be better newscasters or reporters, so it was interesting because *(laughs)* you completely saw the fabrication of news.

Of reality.

Yes, and that probably pricked my interest in any kind of reality work.

Were you bothered by their fabrication of the news?

It definitely, hugely bothered me. It opened my eyes and I started to see the news in a whole different way.

At that point, did you feel there should be a way to depict reality in film without fabricating it?

Well, my interest still was fiction—not only just fiction, but the most extreme kind of fantasy fiction.

So you didn't want it to be real anyway.

It's all psychological for me. My interest has always been in the mind. How film represents people's inner lives in different ways. To me, it's always about insight, the interior, even if it is a documentary. I believe that.

Did you make films during or after your work at the news agency?

I lived in New York for about ten years and then, toward the end of my twenties, I went back to San Francisco. Some of my friends were software developers and they wrote Pro-Tools. It was the most popular audio editing software and affiliated with Avid. They had an Avid system in its nascent stages and they asked me, "Hey, would you be interested in goofing around with it?" So I did. Just based on that skill and knowing how to use it—it was the time when the whole digital editing thing was starting in the early nineties—I began to get work. And with these guys, I opened an editing facility in San Francisco where we did an audio- video / audio-film thing all in one building. One day I got a call from a friend who said, "You guys have Avids, right?" I said, "Yeah." And he said, "Well, do you want to work on this thing for Werner Herzog?" "You're kidding!" *(Laughs.)* The next day, I was editing with Werner Herzog! *Little Dieter Needs to Fly* was the beginning.

In starting that editorial company, did you continue to feel the urge to direct or act since that's what you studied?

I continued to make short films during that period, and it's still what I want to do. I really don't completely consider myself an editor. A film- maker first.

Does something about editing, though, resonate with your personality?

Definitely, and I think that's why I've been successful at it. I look at cinema as a language, and we editors are the people who are the most pro- ficient in that language. We speak it the best. So if you want to learn to speak the language of film, editing is where to learn it. Screenwriting is great too, and I'm not denigrating it, but it ultimately is writing, a step back in the process. A writer does his or her job and has created something that's got a long way to go before it is a film. The director does his or her job and has created something that needs to be edited. You could argue that the cameraman does pure cinema, which you sometimes see in documentary.

But it is still fragmented until the editor—
    Yes, that's the power—or whatever the word is—that editors have. I've always liked that.

Is it important to use the word "cinema" as opposed to "film" or "movie"?
    I'm very old-fashioned in terms of the art element of cinema.

"Art," meaning?
    A transcending experience for me. If it's not transcending, it can still be interesting and still be good, but it's not what I'm interested in. You don't always achieve art, but that is what you are aiming for.

That goal of transcending might eliminate a number of Hollywood films today.
    It sure does.

In a DVD featurette, Herzog stated most definitively, "I do not make documentaries!" Many of his films seem to bridge a Hollywood-type of narrative film within a documentary of a given reality. Given this bridge, what does "documentary" mean to you?
    Well, I think I have worked with Werner more than anyone else and he introduced me to documentary film. As I said, I had no interest in it before. After I met him, we worked on *Little Dieter Needs to Fly,* and when I had gotten involved with it, it was half or more edited already. Here was a documentary with a *dream* sequence in it. That's what I remembered when I first saw it and it made perfect sense to me. It didn't stand out as some weird thing in the context of that film. That opened my eyes to what a documentary could be. Werner looks for things that are more than just surface-level truth. That's boring to him. When you use the language of cinema, that means you can "fabricate" things to tell the truth.

What's an example of that from Little Dieter?
    There's a scene early on when you first meet Dieter as he gets out of his car and slams the door five or six times. Then he goes to his house and

slams that door five or six times. Then he says, "This may seem crazy to you, but when I was a prisoner, I couldn't open any doors and so now open doors are very important to me." Then you walk into his house, and in his hallway, there's paintings of open doors.

Are you saying all that was fabricated?

No, but the whole idea of him slamming doors was fabricated. He doesn't really do that. He doesn't go through his life slamming doors.

Will you spoil the film now by saying that?

Not at all. Werner directed Dieter to do that. And Werner is very happy about that fact and proud of it. That's an example of using film to create something you will not forget. If Dieter simply said to you, "When I was a prisoner, I couldn't open doors," okay, that's interesting, but it would go right by you. Here, though, you see something weird, something different, and you *want* to know more about this man. Is there something wrong with that? I don't think so. I think that really is using film to transcend.

The truth is that Dieter was a prisoner of war and lacked freedom to move. And he did have those door paintings in his house.

That is correct.

Then the enactment of his fear or, perhaps, obsession with his lack of freedom was scripted to make the point real for the audience.

Exactly. Werner just tries it, and many times it's off the cuff. That's how he works. "Let's try it, let's try it." There are many "performances" in Werner's films, a lot of performance-based stuff. Some of them are even bad performances, which I find quite funny.

That may be an opportunity to add humor to a heavy subject.

Like with the coroner in *Grizzly Man*.

Oh, that guy seemed to enjoy his position of working with cadavers while looking rather cadaverous himself! Did he play up his own ghoulish physicality to enhance the storyline?

That's exactly right. He gave a "performance" in the film. Was he *really* like that? He was to some degree. He was important to the film because he was commenting on what happened in the film: a man named Timothy Treadwell, who went to save and live with grizzly bears in Alaska, ended up being killed by one. But the coroner's scene was also an absolutely brilliant underpinning to the entire film. One of the premises of going to that film is that you, as a viewer, are kind of a vampire. You as the viewer want a—what's the word?—salacious experience because you go in there to hear how this guy was eaten by a bear.

I admit that was my motivation to see the film (sighs).
   Yeah, and everyone! Mine as well!

But your editorial choice to presents a lengthy shot on the coroner—almost a full minute, it seemed—was equally intense in and of itself. Did you discuss with Herzog how long to hold on that shot of the coroner?
   I should say first that I have never had a discussion with Werner about aesthetics. He doesn't discuss stuff like that. If I was to ask him, "Why do we have to do this?" he wouldn't have an answer for that—or he won't answer that. So I don't ask those questions. However those shots come about, which could be wrong or right, I always feel those are moments where you suddenly become aware that it's a film. The consciousness of making a film. As a result, there is more honesty about the reality, in a weird way.

Is using such a lengthy shot an editing technique that forces the audience to analyze the character? Or does it make the audience frustrated, like, "Why are you making me sit through this endless minute staring at this odd man?"
   Both. I would also say it's more making you think about *your*self—you, the audience member. It's a moment that makes you uncomfortable.

We are so used to rapid cutting today that a shot with one person talking for a minute makes us squirm. I know I found myself saying, "I need a cut . . . now . . . please!" And you weren't making it.
   (Laughs.) The *whole* idea was we *wanted* to make you feel uncomfortable. This is a massively underutilized technique today. When I have a meeting with producers and show them a cut of a film, like that example from *Grizzly Man* or something from *Encounters at the End of the World*, they're like, "Why that moment?" And my response is, "Well, how did it make you feel?" "It made me feel uncomfortable. It's stupid. Why didn't you cut there?" But that was our goal, and you felt uncomfortable, so it *was* successful, right? *(Laughs.)* We wanted to take

you outside of your comfort zone so that you can have an *experience* with the movie.

Don't you risk losing audiences that way?

Well, here's the beauty of doing these kinds of theatrical documentaries: there isn't much of an audience anyway! *(Laughs.)*

More's the pity.

By that I mean that we never have the pressure that you are under when you are doing a big-budget film. Working with Werner is a different experience from other directors because he's an established filmmaker.

Filmmaking is definitely a global passion for him.

It's his whole life. We have had our conflicts and a very up-and-down relationship, but we've stuck together for a long time. Working for him is both good and hard. But what I appreciate about him in the end is that he is a filmmaker beyond everything else. Given a choice between a big-budget film that will take a year or more to develop and a small-budget film that we can shoot tomorrow, he will always go with the small-budget film because he simply likes to make films. He wants to spend his life making films, not making deals.

When you say you don't question some of his aesthetic choices, does that mean you tried to but stopped?

Yes, we do a lot of things that I don't like or that I wouldn't have done. There are story-point things we can argue about, where I can give him my reasons and he can tell me his reasons and we discuss it. But aesthetics, the look and feel of a film, we really can't discuss. When people ask me why Werner did something, I can only give you my opinion. I don't really know why he does a lot of what he does! *(Laughs.)*

Does that limit you as an editor in what you can contribute to the film since you are following his directive?

But that's what a Werner Herzog film is all about. It's very specific and from having worked with him so long, I'm past the point of even questioning it. I just follow his lead. It's part of my job, as is always the case with an editor. I'm often the go-between, between him and the producers, so they can establish early on that I'm sane *(laughs)*, and then they can ask me those questions and I can help them try to understand. And especially if I agree with their opinion, as I sometimes do, then I have some outside support and I can go to Werner and try to push *him* harder. We actually make two kinds of films. We make films that have *no* outside push on Werner, except for me and his cinematographer, Peter Zeitlinger, who has worked with Werner as long as I have, and to some degree we can push him. Then there's someone else out there who, for financial reasons perhaps, has power. That's a different kind of Werner Herzog film, like *Rescue Dawn* or *The Bad Lieutenant* or *Grizzly Man*. Does that mean that those films are more commercial? Yes, to some degree, but I've always appreciated that frankly I never feel like we're being screwed. I like that other people are pushing because there's more money involved in the film that they have invested in it. *Grizzly Man* was that way. Werner didn't initiate that project; the producer, Erik Nelson, did. So in a way that was a good functional relationship because Werner had a say, but we also had a strong producer.

You and Herzog have also worked on two very clearly distinct types of films: documentaries versus fictional films. What is the nature of the script that you have in each case?

Well, for documentaries, there's no script. Let's talk about a specific film, *Grizzly Man*, for example. Werner obviously understood what the story was, went up to Alaska, shot all the interviews. At that time, we had only seen a little bit of Timothy Treadwell's footage—he's the activist who went to live with the bears. We had only a vague idea that Timothy was kind of this crazy man and the film was essentially going to be all of his video diary stuff that he shot while he lived in the wild. So Werner had to go up to Alaska and collect interviews with people who knew Timothy—and I should mention Werner always shoots a minimal amount of film.

As opposed to?

As opposed to the other kind of director I see in documentary, the person who directs but whose job to me is more producing. He or she shoots hours of interviews with each person, and then I come into the editing room. And that director gives me all the footage—

Hundreds and hundreds of hours worth.

Exactly, and then there's archival film on a B roll or whatever, and we're going to make the film in the editing room. That's the more typical way of documentary making and it certainly can be successful. But it's amazing to me when I get into an editing room that this type of director often has absolutely no idea how a film's going to begin or end, or what the turning points are in terms of how they shot it. They might know this in the story, but they don't know the *film* because they're not thinking filmically. You'd never do that in a fiction film because you have a script, but it seems some people don't think about this in documentaries.

Timothy had been killed long before you made the film. How did knowing the outcome—that he died a gruesome death by the animal he loved— affect how you told the story of his life?

It was actually very difficult to figure that out because there were two important issues. First, once you know the outcome, how do you keep the rest of the story interesting? Fortunately, that issue was immediately dispelled when we started looking at Timothy's footage, because it was just incredibly beautiful. The other issue—which I always considered an issue that made no sense to me, but it did to Werner—was why in this film do we have a German filmmaker narrating this guy's story?

That's Herzog's style, immersing himself in the film?

Well, I know, but if you were making this film abstractly about this man, you would think that Timothy's footage would be enough. Why do we need that narration? And then how do we make the film organic? How do we make it seem like a whole? What I remember most about the process, after Werner had shot all his own stuff, was when we started looking at Timothy's footage—about one hundred hours of it. I was utterly taken aback by Timothy's work. It was not at all what I expected. First of all, I had hated Timothy from the start, from what I had heard about him. I thought he was a complete asshole, and Werner felt the same way. We'd just sit there and make fun of him! Then I started thinking, how can I make a film if we hate the main character? But then over the course of watching Timothy's footage, we completely turned the corner. We started to realize that he was an amazing guy as well as being an asshole *(laughs)*, and having many issues. What we found more and more was that he loved his filmmaking. He was outstanding. Some people just naturally know to put the camera *here* instead of over *there*. Timothy had a brilliant sense of that. And that was when the film began to come together; the two issues weren't issues anymore. A big part of the film was going to be about Werner, a filmmaker with his point of view about nature, and Timothy, a filmmaker with his point of view about nature, kind of meeting in this film, so to speak. Meeting in the middle. But I will never, ever forget watching Timothy's rushes. I kept thinking, oh my God, he's dead, and nobody else has seen this footage and he's talking from the grave. I never got over that. I'll never get over it.

Given the outcome of Timothy's life, you had to establish his death up front and work backward to include these two points of view.

Yes, when the film begins, the very first time you see Timothy, it says he died on such-and-such a date. So you know he's dead, and that informs a lot of the story. This guy is so alive and so weird, but he's already dead.

That was part of the irony of the film—knowing he was dead, but bringing him back to life only to be killed again, so to speak. You later created incredible tension with just a title that said "Hours before his death."

Yes, we showed material from the "last tape," where the camera was actually running at the time Timothy as well as his girlfriend, Amie Huguenard, were attacked and killed by one bear. The executor of Timothy's estate, a woman named Jewel Palovak, wouldn't give us that terrible tape, and I said, "Fine, but aren't there other things on that tape that maybe we could use? We'll just take the last part off and we can work with the rest." And it was absolutely incredible footage, like nothing else in the film he shot. It was almost like he knew he was going to die.

I remember some footage where Timothy just lingered in front of the camera, like he didn't want to leave the frame—as if he sensed doom was coming.

Yes. And so by putting that little title in, "Hours before his death," we were using the "language" of cinema. It made a better story, it was more entertaining, and it upped the level of meaning in the film. But we actually did have to make a creative decision about including Timothy's final footage in which he was killed. The producers were asking, "Okay, how are you going to play that tape?" Well, number one, we didn't want to show it. I thought it would have been disgusting and wrong, and we had to have some responsibility for the families of Timothy and his girlfriend. Werner was also very happy that Jewel did not allow us to have that tape, but he came up with the idea that it would somehow be in the film. So as he talked with Jewel on film, Werner also filmed himself listening and reacting to the tape, and telling Jewel that she must never listen to it and even destroy it.

Yes, in that scene, the camera is on Herzog's back as he listens to the tape through headphones, while we instead are focused on Jewel's tearful reaction as she imagines Timothy's death while looking at Herzog.

I thought that was a brilliant way to deal with the gruesome reality of that tape. It is a classic example of a restriction leading to a better idea, through which you have a powerful reaction. It's a classic example of *directing* in a documentary. I mean, that's a fabricated scene in the sense that it's staged, but it is also really happening.

Herzog is actually listening to the death tape?

He is.

It also serves to pique the spectator's morbid curiosity about what happened to Timothy and reinforce the fact of his death which you established from the start.

It was like Timothy knew he would eventually die with the bears and we wanted to build on that possibility. We connected the "last tape" scene with the massive bear fight that Timothy filmed. That was a huge structural decision to put those two scenes together. You realize how really long that bear fight scene is—hugely long. That is another instance of, I thought, effectively making something long and forcing you to sit there and react. Timothy loved these bears, to the point of wanting to play with them, giving them "teddy bear"–like names. But now we see them in this footage as powerful deadly creatures. If we didn't realize that before, we do now. These are powerful creatures and this is how Timothy died. We just let that bear-fight shot linger and you realize. Then that is also the turning point in the film to the second half, which was more about this guy's psychology and what led to his demise.

This is quite a contrast with a film like Little Dieter Learns to Fly, *where you know what terrible things happened to Dieter, but he is still alive to tell his own story. In that case, Herzog recreated Dieter's actual POW experience running through the jungle and being imprisoned, with Dieter playing himself!*

Which I thought was a really interesting technique. My favorite part in the film actually was the use of chapter titles like "The Man" and "Punishment." We wanted to do the film like a Greek or biblical tragedy. A major moment in the film is when Dieter is standing by a tank of jellyfish floating in water and he speaks about his POW experience, saying, "This is what death looked like to me." And you see this beautiful shot of the jellyfish. Then it dissolves and the title says "Punishment." Next, you see Dieter standing with the military "guards" in Laos—those guards are locals posing as guards and it's actually Thailand, but you know he's supposed to be in Laos. That's my favorite moment, it's the "Oh, shit!" moment. It's not the end of the film; it's the moment of total possibility. I know now what's going to happen. I know now I'm going to hear the story about what happened to this guy and it's going to be horrible. I've been hearing hints of it up until now, but *now* we're going to get the story. That's a phenomenal editorial moment in that film because you just want to know what the hell's going to happen next. Later on—yes, he's running through the jungle and it's definitely staged, and it's also a moment where you're thinking, "Is the filmmaker *really* making this guy go through this?!" So you're thinking on all these levels. It steps you out of thinking about the story to thinking instead about the *film*.

No wonder when he's fleeing through the forest, Dieter says, "This is getting a little close to home here." Curiously, Herzog replicated that whole experience with the actor Christian Bale years later in Rescue Dawn, *which was a fictionalized account of Dieter's story.*

I think the documentary, *Little Dieter Learns to Fly*, is a much more imaginative film, while the fictional film is much more straightforward. For me as an editor, fictional editing is much more fun. Documentary editing can be really brutal, not because of the content but because of the process. When I take on a documentary, it's like *I'm* walking in a jungle all by myself and I don't know what's what for a while. You have to think about it constantly, and it's harder and harder as you get older! *(Laughs.)* You've always got a script in a fictional film. Of course, there's other pressures—financial pressures, people wanting the film to be accessible to large audiences. But the script and story help you know while you're cutting one scene what the next scene is, or you know where it's going to go. However, *Rescue Dawn* was also rather documentary in a stark sense, like all those scenes of Christian Bale being tortured. He was hung upside-down, he did get stuck in a well, he lost forty or fifty pounds.

Thanks to an actor willing to do all that!

Yes, he went through Dieter's experience. That is a big part of how Werner wants to do films, as he did with his earlier films with Klaus Kinski. It's almost like a documentary of a crazy performance.

Nicolas Cage's performance in *Bad Lieutenant* falls into this category. So from an editorial standpoint, you want to keep that energy and bring excitement to the film so the audience, hopefully, will be excited about it as well.

Do certain editorial guidelines help you keep that energy going or is the energy created mainly by the footage itself?

For me, the essential guideline for keeping the energy is to keep the film fresh. I like to cut films as quickly as possible. I'm very much a jazz musician in that way. I'm more of an "improv" kind of editor than a "let's get this splice exactly right" kind of editor. You do try to get it right, obviously, but keeping it fresh is essential. So when you're editing a feature-length film—whether documentary or fictional—you only have three or four viewings where all the circumstances have got to be *right (laughs)*, and you're going to actually be able to "see" the whole film. That time is precious. Then you have to act on that and know what to do with it and be able to mold it at that point.

Does that always involve an audience?

Could be. I get a lot out of showing it to audiences. But I wasn't speaking so much of that. I was referring to personally viewing a film.

Given that you sometimes find yourself in a "jungle" when editing a documentary, is it possible to maintain your energy as you would on a fictional film?

It's harder. It is harder. I mean, I always find something fun in cutting films like *Wild Blue Yonder* or *Encounters*. I think I cut *Wild Blue Yonder* probably in one week in my bedroom! *Encounters*, I probably cut in a month. I think of those films as charcoal sketches.

Sketches do have their place in the art world.

Certainly. Da Vinci largely exists as sketches.

But everyone remembers da Vinci's Mona Lisa *best.*

Right. Other films, like *Grizzly Man*, are the oil paintings where you fill in all the colors and spend a lot of time on them. When Werner's gone, those "oil paintings" like *Grizzly Man, Fitzcarraldo,* and *Aguirre* are what will be remembered most. It used to drive me insane when I first started working with Werner, I couldn't stand that there were so many rough edges and I wasn't able to really—that was the thing he did that drove me insane, just not give me enough time to do what I wanted to do. He'd say, "No, no, no, that's fine, it's fine, it's fine." See, *Grizzly Man* is much more like an oil painting because other people besides me were saying, "It's not good enough, it's not good enough, it's not good enough." I've come to appreciate the charcoal-sketch types of films, although I'm actually not that interested in watching them. I remember them more as a process. Some of those films were personal experiences between Werner and me. I liked some of the films, like *Wild Blue Yonder,* and it had really funny bits, but I wasn't happy with all of it. It's also always a bizarre experience when the film goes from my laptop to the big screen—that's a trip. Then I'm like, okay, that's it, I don't ever need to see the film again. I've had its ups and downs. It's not perfect, it's not even close to perfect, it wasn't intended to be perfect, and I have come around to appreciating that.

What is a perfect film?
I think *Grizzly Man* is an excellent documentary.

Because it transcends?
Without making it be about the wonderful work *I* did *(laughs),* I think that it is perfectly structured. It works as a biography. It has a level of depth you rarely see in a biography. It asks all kinds of questions. It's a film that makes you think on *all* kinds of levels. The footage is beautiful. The music is great. It is totally cohesive, and I think I had enough time to do it right.

The process of writing the music for Grizzly Man *was so fascinating that you made a short film about it called "In the Edges." The score was written in two days by two musicians improvising together as they saw the finished film for the first time.*
Yes, the film had been cut by the time we recorded the music, although I always try to leave room to go back and recut after that. The way the music *was* recorded was like shooting a documentary. You go in with the same attitude as when you shoot an event-type documentary. You don't know what you're going to get. You just have to be there and be a professional and hope that you get what you need. It is risky, but by the same token, because of the risk, you may have the potential to do something amazing. That, to me, is what filmmaking is all about. You talk about the Hollywood aesthetic and all that—we all know it's the same shit over and over again. It's particularly true, I think, in music, where there are only

like eight guys who are writing scores and they're all brilliant, but it's the same shit over and over and over again.

Herzog mentioned how the music ultimately impacted the rhythm of editing Grizzly Man. *Did you have to go back and recut it?*

Yes. I'll give you an example. When I started listening to Richard Thompson's music in our session, I thought, that's so sad. Well, of course it's sad. I mean, the film is sad. It's about this guy who's killed—but somehow it just never hit me. That is, I saw the tragedy of the story, but I'd never gotten the *sadness* until I heard one amazing piece of music Richard wrote and it was so sad. I was like, Whoa! That just gave me a whole other feeling which I wanted to show, and I pulled the narration out in some spots. We just pulled narration out altogether or gave more room to the images to up that feeling in a couple of spots.

Did the words weaken the impact that the image and music made together?

It depends on how you do it. Let's talk about how we work with words, because I'm very proud of the way we do it. I've worked with people who will edit a film and then afterward write the narration, or they will hand you a script of narration—this is typical in television—and you cut the imagery to it. The way we do it is organic—we do it as we're doing the film. Okay, we have this scene, and now we have *this* scene, and we're going to put those two scenes together and then—but they don't go together so well. So we need a transition in there. That transition can be brief, and it can be in words, like in *Little Dieter.* In that film, there are radical instances of Dieter talking on and on and on. In some of those moments, we literally turned down *his* voice and Werner speaks *over* it, saying, "And then he did this and then he did that and then he did this"—and then we bring Dieter back to his normal voice. At the time, I thought, this is absurd! But it's a transition that functions incredibly well and I think the audience appreciates when you keep the story moving.

That reminds me of the end of Grizzly Man, *when Timothy is filming himself cursing out the National Park Service and flailing like a wild man, but you subdue his voice and let Herzog speak over it so it becomes just the image of Timothy's tirade.*

Exactly. But can I tell you about that? That case again comes out of necessity. What Timothy is doing there is calling out members of the

National Park Service by name because they didn't want him to be there, and he's saying "So-and-so is a cunt!" and "So-and-so is an asshole!" and "Fuck them all!" He comes off as a wanker, frankly. The producers were like, "Werner, you *cannot* put this in the film. This is going to be on the Discovery Channel!" And Werner—and I really appreciated this—said, "Screw that. I don't care. This is amazing! I want to put this in the film." So then out of necessity came this idea of, well, what if while it's happening, we just turn down those parts? What would that mean? What would you have to do to accommodate? So Werner spoke over it, talking about Thoreau, Walden, the nature point of view again. So instead of Timothy coming across as a wanker, you see him on a whole other level, in defense of nature. If somebody hadn't been pushing us, we probably wouldn't have done that particular thing. But as in *Little Dieter*, adding narration might be a utilitarian situation where you have to have a transition to deal with something boring, where you say, "I can't handle this anymore!" For other transitions, many times it's a question of "Okay, to get from here to here, what would be good? Well, we've collected all this footage in the back of our minds. Let's see, remember that scene, those couple of shots of whatever? Let's try that in there." And I know that if I put together a couple of shots, the attachment triggers something. It might go off in a poetic direction—I call it poetic. We see something in the imagery, so it's no longer just storytelling. The point is that we can write the narration right then and there and put the images together at the same time. Then we'll tweak the narration later. But it's a long process of trying to make the editing organic.

Does "organic" imply that it is also spontaneous, coming out of itself unexpectedly?

Often. It's analogous to what I said before about being a songwriter or writing poetry. In writing a song, it's usually easy to write the first verse or the chorus, like it just comes out of you. The trick then is to write the other verses to live up to that one. So you try to have these ecstatic moments of creativity. It's not about, "Hey, I had a creative *moment*." It's the incredible amazing process we had and why would we want to change it? I've had experiences with another director who made me recut a scene about fifty times. Well, in the first place, I thought it was the best already! Second, we're watering it down each time. Okay, I understand that maybe the scene didn't have some information, I understand that.

But at some point, you have to *trust* the medium and the creative process of making a film.

Your instinct.

Your instinct in the moment. You've got to viciously protect that.

But what gets you to the point of knowing you can protect your instinct? Is it becoming so familiar with the material that subconsciously you learn how it connects?

First and foremost, freedom is what gets you to that point. You have to have the freedom to try it out. You have to feel safe to try it out. That's what a director has to do for an editor. A director has to give an editor room to be safe and feel safe. I mean, probably half of what I do isn't necessarily good. Fine, maybe more than half, I don't know. But there's always something good in it, and is somebody there helping you find that? Otherwise, frankly, I can work on my own!

Have you ever been left totally alone on a film to do your work?

The Roman Polanski film, I did the final form of the film entirely on my own as an editor. The director, Marina Zenovich, shot a ton of interviews, something like eighty-five, over a three- or four-year period. She interviewed police, lawyers, all the people in Hollywood who worked with Polanski. Fortunately, she had been editing it before I got involved and had made an assembly of what she thought was good in the interviews—there was a structure to it. Then they acquired some archival film, and that's what I was given. So we had about ninety percent of the best of the interviews and amazing archival footage. I told Marina that I had a particular composer I like to work with, Mark Degliantoni—can I work with him? "Sure, let's hear his work." Then she approved of it. You know, she was confident enough in me to let me cut the film on my own. She came in during the last couple of weeks, she had her say, we changed a few things, but generally speaking, once she saw the beginning which I had cut right away, she liked my aesthetic, and that was it. Part of me was like, well, gee, she's maybe not much of a director, is she? *(Laughs.)* But then, having just had a bad experience on another film, I realized it's another totally functional way to work. Just get good people and let them do their job! Fortunately, we shared the same aesthetic and I was trying to live up to that. I was trying to please her, not myself. Of course, she didn't love everything. I had to talk her into some things, she had to talk me *out* of some things! But it was a reasonably pleasant way to make a film. And effective.

What was your shared aesthetic?

We were both huge Polanski fans—I'm saying, of his films. When I was at NYU, I had a real sense of Polanski and his music and films, and so did Marina. We had an amazing common ground. So we wanted to make this documentary about Roman Polanski *look and sound like* a Roman Polanski film!

You also have a writing credit on the film. What did you write?

It was Marina's idea to give the writing credit. Two things were going on with the writing. One, we used title cards in the film—that was my idea, using people's quotations for titles. Then, what you choose to show in a documentary is writing as much as it is editing. It was also, I guess, a "power" issue. It reflects more what you have to do in documentaries as an editor. You *are* writing the film. Some editors may think of themselves as directors, but I would say that we're more writers. There's quite a difference between when somebody hands you a script with the accompanying footage and says, "Edit it!" and when somebody says to you, "I shot all these interviews. Here's the story of what happened. I have no other idea. Go!" You have to come up with the structure yourself.

So you are a writer, not really an editor.

I mean, it is editing. I'm not trying to denigrate what an "editor" does. That *is* what an editor is. But somehow a straight "editing" credit doesn't cover the extent of what you often have to do in a documentary.

Director, writer, and editor rolled into one.

That's what I'm trying to say: that what we're doing is often more important than what we're getting credit for. Even if you have wonderful relationships with the directors, and you have all the freedom in the world to follow your aesthetic, at some point the film goes out and it's *their* film. The Polanski film is Marina Zenovich's film. She deserves it, she worked on it for five years—I worked on it for only four months! But creatively, as an artist—which is also what an editor is—it's hard to let go. All directors tend to do that. Werner does that. It is his film, he will publicize it, and it will be about him, him, him, above everyone else. And what is interesting is that people feel that Werner Herzog films just come out of the side of his head or something!

Like Zeus? (Laughs.)

Exactly! But I beg to differ. Peter Zeitlinger, his cinematographer, and I have a lot to do with Werner's filmmaking.

At least sometimes the recognition comes out in editing awards.

But *Grizzly Man,* for example, was not only *not* nominated for an Academy Award, it wasn't even shortlisted for an Academy Award, meaning that in that year, it was not one of the seventeen best documentaries made in the United States. So that was a completely political thing, a whole other issue, but that is how it's run.

It did win awards at different festivals.

Sure. International documentary societies' Film of the Year. Werner's won plenty of awards with his films. A lot of people celebrate that he is a different voice, and he certainly is.

If you went back to the films you said you wouldn't see again—the charcoal sketches—and reedited them under different circumstances, would you feel differently about them?

That's a great question. I don't know if Werner's ever really said this to me, but I have this feeling that there's kind of this "eighty percent" that you get to with a film. In other words, you pretty quickly get to a point with the edit where you see what this film is going to be. Then there's that other twenty percent where you're going to move this, tweak that, change this and that. But that extra icing on the cake doesn't really matter, in a sense. The film is essentially what it is. I think this is more Werner's point of view actually. Here's a good story to illustrate. If you asked Werner, "How long did it take to edit *Grizzly Man?*" he would say eight days. That's absurd.

What would you say?

It was like three months! *(Laughs.)* Which, by the way, is fast enough.

Then what does he mean by eight days?

In eight days, we made a first cut of the film. And you could see what the film was going to be in that time. But it didn't have all the elements that made it work. For example, the whole idea of the filmmakers' views on nature—Werner's and Timothy's—meeting in the middle, the whole idea of the very first shot of the film establishing the death, the whole idea about how to show the terrible "last tape"—none of those were in the first cut. But the *aesthetic* of the film was there in eight days. So I don't know if Werner somehow lost interest in the ideas that had to be developed after eight days, or maybe he felt reworking the film so much was taking power away from his filmmaking. A lot of times, he wasn't even there for much of the later work or he didn't want to be involved in that process. Of course, he approved of everything eventually.

Maybe he felt he did all he could with the assembly and that was enough for him.

I think after that moment—after those eight days—other people had to start chiming in. But, remember, the film is *his* child. Sure, he loves me and my aesthetic well enough, but I'm still messing with his child! *(Laughs.)* I tell the eight-day story quite often. One time we talked together at a screening somewhere and he said *Grizzly Man* was edited in eight days, and I said to Werner, "I really don't know where you're coming from with that!" I tried to make a joke out of it, but it used to really make me angry because to me, the gist is that he's negating what I did on the film by saying that.

Or else he's giving you much credit to say you're a genius who did it in eight days!

I think that is his point of view. But everything we did that I think made the film work, we did *after* eight days. *(Laughs.)*

You've edited so many documentaries with Herzog and others—a far cry from your college aspiration of directing. Do you want to continue documentary editing in the years ahead?

Well, I think most of the exciting filmmaking you see today is documentary filmmaking. It's the last refuge of what used to be art cinema or low-budget filmmaking. That's why I ended up doing it even though I had no interest in it, because it's where you have the freedom to do your stuff. Most of the documentaries I have worked on were at around or under a million dollars. That means there is simply not the pressure that a twenty-five or forty million dollar film has. But I'm really much more interested in fiction now; that's what I want to do more and more of. I'm not really in tune with Hollywood films for the most part, so I can't see myself doing those. I like the kind of films that Lynne Ramsay makes, fictional but very creative, rich films, and I will be working on her next film, *We Need to Talk about Kevin.* I also want to write and direct my own fictional films.

Does it all boil down to learning film "language," as you mentioned before? That is, by learning the language, you can become a consummate filmmaker?

Learning the language of film is powerful. I once did two science films in England, TV films about DNA, and when I got there, I started looking at the material and I was like, oh my God, this is a total mistake because I don't have the slightest understanding of all this science! How am I going to edit this? But then I realized what my role was. That's why I started thinking on this level of language. I needed to interpret this scientific material into the language of *cinema.* I'm looking for structure—that's the biggest part of language. Look for the structure in the scenes. How does one thing fit with the next organically? There is an architectural element as well. It becomes very three-dimensional. One of my biggest thrills is also in making metaphors in film. In the Polanski film, I made a little gag in one scene, just like a Buster Keaton gag, with three beats. You hear a drum being pounded over somebody's interview, then we cut to a clip from the film *The Fat and the Lean,* where a fat man is beating a drum, and suddenly you realize Polanski is in the scene dancing as the puppet to this fat man's music. And it resonated to what was going on in Polanski's life being told in the documentary, where he had become a puppet to all these people who want to string him up for his crime. I always love it when the "gag" works and the audience gets it. It's not like "Ha ha ha, I'm brilliant!" but "Ahh, you and I are speaking the same language!" And in the documentary, we were showing you clips of Polanski's films all along, so seeing him in *The Fat and the Lean* as the puppet doesn't come out of nowhere. It's organic. In another scene, when Polanski is fleeing the U.S., we didn't have any footage of him in that moment, obviously because he's skipping town. So we did straight-on archival footage to tell the story. We found shots of someone driving a car and we are in the driver's seat looking out the window, then of an airport, then shots of an airplane landing, then of Paris, and so on.

So although it's not his car or his plane, it suggests what Polanski went through and it becomes a film of the filmmaker, so to speak.

And it's psychological, like you are in his head at the moment. It's you as Polanski looking out that car window. So editing all comes down to being fluent and knowing what you want to say. Knowing when to use archival footage to tell the story, knowing when to use music as part of the structure, knowing when to use just one shot, if that's all it takes.

How can using only one *shot for one scene really be editing?*

Well, I spoke recently at an Academy editing seminar. We were all supposed to bring samples from our films, so I showed the beginning of *Grizzly Man,* which I thought was brilliant. It was Timothy's long monologue. Like in a perfect, beautiful stage play, he walks into the frame. In his speech, he encapsulates everything you need to know: that he's somewhat insane, that he's really charming, that he has an interesting story, and that he's eventually going to be killed by these bears. But I forgot one thing. The whole scene was *only one shot!*

And that was your exemplar of good editing?

Yes. Interestingly, the scene used to be shorter and it used to be in the middle of the film. That was another thing we did after our "eight days": we pulled that scene all the way out of the film and put it at the beginning. To me, that made all the difference in the world to the film.

What reaction did you get at the Academy?

The people were like, "What is this? This is *editing?*" Well, it *was* an important editorial choice to make that shot the beginning of the film. For *that* film, that's the perfect opening as far as I, the editor, was concerned. And I stand by it.

7. Editing the Self

ALAN BERLINER

1975 *Patent Pending* (short), dir. Alan Berliner

1976 *Four Corner Time* (four short films), dir. Alan Berliner

- *Line*
- *Perimeter*
- *Intersection*
- *Traffic Light*

1976 *Color Wheel* (short), dir. Alan Berliner

1979 *Lines of Force* (short), dir. Alan Berliner

1980 *City Edition* (short), dir. Alan Berliner

1981 *Myth in the Electric Age* (short), dir. Alan Berliner

1983 *Natural History* (short), dir. Alan Berliner

1985 *Everywhere at Once* (short), dir. Alan Berliner

1988 *The Family Album*, dir. Alan Berliner

1991 *Intimate Stranger*, dir. Alan Berliner

1996 *Nobody's Business*, dir. Alan Berliner

2001 *The Sweetest Sound*, dir. Alan Berliner

2006 *Wide Awake*, dir. Alan Berliner

2010 *Translating Edwin Honig: A Poet's Alzheimer's* (short), dir. Alan Berliner

2011 *Playing with Fire* (short), dir. Alan Berliner

2012 *First Cousin Once Removed*, dir. Alan Berliner

AWARDS

1986 Grand Prize Winner, Ann Arbor Film Festival, *Everywhere at Once*

1987 First Prize Blue Ribbon, American Film / Video Festival, *The Family Album*

1987 Golden Gate Award, San Francisco International Film Festival, *The Family Album*

1987 Whitney Museum of American Art Biennial Exhibition, *The Family Album*

1992 First Prize Blue Ribbon, American Film / Video Festival, *Intimate Stranger*

1992 First Prize, Nonfiction Category, USA Film Festival, *Intimate Stranger*

1992 Special Jury Award, Cinema du Reel Film Festival, *Intimate Stranger*

1992 Audience Award, San Francisco International Film Festival, *Intimate Stranger*

1993 IDA Award, International Documentary Association, *Intimate Stranger*

1997 International Film Critics Association Prize, Berlin International Film Festival, *Nobody's Business*

1997 Golden Spire Golden Gate Award, San Francisco International Film Festival, *Nobody's Business*

1997 Caligari Film Award, Berlin International Film Festival, *Nobody's Business*

1997 Audience Award for Best Documentary Feature, Florida Film Festival, *Nobody's Business*

1997 Grand Prize, Visions du Réel Documentary Film Festival, Switzerland, *Nobody's Business*

1997 First Prize for Innovation in Documentary, Festival dei Popoli, Italy, *Nobody's Business*

1998 Emmy Award, *Nobody's Business*

Editors hired to cut directors' visions admit to living with the film, daily and obsessively, as if it were their own. For an editor who is also an independent filmmaker, the obsession is both inexpressible and perfectly articulate. As writer, director, cinematographer, editor, sound editor, and producer, Alan Berliner's life is inseparable from his films and vice versa. He keeps personal journals that capture the midnight thoughts of a film-maker who sleeplessly deliberates over "four words too many" or "two frames too long" to create his life-works. So blurred is the line between life and film that Berliner has even made a film about his insomnia!

Berliner perpetuates the editor's reliance on poetic metaphors to explain the art, craft, and mystery of editing: his process is like chemistry, archi-tecture, music, stamp collecting, evolution, and mountain climbing. His work environment mirrors the intricate, layered organization of his editorial mind as his studio is part museum, part archive. His enormous personal library of sounds, images, and objects are cataloged in spectral-colored boxes; shelves upon shelves hold cross-referenced files of newspa-per clippings, correspondence, and tens of thousands of *New York Times* photographs. Space is filled with boxes of old American home movies and sculpture made from discarded film reels. Through the innovative use of "found" material, sounds, vintage footage, and interviews with sup-portive (but sometimes reluctant) family members, Berliner has created a series of visually intriguing, highly respected, and poignant cinematic records of family history, memory, and identity—films which are exem-plars of the power of editing and all the metaphorical connections it offers an audience.

Although Berliner has been making personal films for decades, he epito-mizes the innumerable possibilities, because of the digital revolution, for aspiring filmmakers in the twenty-first century to express themselves in "homemade" films. As a teacher, Berliner encourages students to trust their instincts and find connections that "make the mind smile." While the process of editing, particularly for an independent filmmaker, is not unlike walking down darkened streets of an unknown geography, for Berliner and all who take the trip, serendipity and creativity prove to be perfect guides.

In an article you wrote, you said that even as a child, you thought like an editor. What did you mean by that?

On the most basic level, what I'm doing now is directly related to the way I did things as a child. When I was perhaps nine or ten, my grandfa-ther began what would become a weekly ritual of bringing me envelopes stuffed with postage stamps from all over the world, that he had gathered and saved from his extensive international correspondence. As my collec-tion began to grow, I used to love the serenity of going into my bedroom, closing the door, and spreading those myriad tiny images out in front of me across the bed. But unlike most of my other stamp-collecting friends at the time, my pleasure didn't involve filling up the pages of a stamp album. It was enough for me to savor them, make little sequences of them, organize them by subject, country, color or whatever other criteria I had in mind that day, and then put them back in the box. I've always imagined that this simple hobby somehow catalyzed and stimulated a kind of visual sophistication from a young age. It also established my comfort level working with large quantities of images, doing so in a room all by myself— and having fun doing it. A few years later, in junior high school, I developed a unique way of writing term papers and essays. I wrote all my thoughts out on legal-sized paper, generating pages and pages of information in longhand. I would then staple all of those pages together end to end, and roll them up into a scroll, which I would take to the longest corridor of my house and spread across the floor, all the way down the hall. With pen, paper, scissors, stapler, scotch tape, and research books by my side, I then got on my hands and knees and began "editing." If I needed to generate additional material, I would write it out by hand on a new piece of paper and Scotch-tape or staple it into the scroll. If I wanted to remove information, I would cut it out with my scissors and "resplice" the scroll back together. At the end of the day, I would roll up the scroll, ready to begin the process again the following day. Cinematically speaking, my final rather messy "edited" scroll was nothing less than a "spliced workprint"! I guess you could call the final typed-up version the "answer print." Of course if I was in junior high school now, I'd be writing on a computer, and none of this story would make any sense to me.

Did your family understand what you were doing?

I don't remember anyone paying any particular attention, except maybe when they had to climb over me as they walked by. But the interesting point was that even as a child, I needed to have a holistic sense of the entire thing, especially something I made, you might even say "sculpted" with my own two hands. I did all of it intuitively; no one taught me to put ideas and information together like that. Looking back on it now as a filmmaker, I see it as an absolutely protocinematic editorial process in both conception and execution. I also remember that it made perfect sense to me at the time.

How did your education help you develop film as a form of personal expression?

I have a BA in avant-garde film and experimental cinema from the State University of New York at Binghamton, one of the few places in the country where film was taught as an art form, without any connection to broadcasting, theater, radio, television, journalism or fiction. Without any connection to any commercial motivation or Hollywood ambitions. We were oriented to think of ourselves as artists, and to think of cinema as a cousin to the rest of the arts—music, architecture, painting, and sculpture—and a kindred spirit to poetry. In fact, we weren't even taught all that much about the technical aspects of filmmaking. It was more about learning what you need to know in order to do what you need to do. From there, I received a special graduate fellowship from the School of Art at the University of Oklahoma, home of another experimental filmmaking program, where I received my MFA degree and taught film production courses before returning home to New York City in 1979.

Did you study editing in college?

No one ever actually taught me *how* to edit. I've never taken a class on montage, for instance. I did study exquisitely edited films by filmmakers like Vertov, Eisenstein, Pudovkin, and Welles, and avant-garde masters like Kubelka, Connor, and Snow in college, but it was all purely analytical, not practical. I remember being especially intrigued by the way we would sometimes use what was called an "analytic projector" to study a film in class. An analytic projector allows you to stop on any frame, run a film at different speeds, and go forward and backward one frame at a time at will. We would study various scenes and "cuts" in films like *Citizen Kane* or *Man with a Movie Camera,* going back and forth over and over to see and discover the logic and aesthetic thinking at play. The idea of making films that could be studied on an analytic projector one day always stuck with me, and has somehow played a role in my aspiration to make films in which my own decision-making process could, would, and should withstand the rigors of that kind of careful, probing examination.

How did this training help with later work experience?

In both Binghamton and Oklahoma, students were expected to make films completely by themselves: we directed, shot, edited and negative-matched—whatever was necessary to complete our own films from beginning to end. When I returned to New York and started looking for a job, it felt strange and rather limiting for me to think about working in any one particular aspect of filmmaking because I loved the entire process so much. As it turned out, the few connections I did have within the New York film industry were in editing, so my very first job interview was for the role of assistant editor—not that I knew what an assistant editor actually did. Although I had both undergraduate and graduate degrees in film, both with highest honors, I didn't know a thing about how a professional cutting room was set up; I didn't know anything about the industrial protocols of how real films got made. Most importantly, I didn't know a word of the professional lingo or jargon that editors speak. To be honest, I didn't even know what I didn't know. The very first job I got was working in the postproduction editing world of ABC Sports, for a program called *The American Sportsman*. Although I had initially applied for an assistant editor job there, the supervising editor, a really nice and talented man named Ted Winterburn, told me that there were no openings. Much to my surprise, a day or two later, Ted called me back and asked if I would be willing to work as a sound-effects librarian. Considering that I had no idea what an assistant editor did—applying for the job in the first place was part naïveté, part youthful folly—being offered a sound-effects librarian position was the luckiest consolation prize I've ever received. It was also one of the most synchronistic moments of my life. I've always been an extremely organized person, so the idea of being a "librarian" seemed far less intimidating and potentially embarrassing than pretending to be an assistant editor.

Were you worried about not being able to continue making your own personal films?

The one thing I did know was that I needed to keep working on my own films, even though I was no longer a student and now had to work to pay my rent. I always thought of it as a good news / bad news situation. The bad news was my loss of freedom—that my time was no longer my own. The good news was that I was now around flatbed editing machines, sound dubbers, mixing studios, and other editing tools and supplies all the time. It didn't take me long to realize that if I didn't abuse the privilege, I could work for ABC by day, and stay after hours to work on my own projects at night. When their day was over, my night began. Another way of saying it is that when my job was over, my *work* began.

What did you do as "librarian" at ABC Sports?

A virtual mountain of sound effects recorded from all over the world, primarily from nature and nature-related sources and activities, was waiting to be listened to, annotated, and cataloged. For nine months, that's just what I did. I'll never forget coming home and being asked what I did at work that day, and I'd tell stories about how I'd listened to waterfalls, or exotic Arctic winds, or thirty-three variations of fire. Then there were days filled with the sounds of monkeys, whales, dolphins, camels, elephants, hippos, endless crickets—just about everything that lives in forests, jungles, deserts, and oceans. I once spent an entire week listening to the sounds of footsteps: through grass, through leaves; on sand, snow, gravel, metal, wood, linoleum, carpet; up stairs, down stairs, people wearing high heels, sneakers, shoes, barefoot; one person, two people, five people, crowds of people—you get the idea. It was an incredible education in close listening and recognizing nuances of difference between sounds that were often only slightly dissimilar, all the while finding ways to translate those distinctions into words. In the end, I must have annotated several thousand sounds. The wonderful thing about that job was that I was left virtually on my own, without any pressure, and had both the time and freedom to secretly learn the lingo, protocols, and culture of the industrial side of filmmaking—and get paid while doing so. I even became a member of the motion picture editors union!

Did you observe other editors at work?

Yes. For nine months, quietly and innocently, a part of my day would be devoted to observing various editors going about their work. From time to time I'd nonchalantly ask them what they were doing and why they were doing it *that way.* All of this came in handy when my work on the sound-effects library was finally complete, and Ted told me I would now be assigned to the position of assistant sound editor. After one year of assisting others, I was "promoted" to the position of sound editor. In many ways, I had become extremely valuable to ABC Sports because I had absorbed an entire library of sounds and could now suggest specific sounds, and combinations of sounds, to the sound and picture editors who worked there, if and when they ever needed help. To this day, Ted has no idea that I knew next to nothing about the editing industry when I first walked in the door. That is, until he reads this book!

Was this the first time you had worked so intensely in sound?

Yes, it was all new to me and I was hungry to learn, which is why I think I grabbed onto sound so easily and so quickly. Another amazing thing about the job was that the producers at *The American Sportsman* took "sound" very seriously. They wanted the soundtracks for the films we were making to be extremely textured, full of nuance, and—especially because it was an "outdoor" series—extremely precise in its aural representation of nature. And they spared no expense. There I was, not even two years out of school, preparing anywhere from fifteen to twenty-five tracks of sound every few weeks for mixes with the legendary Lee Dichter, perhaps *the* best sound mixer in New York City. Without truly appreciating the ramifications at the time, I was working at the highest professional level, often under intense deadline pressure, and preparing for mixes that were observed and scrutinized by several layers of people who sat in judgment. All this gave me confidence and proficiency with the skills and tools of filmmaking. But most importantly, this situation facilitated the continuation of my own personal filmmaking, and I was learning things that would enable me to grow with my own work. I also had access to a first-class sound-effects library, which I made extensive use of. During the five or six years that I worked for ABC (at some point, I starting working freelance for ABC News), I completed a series of short abstract "found footage" collage films that explored the relationship between sound and image rather intensely. In retrospect, my innate sense of organization, an ability to work long hours with both focus and patience, and a willingness to believe in myself amid the uncertainties and insecurities that are intrinsic to the process of making films, made me a perfect fit for the world of editing. This has become the primary aesthetic force behind all of my own films ever since.

Can you talk more about your relationship to organization?

Over the years I've met really good editors whose personal lives and even their aesthetic sensibilities were truly "chaotic." They've somehow managed to use the editing room as a special haven for creating inspired and cogent film logics. I also know extremely structured people whose overly linear thought processes often get in the way of their ability to create lyrical and/ or abstract metaphorical film logics. Ironically, most organized people will tell you that chaos and disorder are important parts of their process; there's always a balance, a dialectical dynamic that gives shape to their lives. My own sense of organization is a part of an intuitive process I live and breathe both inside *and* outside the editing room. I've always been attracted to detail and have never shied away from a project because there was too much information or material that required organizational triage before anyone could begin working with it. On the contrary, I love being surrounded by lots of media, information, ideas, and materials—the more the better. One of the things I realized about myself at an early age is that I am a natural collagist. And so over the years, I've done what collagists tend to do: I've surrounded myself with things that I might one day want to put together. My studio is filled with film images, sounds, found photographs, old photo albums, slide transparencies, newspaper clippings, newspaper photographs, magazines, odd and unusual objects, materials, and media detritus of all kinds—all organized in boxes and drawers and labeled with a librarian's sense of care and order. Editors are part librarians anyway, because they need to know where things are in order to make use of them quickly and efficiently. Having an idea but being unable to test it or act upon it is not editing—it's frustrating. And so I've spent a great deal of time and energy creating systems of organization that allow me to make connections and associations between things (and the ideas behind them) quickly and fluidly—that help me to "act at the speed of thought."

In organizing the material, you are also creating atmosphere. For example, people might use black-and-white boxes to store film, but you use rainbow colors.

I do that instinctively. I also want my process to resonate with a certain visual elegance both inside and out. I'm a big believer that process and product are directly related; that many of the intrinsic "givens" we often take for granted about *how* we do things contribute in very subtle but often significant ways to *what* we do. There are times when I let my studio become cluttered and disheveled, because I know that the act of cleaning it up and restoring order will have a positive impact on my work. I don't know how many times simply moving a piece of furniture or changing the composition of my bookshelves has literally given me a new sense of clarity—and the boost that comes with it.

Are your thoughts sometimes cluttered and disheveled?

Sure. Sometimes you have to get lost in order to find your way. Thought by its very nature is extremely messy and malleable. I don't think anyone finds the road to good ideas in a straight line, let alone on their first try. There's always a trail of discarded concepts and "bad ideas" that got you there. In fact, I'm a big believer in bad ideas, and will never be afraid to celebrate their role in my work. For editors, a willingness to acknowledge the importance of bad ideas implies both the ability to be self-critical *and* the resiliency required to respond to that criticism by having better ideas. Your thought process must be flexible, active, and open to your own suggestions, because editing is inherently a responsive endeavor. Over time, by engaging in an open and honest dialogue with your film, slowly but surely the film itself will begin telling you how it needs to be made.

Can you talk about your early abstract collage films from the 1980s?

I began building my own personal library—I refer to it as my "image bank"—of 16mm film and sound effects (ABC let me make copies of their entire sound-effects library) ever since I started making films in the mid-1970s. Between 1980 and 1985, I completed a series of four short collage films, *City Edition, Myth in the Electric Age* (with voiceover by Marshall McLuhan), *Natural History,* and *Everywhere at Once.* Each of them is a rather dense collage film exploring the territory of what we used to call "sound-image relationships." While making these films, I developed a working process loosely based on an analogy with molecular chemistry. I began each film by simply looking through my image and sound library to discover interesting and compelling visual and aural connections, thematic associations, and musical dynamics, whether image-to-image, sound-to-sound, or especially sound-to-image. I would then isolate these cuts into what I call "molecules," set them aside, and continue making more. During the fledgling stages of stringing these molecules together, I'd start to think about the "valence" of a particular image or sound—its potential "bondability" with other images and/or sounds. Then I'd begin making notes about the qualities that defined each shot's beginning and ending—its "edges," based on color, movement, shape, graphics, theme, and other cinematic dynamics that could help me link molecules together into longer sequences that I call "compounds." After much trial and error—and a lot of bad ideas!—these compounds grew into longer and longer chemical equations that eventually coalesced into a finished film.

You often reuse the same images and sometimes the same sounds in different films. For example, I recognized shots from your short films as well as from Intimate Stranger *and* Nobody's Business *in the more recent* Wide Awake.

I've always been fascinated with the idea of recycling images and sounds I've used in the past and giving them new meanings by recontextualizing them—a different sound over the same image, a different image under the same sound, the same shot incorporated into entirely different montages—all in an effort to illustrate and play with the plasticity of editing. Once I finish a film, I take it apart and put all the sounds and images back in my archive, where they await the demands and explorations of my next film. By now, at least a hundred different images and sounds must have appeared multiple times throughout all my films, establishing a kind of "genetic" continuity between them as well as creating multiple layers of references and connections between and among them all. Another key element I learned from making these short films is that, for me, sound and image almost always have equal weight, equal importance. When I'm working on a film, it is equally possible for a sound to suggest an image or a storytelling strategy as it would be for an image to suggest a soundtrack. And so I treat sound and images with equal respect—which brings me to the idea of proper naming in the editing room.

Naming, with multiple levels in mind?

In a way. What you call something—how you describe it—and the consistency of the vocabulary you use in the editing room will ultimately determine a great deal about the character and quality of your editing experience. What you call something is crucial to the process of determining what you might end up doing with it. Naming something also profoundly impacts how your associative memory will be able to link to it, connect with it, and generate new (or old) contexts for it. Not only that, but calling a shot, a sound or a sequence with an appropriate name will also help you remember it. And that's important, because amid the throes of intense editing, important elements and details can often get lost in the crowd if they're not given names that facilitate an active—and memorable—engagement with them. For me, the secret to all of this is "specificity" and "visibility" during the process of logging. As I used to tell my son Eli when he was younger, you first have to lay out all the pieces of the jigsaw puzzle face up in front of you before you can begin putting the puzzle together. Transposed to the editing room, this means having the patience, taking the time, and caring enough to create as many categories and subcategories as possible—being as *specific* as possible, so that you break down your raw material into as many discreet and individualized pieces (and by that I mean bins, clips, and subclips) as possible. By making all the component *parts* extremely clear and visible at the beginning, it's easier for me to see *the whole* on my journey to the finish line.

All of this sounds very time-consuming, even laborious. How do you keep it from becoming an obstacle to the very fluidity you're aiming for?

When you're as process-oriented as I am, you need to find ways of keeping things from getting too laborious or bogged down in detail. I often tell myself—because I truly believe it—that breaking down and logging the material is actually much more difficult than working with it. But there's also a tremendous amount of discretion and play involved. You're in a position to define terms, and create a uniquely descriptive shorthand that reflects your relationship to, and understanding of, the characters and themes of your subject. At this early stage, I'm always finding ways to amuse myself as I climb my way up the huge mountain of material standing in front of me. I make up little games with myself as I go along. I avoid doing things based on alphabetical or chronological order. I give people, places, and things nicknames. Everything is done with a kind of playful diligence. I'm someone who believes that editing should be fun. That making discoveries and finding connections are fun. That storytelling is fun. Then again, as someone who's often been described as a "perfectionist," I'm always trying to balance the parts of me that need to be precise and controlled with those that aspire to be playful and unpredictable. Sometimes it's hard.

Do you feel overwhelmed by that?

Sometimes, for sure. After I finished my first hour-long film, *The Family Album*, I lost sleep because I felt that one shot was two frames too long. I fixated on it for days. And there was one voiceover line that I felt went on four words too long. That bothered me a lot too. I think many good editors have a strong obsessive-compulsive component to their personalities—the cause, or maybe it's really the effect, of prolonged and intense concentration, and a deeply-felt sense of caring. And there's certainly nothing wrong with that. I used to feel extremely fragile after I finished a film. If something fell short of my expectations, or if certain filmic problems still felt unsolved or unresolved, I got very distressed. I've learned from experience, though, to accept that I will probably always fall so many degrees short of my own idealized sense of "good" and "great," let alone "perfect." It's part of maturing as a filmmaker, accepting the limits of human nature and the limits of technology. Besides, with filmmaking, so many things are out of your control. It was hard for me to accept that I couldn't keep a shot of the sky from being too blue, regardless of how many times I complained about it to the colorist. Or simply that amid the 227 details that made their way onto my list in the final days of finishing a film, 1 additional, even essential item—or maybe 7 of them— somehow escaped me. That's called being human.

Let's go back to The Family Album. *Because home-movie scenes tend to be very short, there must be hundreds of shots—most of them just a few seconds long, not to mention hundreds of small pieces of sound, all collaged together. That's a lot of detail to keep track of.*

In many ways, *The Family Album* is very much all about editing. One critic wrote that it "resembles a sort of *Man with a Movie Camera* [1928, Dziga Vertov] goes to the American nuclear family." It's an elaborate collage of old and anonymous 16mm American family home movies from the 1920s to the 1940s, juxtaposed with mostly anonymous family audio recordings and oral histories to create a film that grapples with home movies as tools—and gestures—of personal history, memory, and identity. As idealized representations of family life, home movies manifest our collective need to present a false front to posterity. They ooze with joy, celebration, and the pleasures of leisure time, avoiding and denying the more gritty stuff of real-life experience taking place in front of or behind the camera. One of the most representative juxtapositions in the film is of a man and a woman in a car looking into the camera. The smiling woman puts her hand to her nose and twirls her fingers while the voiceover says, "I always looked like I was happy to the public, but it just was never like that in the home."

Yet the film seems to cover all *of life, not just moments.*

The film follows the intuitive logic of the life cycle, with all home-movie imagery structured from birth to death. The addition of a wide variety of emotionally and psychologically discordant sound elements allows me to create layers of irony and counterpoint between what you see and what you hear. In the discrepancies between these two completely separate and unrelated realities arises a multitude of little fictions that become both personal and archetypal at the same time. In effect, the film, like life itself, becomes more complicated as it progresses, introducing issues of jealousy, insecurity, guilt, divorce, alcoholism, ambivalence, suicide, the indignities of growing old, and the inevitability of death. But my deepest and highest aspiration for the film, especially from this distance so many years later, is that it resonates with a profound love of humanity in all its shapes, sizes, and myriad foibles.

Did you want an overriding playful tone throughout The Family Album *despite dealing with some serious subjects?*

Because there are images and sounds taken from more than seventy-five different families in the film, there's an extremely broad canvas of religious, race (I did manage to find some rare African-American family home movies), gender, ethnicity, and class issues swirling around. This incredible diversity of source material gave me freedom to move from the playful to the serious and back again—often from shot to shot, from moment to moment—just like it happens in life. Ultimately *The Family Album* is about the role of family in our lives, and there's nothing more complicated than that. But even if you approach the idea of family as a bourgeois capitalist institution, the film can and should still resonate with you. After all, when it comes right down to it, each of us was once a vulnerable and impressionable child in someone else's arms, trapped inside the maze of someone else's best and worst intentions. That is one thing we all share.

Some images reach into deeper levels of thought. For instance, when you set the audio of the funeral against an image of a boat on the water, I couldn't help but think of the Greek myth of Charon carrying the soul to the other world on his ferry.

Since I didn't have any footage of a funeral but did have an audio recording of a funeral ceremony, I was able to poeticize the subject by using a series of very evocative, mysterious, and grainy shots of someone in a small boat, alone in the middle of a lake, rowing his way across the horizon. There is also a fragment from a funeral prayer on the soundtrack, referring to some distant shore: "As a drop of water in the sea, as a grain of sand on the shore, so are man's few days in eternity . . . the good things in life last for limited days." I was just making what seemed like the most powerful connection I could, given the limitations of the home movie imagery and the "found audio" I had to work with. Of course, you rarely see funerals or cemeteries in home movies; they are, after all, sad occasions, sad places, and basically at odds with the joyous imperative that motivates us to take home movies in the first place. In the many hundreds of home movies that I saw during the making of *The Family Album*, I did not see one single image of a funeral. There are some shots of people in a cemetery dancing on top of tombstones, but I see that as just another example of someone trying to put a home-movie smile on the face of death.

If home movies are idealistic, do you think audio is realistic?

Much more so, I think, although I've encountered many different attitudes from people when it comes to relating personal history or revealing inner thoughts during oral histories. Some find it hard to lie but at the same time find the truth painful, so they solve that by avoiding difficult issues. For some people, doing an oral history is an occasion for revelation: "You know, I've never told this to anyone before, but . . ." It's a kind of absolution. Of course, all history, and in some way all memory itself, is revisionist. It depends on who's telling it, their point of view, their motivation, and especially who they think might be listening—now or in a distant future.

With all the footage and sound you had, how did you choose what to use and what to leave out?

For me, editing is about being responsive and open to making discoveries. The key word in making discoveries is "noticing." What catches my eye? What tickles my thought? What moves my gut? What makes me smile? The more you notice, the more connections there are to be made. I always construct my own films as I go along, building up from my initial "noticings" until the film takes on a heartbeat, a pulse, and ultimately, a personality of its own. I've found that making just one good editorial discovery each day—and by that I mean one cut, one idea, one decision that feels, looks, and sounds good enough to last all the way to the finish line, "a keeper," even if it's the addition or removal of a single shot—is enough to keep me happy, focused, and engaged. As long as I feel the film is getting a little better every day, I'm ready, willing, and able to string together enough of those days into weeks, weeks into months, and months into years if necessary, so that the film can evolve from this slow and steady string of daily accruals. Kind of like the way a bird builds its nest. Twig by twig. Day by day.

Are there different kinds of "noticing" throughout the course of editing?

Absolutely, but for the sake of clarity, let me substitute the word *listening* instead. Just like we can notice with our ears, we can also listen with our eyes. Many different modes of listening are called for during the course of editing. At the beginning, you're listening while you digitize your material, you're listening while you log your material, and you're even listening while you read your transcripts. What are you listening for? When every idea you've had, every image you've shot, every bit of research you've done, every aspiration and fascination you have about your subject is shouting out for your attention, you're listening for the quiet truth inside your material. You're listening for the thread of a melody, a direction you can quietly follow without getting overwhelmed by all the noise. I said it before and I'll say it again: "If you have the patience to listen, the film itself will tell you how it needs to be made."

It sounds like a process of refinement.

Absolutely. It's a perpetual process of refinement. From the very first day of editing, I'm looking to assess what's working and what's not, and trying to understand and articulate why. Every day is an opportunity to make what's bad good, what's good better, what's very good even better, and keep what's great, great, without mucking things up. I always reserve the last week or two of a project for something I call "polishing." It's when I deal in the minutiae of editing. Sharpening the edges of shots. Assessing whether something needs to be slightly faster, slower, longer, shorter, rougher, smoother, louder, or softer. The mind's eye becomes an ever-finer sieve, often dealing with one- or two-frame increments. You can do a lot with a few days of intense noticing and listening at that level.

In keeping track of these minutiae, do you ever write a script of what you are filming?
Never.

Notes of how to divide the film into chapters?
Never.

Outlines?
No.

Treatment?
I've never written a treatment in my whole life. I wouldn't even know how to go about it.

But you keep track of what you have to cover to develop something logically. Is there a way to explain that to novice filmmakers?
Think process. The process of making decisions; the process of growing with something over time; the process of making something better over time; the process of learning to trust your own instincts. It's important to acknowledge that it's okay to get lost. It's okay not to know where you're going when you start out. Filmmaking is not a paint-by-numbers game. It is, of course, important to have a sense of direction, to draw a rough map of the territory you're traversing. But I recommend an unabashedly open mind, especially at the beginning. From time to time, students will come to me and tell me they're stuck, that they don't know what to do with their film, and I often tell them, "Just throw something against the wall and see what sticks. Even if you think it's horrible, you now have something to talk about, to reflect upon. You now have some questions to ask, or more appropriately put, some questions to answer: what makes it horrible? What might you do to make it a little better? Is there anything about it that you like? How can you build on that?" It's about initiating a process, a feedback dynamic—a dialogue—with your film that will eventually take on a life of its own.

Can you teach that?
You can certainly try. I once developed an exercise to teach the importance of context in editing, something I call "The Postcard Experiment."

I ask each student to bring in a horizontally-oriented postcard picture, whether a photograph, an illustration, something they bought or received in the mail, personal or commercial—so long as it's not one of those "I ♥ New York" tourist postcards they sell in Times Square. Then I randomly choose one person to put his or her image up on the wall to represent the first shot of an imaginary film that everyone has to invent on the spot. What's the film about? What does the first shot suggest? What does it tell us? How does this image orient us in time and space? Then I randomly pick someone else to put a postcard image up next to the first image. Now you're the second shot in the film; repeat in your own words what the first person said, and then move the sequence forward, sideways, diagonally, or any other way you choose, just so long as it's suggested or supported—perhaps a better word would be "imagined"—by your "shot." What connections can you make between the two images? What contexts do they share? I then continue through the entire class, randomly picking people one at a time to add their images to what has now evolved into a surreal yet strangely logical storyboard—a cinematic "exquisite corpse." At his or her turn, each person has to retell the entire flow of the "narrative" (though that's not always the proper word to describe it) from the very beginning—in many ways, it's also an interesting exercise in memory—up to and including the very last person, who somehow has to bring closure to the entire flow of thought. The postcard experiment is also a great way of representing some of the basic underlying tenets of surrealism in cinema—I'm thinking of films like *Un chien andalou* by Luis Buñuel, *Entr'acte* by René Clair or *Ballet mécanique* by Fernand Léger. You'd be amazed at the connections that people make, at the diverse themes that get interwoven, at the playful (and by that I mean fun) thinking that's demanded by this "game," and the genuine feeling of satisfaction that comes to each person solving his or her particular piece of the puzzle. In the end, it's all about discovering how context creates meaning and how the mind can reach in many directions at once to make sense out of nonsense and bring order to randomness, something we all do every day of our lives without realizing it. We just don't call it editing.

Much of editing seems to be open to unconscious forces, perhaps even including chance. I was intrigued that at the end of The Family Album, *you actually listed "Serendipity" in your credits. Can you comment on how "accidents" or "serendipity" impact the editorial process?*

Accidents in filmmaking are often magic by another name, and good directors and good editors must be willing to change and adjust their thinking in response to them all the time. I'm thinking of an example from *Wide Awake*, a film I made in 2006 about my long and problematic relationship to sleep—or the lack of it. At one point near the beginning of the film, there's a scene of me walking away from the camera down a long Las Vegas hotel corridor, slowly dissolving into the distance until I can barely be seen. The initial shot was taken almost on a whim, with no preconceived thought in mind—at least none that I understood at the time. Late one night as we were getting off the elevator and going back to our hotel room after shooting some parts of a sleep conference (none of which is used in the film), Ian Vollmer, the cameraperson, and I were struck by the sheer beauty and dramatic depth of this long, ornately carpeted orange-colored hallway, perhaps more than two hundred feet long, and I suggested—for no particular reason—that we get a shot of it. After we shot it "empty" (remember it was almost two in the morning), I suggested that we also take a shot of me walking down the hallway to the very end and back. It was all done playfully. No intent, no purpose, no meaning—a throwaway shot if there ever was one.

Meaning you had no idea you would create a sequence from it—or that you would even encounter such a corridor in the first place?
    Yes. In fact, when I got the footage home, I basically forgot about it. I don't even think I logged it. Then, months later, in the course of editing, some unexpected synapses began firing. I was working with a "relaxation tape" that I had recorded off a New York City hospital telephone insomnia hotline, in which a soft-spoken voice says, "Breathe in. Breathe out. Now . . . walk with me down the stairs, we're gonna walk out into a beautiful garden. Take one step down, and then two, then four, half way, five, six, seven, we can almost see that door." And then it continues to count down the number of steps it takes to get to a door that one imagines will open up onto this transcendently tranquil garden of sleep. The "guided imagery" of those words—the steps, the door, and the beautiful garden—somehow made me think of the shot of myself slowly walking down that long corridor in Las Vegas. Suddenly I began to see that shot as a potential metaphor for the idea of drifting off to sleep. Yet, as I know very well from personal experience, someone with insomnia doesn't get through that door very often, and therefore will likely feel more frustrated than relaxed, which in turn led me to search for archival shots of someone struggling to open a door, or shaking a doorknob, or banging on a door, "Let me in, let me in!" It also led me

to search for shots of "No Trespassing" signs, "Do Not Disturb" signs, and other shots that allude to the anxiety of not being able to get through that door and into the garden of sleep. Quite unexpectedly, I had stumbled upon a series of metaphors for the frustration of insomnia, all because of a throwaway shot taken in the middle of the night in a Las Vegas hotel.

What impact does such a metaphor make on the audience then?

First of all, it makes them think outside of traditional storytelling conventions. You're giving the audience an opportunity to make connections on their own, and in the process, think about insomnia in ways they probably never have before. I think people enjoy it when images they see everyday suddenly take on new meanings, especially as metaphors. It makes the mind smile. And when a mind is smiling, it's more nimble, more active, more open to possibilities. For me, this is where editing serves its most important function: if the audience can feel the touch of your invisible presence, especially if the close attention they're giving the film is rewarded with the discovery of meaningful connections and metaphors that resonate with their own experience and understandings—emotionally, intellectually, and viscerally—then you're creating a bond of trust. A bond that is, in effect, a contract with the audience. By pushing myself to find unique ways of merging form and content in each of my films, I am catalyzing the audience to work with me, play with me, and join me to see things differently.

I'm reminded of your use of the typewriter sound as a storytelling device and as a metaphor in Intimate Stranger.

Let me give you some background before I explain why and how the sound of a typewriter became the driving force of the film. *Intimate Stranger* is a portrait of my maternal grandfather Joseph Cassuto, who died—the victim of a hit-and-run car accident—in the middle of writing his autobiography. My grandfather had meticulously saved thousands of photographs throughout his life, along with virtually every letter and document he had ever received, and virtually every letter he'd ever sent (he used carbon paper in the days before xeroxing); in many cases he even saved the envelopes! When I first encountered this treasure trove of material (fifteen large boxes) gathering dust in the back of my uncle's office almost sixteen years after his sudden death, I felt like a private detective, combing through the known and the hidden, the obvious and the secret, in search of the revelations, contradictions, and similarities of someone who, like me—or, should I say, I like him?— liked to surround himself with overwhelming amounts of material and information.

How did you respond to discovering the inevitable "secrets" that all families have?

Making personal films about "the family" is complicated. From film to film, my relationship to my close and even extended family members is constantly changing. I'm alternately and simultaneously son, brother, grandson, nephew, cousin, husband, father, friend, or in the case of *The Sweetest Sound*, the "namesake" whose perspective is being explored. In *Intimate Stranger*, I put myself in the position of grandson making a biography of his grandfather, a so-called "ordinary person," who happened to think that his life was interesting enough for the rest of the world to know about. The only problem was that his own children, including my mother, were incredulous as to what, if anything, made his life all that fascinating. As my uncle Al says in the film, "He led an interesting life, but a lot of people lead interesting lives. He was just an ordinary man." And so I chose to take the journey inside the life and the labyrinth, also known as the "psyche," of my mother's family— history, secrets, patterns, unspoken truths, and myths—in order to understand my grandfather's legacy, both to his family and (as he apparently believed) to the world. Making the film made me realize how films about the dead are really about the living, and how this thing we call a "legacy" is actually a living, breathing set of emotional qualities that resonate long after a friend or loved one is no longer around. But my first challenge was to find a storytelling strategy that would allow audiences to see my grandfather's life—regardless of whether they found it interesting or not—as a kind of mirror of, or window into, aspects of their own lives.

And the typewriter?

Now, on to the typewriter . . . specifically a *manual typewriter*, which was the tool of correspondence in both my grandfather's business *and* personal lives and, of course, the tool he used to write his autobiography. The notion of using the typewriter as a storytelling motif was not so much *an idea* I had as it was *a connection* I made between typing and editing; between a blank piece of white paper and an empty white movie screen on the wall. I started to think about ways of transposing and synchronizing the clickety-clack sound of fingers hitting the individual keys of a type-writer as the basis for a rhythmic montage of images—photographs, letters, stamps, and hundreds of documents—that I as filmmaker would type (and by that I mean "edit") on the surface of the blank white page, the empty white screen. In order to accomplish this, I first recorded the sounds of someone typing a few sections of my grandfather's autobiography on his old manual typewriter. I then analyzed the number of frames between each typewriter keystroke (between each letter), and then the number of frames between words, generating an elaborate "score" that I used as a template to photograph sequences of pictures, letters, and documents on a copystand in my studio. I spent countless days on that copystand, rigorously following the score by clicking off individual frames on my Bolex camera: five frames, eight frames, nine frames, three frames, seven frames, and so on, one image at a time. It took forever, but in the end, this unity of form and content—between sound and image—brought the act of editing a film biography into metaphoric contact with the act of writing an autobiography. It also allowed me to shape an incredible amount of material into rhythmic sequences that became a kind of music, and with it, allowed me to think of and treat the typewriter as a kind of musical instrument. I also made use of the sounds of the space bar, the shift key, the small bell that rings at the end of each line, as well as the sound of the carriage return lever—accompanied by the image of a thick white line moving left to right across the screen, which I used in the film whenever I wanted to indicate a new idea, a new "paragraph" or a new "chapter." By weaving all of these elements together, I also in some way united all of my various roles—as filmmaker, editor, writer, animator, musician, biographer, and "grandson"—into one.

In Nobody's Business, *you're all of those things, but this time you're "the son."*

Like *Intimate Stranger* before it, making *Nobody's Business* was also a labor of love. It was my chance to confront the saddest and most compelling character I knew—my father, a man who lived alone in a New York City senior citizen home, seemingly defeated by the circumstances of his life. After reckoning with the legacy of my deceased grandfather, and through him, the story of my maternal family history, it now felt right to try and make a portrait of my very much alive—though very wounded—father, and complete the genealogical circle by exploring my paternal family history. The only problem was that my father had no interest in being the subject of a biography and couldn't care less about his family history. Throughout the film, he questions the very nature of my project: "I'm just an ordinary guy who's led an ordinary life. I was in the army, I got married, I raised a family, worked hard, I had my own business. That's all. That's nothing to make a picture about." And so *Nobody's Business* is a document of my attempt to interest my father in the meaning and significance of his own life, despite his resistance to me virtually every step of the way.

What about the shots of the boxers in Nobody's Business? *That's another use of a central storytelling metaphor.*

Over the years, my father had jokingly described some of our conversations as a kind of "verbal sparring," and so I had the idea early on of using some old archival boxing footage as a far-reaching metaphor for the Oedipal drama of our relationship, the collision of generations, and the way that words and ideas can function as punches and counterpunches in the course of a conversation—in the life of a relationship. My first inclination was to structure the film as a fifteen-round title bout, with title cards announcing the start of each round. The more I thought about it, though, the more I realized that doing so would put an unnecessary emphasis on keeping score; the audience might get too involved in the game of who's winning and who's losing. I was much more interested in representing the resiliency of the battle, a kind of nonstop perpetual exchange, more in tune with the real dynamics of family life. You'll notice that there are no knockouts in the boxing footage, just a lot of punching, scuffling, and holding on. I'll never forget the first time I put words and expressions with emotional power like "Don't push me" or "You keep on hounding me and pounding me" over the boxing footage. It was amazing to see how their meanings would shift when juxtaposed against such rugged physical imagery. In an attempt to be fair to my father—after all, I'm the filmmaker, and I have all the power as editor of the film—I made it a point to include several of his verbal put-downs and admonishments of me over the boxing footage. For instance, when I asked him about his divorce from my mother, Regina, something he did not want to talk about, he declared that it showed my "lack of under-standing . . . lack of sympathy . . . lack of empathy . . . lack of feeling . . ." for what this meant to him. Those words hurt me, but I included them so he too could land some punches. Later, at the end of the film—again over boxing footage—when I told him that he's never more alert and more alive than when we have these conversations, and that the film was an expression of love from me to him, he replied, "Bullshit!" It hurt me to hear him say that, but it was important to empower him with the ability to punch me in this instance as well. I suppose the boxing metaphor finds its final poetic poignancy in the idea that my father is "the champion," because throughout the film, I am indeed very much "the challenger."

In terms of the challenges of making such physically intricate films, I imagine that digital technology has made your editorial process easier. What was the first film you edited nonlinearly?

All of my films up to *Intimate Stranger* and *Nobody's Business* were shot on film and cut on Steenbecks. *The Sweetest Sound,* my film about names, was shot on motion-picture film but edited on an Avid Media Composer. The central thread of the film revolves around my search for all of the people in the world who shared my name—I found twelve of them, I mean *us*—and a dinner I hosted for our gathering at my home in New York. Because of the crucial role of computers in my research for the film—I couldn't have made that film in a precomputer era—I decided to use its visual and aural vocabulary—mouse clicks, computer keyboard keystrokes, the sounds of dial-up Internet, and a variety of other recognizable computer graphic icons and symbols—as the metaphoric language that motivates the storytelling of the film. In some ways, I thought of *The Sweetest Sound* as an updated technological version of the manual typewriter strategy I used in *Intimate Stranger.*

How has digital technology altered any aesthetic choices you make in the editing room?

Of course there are many, many advantages of editing on nonlinear editing systems and I wouldn't ever want to go back to editing on my Steenbeck (which I still have). There is, though, one subtle but significant difference: the simple act of rewinding, fast-forwarding, or searching for a shot on a roll of film. Back in the day, there was something special about the quality of concentration involved in gazing at a stream of imagery as it quickly zoomed by on the flatbed—just fast enough, but also just slow enough to clearly "register" each image. On the surface, the act of rewinding film would seem passive, almost meaningless—something that would not appear to have anything to do with the cerebral part of editing. But when editing went digital and images could be found instantly, in microseconds, we lost some of the possibility for serendipitously chancing upon and stumbling across shots we never imagined could or would work in our film—and I must say I miss it.

But there are obviously compensations?

Yes. That said, the most astounding thing about nonlinear editing—aside from the sheer speed and power of computers that allow us to literally "act at the speed of thought"—is the ability to make and save multiple versions and alternate cuts of what we do. I can make a version, save it, copy it, and then change it as often as I choose, keeping track of every version along the trail of my process—to be referred to as needed. When I made cuts on 16mm film, and by that I mean when I used an actual splicer to physically cut pieces of film and magnetic track, and then tape-spliced them back together with special splicing tape—clear for picture and white for track—I had to be extremely diligent and focused, because an overspliced workprint could get really ugly, fragile, and difficult to work with. It made you think twice before making a cut, and generated an unconscious awareness of getting it right the first time, because if you didn't, splicing one-, two-, and three-frame "extensions" back together at the head or tail of a shot made the practical side of editing a lot less fun. My most enduring memory of editing with 16mm film is the experience of sitting at the Steenbeck with several long strips of film around my neck, somehow feeling a bit like a tailor, all the while feeling a mysterious yet very real connection with my paternal grandfather, Benjamin Berliner, who *was* an actual tailor. Both of us "custom" tailors—he with strips of cloth and fabric, me with strips of sound and image.

As you speak, are you thinking now as an editor or a filmmaker?

At this point in my life, there are no real distinctions between the two. Over the years, my process for generating ideas, enacting them, and putting them together has become extremely integrated and fluid. When I'm out shooting, I'm already thinking ahead about how I might edit the footage. When I'm editing, I'm continually generating thoughts for new images to shoot, new archival images to search for, new music to listen to, new words to write, new books to read, and new connections to ponder. It's a never-ending feedback loop in which the different roles I play are able to communicate with one another seamlessly. And that includes the ability to be critical. In order to do what I do, I also need to be my own harshest critic, and no part of me is immune from that—producer, director, narrator, writer, cinematographer, consultant, researcher, biographer, historian, anthropologist, private detective, and/but especially *editor*—the one who puts it all together. It doesn't matter how much it cost, how long it took, or how happy I felt after making it—if the shot, the scene or the sequence doesn't work, it's out.

The editor always wins, it seems.

I'm not afraid to tell you—as I'm sure you've already guessed—the editing room is my favorite place to be. I'm never happier than when I'm working on my own films, lost in the process of trying to make each film as authentic and compelling as possible. I strive to make films that blur the boundaries between experimental and documentary—films that inspire audiences to think about their own lives in ways they never have before; films that push and inspire me toward the edges of my own abilities. When all is said and done, I want to find *ways* of telling stories that are as interesting as the stories I'm telling.

8. Pointing to the Middle

EMMA E. HICKOX

1992 *Miracle Beach,* dir. Skott Snider

1994 *The Crew,* dir. Carl Colpaert

1996 *Dead Girl,* dir. Adam Coleman Howard

1997 *This World, Then the Fireworks,* dir. Michael Oblowitz

1998 *The Brylcreem Boys,* dir. Terence Ryan

2001 *The Breed,* dir. Michael Oblowitz

2001 *On the Borderline,* dir. Michael Oblowitz

2001 *Tangled,* dir. Jay Lowi

2002 *A Walk to Remember,* dir. Adam Shankman

2002 *Blue Crush,* dir. John Stockwell

2003 *Honey,* dir. Bille Woodruff

2004 *Modigliani,* dir. Mick Davis

2005 *The Jacket,* dir. John Maybury

2005 *Kinky Boots,* dir. Julian Jarrold

2007 *Blood and Chocolate,* dir. Katja von Garnier

2007 *Becoming Jane,* dir. Julian Jarrold

2007 *How about You,* dir. Anthony Byrne

2008 *The Edge of Love,* dir. John Maybury

2009 *Pirate Radio,* dir. Richard Curtis

2010 *Worried about the Boy,* dir. Julian Jarrold

2011 *Rock of Ages,* dir. Adam Shankman

If Emma E. Hickox's allusion to editing as touching the heart seems familiar, it should: her mother, Anne V. Coates—award-winning editor of *Lawrence of Arabia*—referred to that quality as driving her editing process in her interview for the first volume of *First Cut.* Yet not remembering what her mother said, Hickox speaks assuredly of finding her own inspiration about film from "the middle," the emotional site within one's being that makes editing successful. Drawing from an impressive résumé across myriad genres, Hickox admits her dread of losing an audience during a preview and her desire to help audiences suspend disbelief to stay with the movie, even after it has ended. In particular, her concern with the impact of images on impressionable audiences raises important issues which editors working on violent or graphic films should bear in mind. Hickox's versatility in editing comedies, dramas, thrillers, and romances is manifested in her knack for "clever cutting," which helped her shape—perhaps even save—a number of sequences in *Pirate Radio* and *Blue Crush.* She also discusses the use of superimpositions to overlay emotions onto characters and scenes in a uniquely filmic way. This versatility is further evident in how Hickox has worked on both sides of the Atlantic to cut films targeted specifically to British or American audiences.

Given her family role model and her own artistic instincts, Hickox has finally embraced a profession that she resisted for most of her growing up. As an editor, she now considers herself a member of the universal tradition of storytellers who offer entertainment, information, and comfort to the human community. Hickox elevates the storytelling responsibility of an editor to an almost genetic level, inherent in the DNA. Along these lines, perhaps her very young daughter Matilda—whom Hickox considers her "greatest production"—will one day fill the shoes of her mother and grandmother.

I watched a bit of *Blue Crush* and *The Jacket* last night, and I saw all the things I wanted to fix! You know, if you've cut a film, you never take your editor's hat off. *(Laughs.)*

How much of the editing do you remember doing once you finish a film?
I don't remember most of it. I really blank it. Once it's done, I walk off and my brain compartmentalizes it miles away. When I begin my first cut, I always watch the dailies, write down notes, and get very brainy about it. Then I start cutting and come out the other end to find I've completely

ignored my notes and the scene's just done its own thing. I think, oh, I don't remember doing that, but, okay, I like it.

Is some intellectualizing going on as you approach your first cut?

When you look at the dailies, there is. You definitely look with your brain because part of your job is to see if you need to call production about anything. You know, "This guy's wig is wonky" or "That make-up isn't good" or something practical like "Did you know the light was in the background of every single take and we're going to have to remove it digitally? Or do you want to reshoot it?" I watch dailies with my brain for technical things like that. Plus performances, to make sure there's nothing where I can think "Hmm," and then have to call the director to ask, "Is that what you intended performance-wise?" And the director will either say, "Mmm, no, I was worried about it as well. Cut the scene together and show it to me," or, "No, no, no, I have this in mind," and then I can say, "Okay, great." The next time I watch dailies is the next day, and I take a more creative standpoint of story and emotion, where the characters are coming from and where they're going to. I always watch all dailies twice.

Sounds like your conscious brain begins to dissolve through that process.

Yeah, and your creative juices start flowing.

Where do those "juices" come from?

I don't know. That's like asking you as a writer, where does writing come from?

I point to the back of my head for some reason. (Laughs.)

If I had to point, I would actually point to my heart. It's more from the middle. At that point, I cut from the middle of me rather than from the top of me.

Do you think having been exposed to editing from childhood might have given you an intuitive sense of how it's done?

Well, I have to say editing chose me, I didn't choose it. I did grow up with film because you know who my mother is, and my father, Douglas Hickox, was a director. But the one thing I *didn't* want to go into was film because a rebel part in me said, "I'm going to do something more impor- tant. I'm going to do *theater!*" *(Laughs.)* I got my theater degree in

England in 1986, started directing theater, and then discovered, after all, I didn't like it that much! It just seemed to be all storms in teacups. From a director's standpoint, actors were difficult to deal with. Not to mention I was earning no money at all. It was a difficult time for the arts in England, and I mailed out a million résumés and pulled as many strings with my parents' contacts as I could, but no one replied. To earn some money, I got a job helping friends decorate and I remember chipping away paint on windows, thinking, "What am I doing? What am I going to do with my life!?" Then at the time, my younger brother was working in the U.S. for my mother as a runner for the film *Masters of the Universe.* My mother's then-assistant, Chris Cibelli, called me and said, "Your brother is going away on holiday. Do you want to come in and run for us for two weeks?" I said, "Sure, why not?" And there was nothing to do there—they were waiting for visual effects to come in, so I'd kind of sleep underneath the coding machine and think, "Great, I'm earning a hundred bucks this week 'cause in the theater down the road, I'm earning nothing!" Then about two months later, out of the blue, a woman named Corey phoned: "Hi, I'm looking for an experienced apprentice editor and Chris Cibelli mentioned you." I thought, that's a bit odd. I didn't want to embarrass Chris, so I said, "Sure, tell me more about the job." And I remember thinking, I feel weird, I don't want to be in the editing room, that's the one thing I *don't* want to do. But I had rent due and I asked, "How much are you paying?" She told me how much, and I was like, "I am *the* most experienced apprentice editor you have ever met and I will be there on Monday!" Well, I thought, they'll fire me after two weeks once they find out I know nothing, but at least I'll have two weeks pay, rent money, and a fortune compared to the theater. Then I called up Chris and asked, "Why would you say that? I don't even know how to sync dailies!" He said, "Emma, you're a natural." I said, "How can you say that? I slept under the coding machine!" And he said, "Trust me, you're going to be a really good assistant." So I asked, "Can I come by and practice syncing dailies with you?" *(Laughs.)* I did and he talked me through it. Thank God Corey set me up with my own room so they couldn't see me trying to figure everything out. When the first dailies came in, Corey sent me off with them and I was literally swimming in film. I tried to remember what Chris showed me and I came out of the room with my wobbly roll of film and sound and tape all over it, thinking, okay, I'm going to get fired on my *first* day! I handed it to Corey, who sweetly said, "Oh, it's quite loose." The center nearly dropped out of it! She put it on the Steenbeck and it was—I cannot tell you how—in sync! "Good job!" she said, adding, "You do need to speed up a bit, though." It had taken me three hours to do one roll instead of the usual forty minutes. "Okay, I'll speed up." I kept the job and she never found out I didn't know anything!

Did that experience convert you from theater to film?

Yes, I loved it. I *loved* being an assistant. In fact, I miss being an assistant on film—I wouldn't like it on the computer, but on film, I loved being an assistant. It's black-and-white. You've either done something right or you've done it wrong. As an editor, it can be such a gray area, such a matter of opinion. Someone might say, "I want more close-ups on the girl," but someone else might say, "I need more close-ups on the guy." It comes down to whose story someone happens to be more interested in when watching the film. Corey kept employing me and then I very luckily fell in with Frank Morriss, who edited John Badham's movies back then. He was a fantastic mentor and he let me cut, which was the most magical thing because if you cut film up, it got all spliced and ugly. But Frank believed in getting his assistants cutting, which is something I have continued as an editor with my assistants. It's really important to learn about notes, about directors, about pushing ego out of the way. Even if you think something is the best it possibly can be, others will have opinions that need to be taken on board.

Was it hard working in both the States and in England?

It was, but what I loved about working in the States was the attitude of, "You're enthusiastic, you're willing, just turn up. And if you mess it up, you can walk away. If you don't mess it up, fantastic, you can stay."

By implication, that's not true in England?

It's not. Certainly when I was younger, it was much more, "You have to earn your stripes and *then* turn up," and you have to be very lucky to even make anyone a cup of tea. Like I said, I sent out letters to people who worked with my parents, and yes, some of it was cold calling, but I didn't even get a reply of "Thank you" or "Maybe in the future." *No* answers. I even had a degree and had earned my stripes, but that enthusiasm to say "Just go for it and if you mess it up, it's okay" wasn't there. That's why I was able to start editing so quickly in the States because you could just get in with the right editor. In England, you expected to be an assistant for a long time before even *thinking* about cutting a frame of film. I mean, my mother still doesn't let her assistants cut because she was brought up in that school of editing where assistants didn't cut.

More like a five-year program before "graduating," so to speak.

Yes, you had to earn it. I mean, it's easier now for me to be very generous in the cutting room because it's all on Avid, so I always say to my assistants, "If a scene comes in that you really want to do, just tell me." On *Worried about the Boy* recently, a scene came in between the young Boy George and his father, set in 1986. The father sits on the bed and asks him, "What's the matter?" and George says, "*Nothing's* wrong with me," although he's wallowing in drugs. And my amazing assistant, Anna Dick, came in and said, "I'd really like to cut that scene." I said, "Great," so I put it aside for her. I then got a call that night from the producers who were worried because they thought the boy playing Boy George was over the top, so could I cut it together ASAP because they needed to look at it. Talk about different opinions: the bit they thought was over the top, I thought *wasn't* over the top, but there was *another* bit I thought was slightly over the top and they didn't! Anyway, I cut the whole scene together, and cut a second version without the worrisome bit so they could see how it worked. Then I told Anna, "Listen, I've got to do the scene because they need it by tomorrow and it's a problem scene for them. But don't look at what I do and do your own cut. I'd be really interested to see your version." I sent off what I did and everyone calmed down. Interestingly, Anna cut the same scene slightly differently, going into close-ups a bit sooner than I did. See, anyone can cut the same scene based on their emotional feeling for it, and it doesn't mean that it's bad or worse or better. Just different.

But there are things you can do wrong in editing.

Definitely. For example, if somebody's on one side of the room and suddenly you cut and they're on the other side of the room and you haven't shown them walk across, that could be a mistake. My basic rule about editing is if you break the suspension of disbelief, you've done it badly. As long as you don't break the suspension of disbelief, you can pretty much do anything you want that emotionally suits the movie. But if it doesn't emotionally suit the movie or if a physical cut just looks stupid, your brain automatically goes: "That's wrong." In short, if you have to fight to return your audience to the film emotionally, you've done a bad job.

How do you know an audience is suspending their disbelief?

They're never looking at their watches during the movie! *(Laughs.)* They have suspended their disbelief and are only thinking about the world of the story we're telling them.

So it's both not getting bored as well as believing that the story is real?

I don't know if boredom makes people look at their watches, but I know when I preview, that's the one thing I look for—is anybody looking down at their watch? I then register that part in the film, but you know what? It's usually not the part of the film that you're in, it's actually the bit that comes *before,* and somehow you've lost them there. Instead of thinking about the movie, you've made them start thinking, "Oh, I'm meeting So-and-so for dinner at ten-thirty."

Or they start sending a text message.

Worst-case scenario! Somehow their life has come back into their thinking because you've lost them. And my job—hopefully the job of all moviemakers—is to tell a story that's so intriguing, interesting, dramatic, funny, whatever that particular genre is, that an audience can leave their worries and their lives at the door for ninety minutes or two hours, then leave the movie and take at least a half-hour before getting back to their worries because they were so much a part of the story.

You hope they maintain that suspension of disbelief even after they've left the movie?

Yes, in an ideal world, it's lovely. A few movies have done that to me, where I float out afterward just going, wow! And you slowly come down to reality. I love movies where four people, say, will see it and go out to dinner afterward and ask, "What's your take on that film?" That's why I love *The Jacket,* because at the end so many people said to me, "Oh, I *know* what you intended." And I'd say, "Really? Brilliant. Tell me."

Considering you had four *possible endings for* The Jacket, *who could tell what the intention really was? The DVD extras featured three alternate endings to the one that made it in the film and all had one key difference that changed the outcome entirely.*

Vastly different endings. The final ending we used was open-ended and could mean a number of things. I'm happy with it that way, but I think audiences would have liked it tied up a bit tighter. The ending of a film is always the result of the whole, so the ending that we finally used came out of that version of the movie. The script really had only one ending, but the alternates came about because when we showed it, some people were like, "Oh, we're not sure about that ending." So John Maybury, the director, and I went into the cutting room and tried different things—that's the joy of editing, you know. Maybe we needed to let the audience show that Jack Starks, the Adrian Brody character, actually died at the end. Maybe we needed a little more of *Jacob's Ladder* at the end, meaning that the movie had taken place in the split second Jack was dying in the tent during the Iraq War, and so the whole film was his journey into whatever lies on the other side of death. I love experimenting, but it's also scary because you can either make or break the film with its ending. That's the big difference for me between reading a book and watching a movie. If I read a great book but it lets me down at the end, I don't mind. I'll still tell people to read it because the rest of the book was so great. But if I see a movie that's been fantastic until the end, I won't want to see the movie again and I won't tell people to go see it. The ending is *so* important. When I read a script that doesn't have a good ending, I won't do that film—if I am fortunate enough to be in a position to turn work down—because I know the problems we'll have with a bad ending. And I know it'll be me who has to try and solve those problems! *(Laughs.)*

Why such a difference between a book and a movie? Is it because there's greater detail of storytelling in a book that makes it more satisfying?

That, and it might also be that a book is about the whole journey. You pick up a book and put it down over a period of days or weeks, while the movie is more about an immediate experience and you want to feel immediately satisfied, especially when it ends. I also find that when I read a script, I often react emotionally to it and it works well on the page. But as soon as it's up on the screen, it's rare that the original story stays in the same order on film as it did in the script, especially if you've got flashbacks and time shifts. When it's up on the screen and you're seeing it as opposed to reading it, you're seeing it not in your imagination, but how it actually is being depicted. We nearly always end up reconfiguring the story once it turns into a film.

"Imagination"—that may be the clue here. In a book, the visual is conveyed through words and your brain has to fill in between the words to create those visuals. But with the purely visual and audio of a film, the audience has to accept the story—and perhaps use their imagination less. So the film better make sense or it won't work.

I have a habit where I won't read the script deeply if I can help it before I cut. Of course, I'll read it once for the interview, and when I get the job, I'll read it once more because I've been asked to see if there's anything in it I want to fix. But then I'll try not to read it again because I don't want to get too set of an idea in my head of how I "see" it. It may have to do with that verbal/visual point you mention. Moreover, it's not about how I see it, but how the *director* sees it. My job is to take his or her vision and make it the best version of that vision I possibly can.

Does the writer remain an integral part of the process because of potential rewriting?

Every script is different. If the script's been a bit wobbly, then we will sometimes bring the writer back in, especially if we have to do reshoots. Some writers already have a relationship with the director and take part a lot, while some writers I never see or hear from. Every single film is a completely different experience, depending on these relationships. I always get frightened when the writer comes to see a cut. I can imagine how much heart and creativity went into the script, and here I've gone in and cut out lines and moved scenes around so cavalierly! I've never had a writer come up and hit me, so I can't have done too badly *(laughs)*. But it must be shocking for a writer who knows the script very, very, very well and envisioned it in a particular way, only to have to let go of it when it's handed over to a director.

Do you think editing a fiction film is a form of writing?

It is a form of storytelling which is visual and verbal and musical and soundscape. We're definitely storytellers using those tools. It would be the same if I were a painter, I'd have to know how to mix oils and which brush does the best strokes for what I'm looking for. But then eventually, you stop thinking about brushes and colors and tools, and you start working with the creative side of your brain. Or like driving a stick-shift car. At first, it's all about when do I put my foot down? When do I shift? And before you know it, you're driving and drinking your take-out coffee, putting on your make-up, and not thinking anymore about the stick-shift. It all reaches into a deeper part of our thinking and creativity. At the risk of sounding pretentious *(laughs)*, I think filmmakers are part of a great ancient tradition of sitting around the campfire and telling wonderful stories. The great storyteller within a community or village would tell the same story over and over, but give it a different flair each time. That's why with movies, audiences and critics might say, "That's a story that's been told before." They're *all* stories that have been told before, probably for thousands of years in different forms. And each storyteller's job is to tell that story in such a way that the listener or the watcher experiences it in a new way, and enjoys that the story is familiar but somehow still new. Even children love the familiarity of a story they know well. "Read me *Peter Rabbit*—again!" *(Laughs.)* In a way movies are so predictable, and so are those ancient stories because you love the telling and you love that you know what's going to happen next. It makes you feel safe on some level. I don't think going to movies will ever die out, even though people keep saying with the digital age . . . whatever. I think we still love the community experience and being told a story together to laugh and cry with it. I believe it's very much in our DNA.

Sometimes a reviewer will say, "It's the same old story, nothing new"—and it's often not a grateful nod to ancient tradition! Does that criticism suggest that the filmmaker and/or editor haven't discovered a novel way of retelling the same plot?

It is actually a strange phenomenon in film. A movie like *The Jacket* is very unpredictable, it doesn't have an ending that's tied up, and it's everything audiences say they want if you ask them: "I don't want to see a predictable movie." But in previews, we got quite low scores because the ending was *not* predictable. Then there's a more schmaltzy movie like *Blue Crush*. Our preview audiences even wrote notes complaining about how predictable the ending was, yet we got high scores! I still think it comes down to the fact that audiences want a safe, predictable story because our lives feel so unpredictable. However, someone like director Christopher Nolan took huge risks with his film *Inception*—he sort of disproves my theory about success and predictability, but I think he's also the exception that proves the rule. *Inception* is a major success, but it is not predictable under any circumstance and has a very open ending. It's a rarity because of that.

But The Jacket *certainly filled a similar mission.*

It did, but it also didn't do that well with audiences, although it's become cult on DVD. It was sold slightly more as a horror movie, which it really isn't, so audiences were expecting something they didn't get. But how do you sell a story like that? What genre is it? War? Thriller? Horror? Drama? Science fiction? It was called all of those!

I was going to say a film's publicity may well factor into its success, or perhaps the time in which a film is made may not be the "right" time for it.

True. Directors like Steven Spielberg and James Cameron, both great storytellers, somehow have their finger on the zeitgeist or pulse of what audiences want at a particular time.

That's the case for many artists struggling to work in a time that's not ready for them. I think of Modigliani—a subject of one of your films. You have indeed cut in a variety of genres—from biography to comedy to romance to drama to horror. Could you talk about the editing challenges inherent in different genres?

Each genre is a unique journey, but again I'm not that conscious of making that journey. Thank goodness, otherwise I would never cut a comedy, for example. I don't sit down and start cutting with the words "I *must* make this funny." I hope that the script will be funny and the performances will be funny, and then I hope my editing will enhance all of the above and maybe even find a bit more comedy to squeeze out of it.

Can editing enhance comedy?

Definitely, because you can tread on a joke accidentally and editorially by trying to be *too* clever with your cutting. By not cutting to the right reaction, you take the air out of the joke before the audience has had a chance to laugh. But equally, if you cut to pause for a laugh and it doesn't happen, then you are in serious trouble. It's like walking a tightrope!

How are you "clever" with cutting?

Clever with cutting is using the footage that you have to solve a problem or tell a story that the footage wasn't necessarily meant for. A really good example of that was *Pirate Radio*. Actually, that's the name of the film released in America; in England, it's *The Boat That Rocked,* and each is a slightly different movie. Because *Pirate Radio* was cut for more of an American audience, we took certain scenes out because American audiences wouldn't necessarily find them funny or didn't find them funny when we previewed it, whereas in England they found those scenes hilarious. Oh my God! You know how long my first cut for that was? Over five hours. Hence, it ended up being such a long movie. There was so much funny footage from *The Boat That Rocked* that didn't even make the DVD extras. We cut out thirty-something scenes. I had to remove whole character arcs because the script was too long. And I can understand why it was too long because it was so joyful to read, with eight characters, each of whom had a major character arc in the movie. Also the actors were always improvising, and so in my first cut, I tried to keep as much of that in as I could. But back to what I was saying about being clever with the footage. In the English version, the broadcasters go ashore to London for a stag night because one of them is getting married. For the American version, we decided to keep them on the boat the entire time, even for the stag night party. But we had no footage for a stag night on a boat because it was not originally shot with that intention. So I had to find and steal footage from lots of other boat scenes that could relay the idea that the broadcasters had a party on the boat, and then I had to create a mini-montage of footage that made the audience think the party never left the boat! You see, so much of being an editor is doing just that, and hoping that the audience will never suspect something wasn't shot exactly the way they see it.

Now that is clever cutting!

That was the problem I was given to solve. For the American version, the filmmakers did not want the characters going ashore, but they still wanted the stag night party. And all I could do was sit there and go, "Crikey! Crikey!" As an editor, only you can do that kind of problem solving because no one knows the footage as well as an editor does. Occasionally, I'll work with a director who knows it as well as I do, but it's my job to have filed all the footage efficiently in my head. So I'm lucky—that's probably why I am an editor, and I'm sure I inherited my amazing visual memory from my mother. I have a hopeless memory for names and other things, but visually, I never lose keys and I remember all my footage! Look, I feel a great way to describe my job is that I am a panhandler sieving for gold nuggets. I get feet and feet of film, and it is my job to sift through and find the perfect moments. In, say, *Rock of Ages* which I am cutting at the moment, there is a concert scene where Stacee Jaxx (Tom Cruise's

character) sings "Pour Some Sugar on Me," and it is three minutes, sixteen seconds long—and I received four hours of dailies on multiple cameras for that one scene, so you do the math! That means I have about seventy-five choices for every moment of that song, and it is my job to go through the footage and find the perfect nugget of gold for each of those moments and put them together so they make sense—and the same goes for conversational scenes. It's all about the nuggets!

Not just gold nuggets, but perfect waves too, as I imagine with a film like Blue Crush.

When I think about *Blue Crush,* I was getting on average seven to ten hours worth of dailies *a day,* so I could only watch the new footage each day one time when it came in, and then only a second time for cutting, and by then it had to be imprinted on my brain or else! If you're fishing through that amount of material and not remembering what you're looking for, you're going to be cutting forever. There was a scene in *Blue Crush* where Kate Bosworth's character teaches her boyfriend how to surf and he catches a wave. That footage was shot just before the crew finished shooting because they realized they didn't have a shot like that. Now imagine all the water footage I received—every take was different. I mean, *every* take. It was all phenomenally beautiful footage, but there was no repetition at all. The ocean was its own boss, you know, and the water was always a different color, the waves were always moving, even the sky was always a different shade of blue. Now I remembered I had a take of the actor himself falling off the surfboard, and he had waved his arms in the air as he fell backward. I *knew* I'd seen it and it was something shot at the *beginning* of the film—four months before! It took me *two* days to find that shot, but I did. It had gotten to the point where my assistants were saying, "Emma, maybe that shot doesn't exist! You're using editor's memory." You know, there's a thing called "director's memory," where the director says, "I know I shot it!" And someone says, "You didn't." But he insists, "I know I did!" So two days later, we found that shot of the actor falling and waving his arms, and I was like, "Whew! I knew I'd seen it." Either that or I was going mad. *(Laughs.)*

Bottom line, you had to make necessary connections that weren't there before.

Definitely making connections. Another example of "tricksy" or "clever" editing came up when I was interviewed by Richard Curtis for *Pirate Radio.* He had actually watched all my movies, which is rare for a director to do, and he asked me very specific questions about scenes. For example, he said, "In *Becoming Jane,* when Jane Austen's brother arrives at their house with James MacAvoy's character, why did you choose to *jump-cut* the scene like that?" And I stared at him, thinking, "God, why did I?" Finally I said, "Oh, I know. The movie was too long. It was really important that the characters arrive at the house and set up their relationships. Julian Jarrold, the director, wanted to keep the scene, but the producers were saying it was too long and maybe we should lose it. So I said let's just jump-cut it together and get the best of both worlds that way! And everybody liked it." So there again, the editor's job is to listen to everybody's notes and use your art to tell that story. That is also a good example of something that might *not* work if it meant that the audience bounced out of the film because their brain was saying, "Ooo, look! A jump cut. Let's see, I've got tea with So-and-so at five o'clock . . ." That would not be good editing. The trick is to jump-cut so that nobody really notices, but they get the *feeling* of what's going on in the scene and move forward with the story. In fact, I thought Richard Curtis didn't like the jump cut, but he said, "No, I thought it worked really well. It's sort of the thing I want to try in *Pirate Radio.*" There are certainly other times jump cuts would never work at all, and the secret is to be "grown up" enough as a moviemaker to know that and try something else.

In other words, the needs of the story must be addressed above all, and each genre poses different demands on that story to be met editorially.

Absolutely. Part of the reason you see so many genres on my résumé is because I don't want to get pigeonholed. The only genre I don't cut anymore is horror because I can't get the nasty images out of my head. *The Breed* was pretty nasty with gore, and the worst thing about editing that genre is that you get really into it and try to make it as nasty as you possibly can because you know that's what your audience wants.

But you want to avoid clichés too.

Do you? Again, it goes back to the idea of familiar story. I think people who go to horror or gory movies love the cliché. When I tell people to go see *Inglourious Basterds* because it was amazing, they're surprised: "Gosh, Emma, it's so gory." And I stop and say, "It is?" But Sally Menke's editing was so beautiful—that opening scene in the farmhouse wasn't gory at all, but the tension was so palpable, just *so* on every single beat. It's immaculate. If I were to ever teach editing, I would use that as a perfect scene. Of course, later on when Brad Pitt and his comrades scalp the Nazis, I know what's coming and close my eyes and block my ears—sound effects freak me out as well! I don't need those gory bits to appreciate an incredible movie like that.

Do such bloody scenes fulfill the expectation that audiences have to be titillated in that genre?

That's a hard question to answer, especially when I think about Quentin Tarantino's *Reservoir Dogs*, where most people say, "It's so disgusting when the guy's ear is cut off!" But it isn't—you don't even see it! At that point, the camera pans away, you *hear* it happen, and then the camera pans back. But everyone *feels* like they've seen it. Now that would be my ideal world to work in the horror genre because I have a very weak stomach for it. I'm not one of those *Saw* people—how many sequels are there now? Sixteen? *(Laughs.)* There must be some intrinsic need for blood and gore within lots of human beings that I'm missing. I do worry about the effects of television and films on people in what you show and what you don't show. Curiously, I read some market research that said if a boy and a girl are going on a date, the movie they're most likely to agree on seeing is a horror movie, and part of that is because if they fancy each other, the adrenalin rush they get from the horror movie means they're more likely to score at the end of the night! *(Laughs.)* Is that true? I don't know, but usually the boys aren't going to say, "Let's go see a rom-com!" because they'll feel like sissies or they're worried their dates will expect them to get married. And girls won't say, "I wanna go see an action movie!" because they probably don't. With a scary movie, you have an excuse to hold on to each other! All that to say that I do think about audience psychology when I'm cutting. I read a brilliant book called *Lost Boys: Why Our Sons Turn Violent and How We Can Save Them*, by James Garbarino, PhD, which talks about the psychology of images, as in video games, and how they affect children. It said that in World War I, the army was teaching young boys to bayonet and shoot, but when they went out into the field, they froze and couldn't fight, and so they were losing and dying. The Army figured out what the problem was: the targets were round. When they designed *human*-shaped targets, that made the difference between the boys freezing and actually being able to kill someone. What does that say about the power of an image and its effect on our children? As a moviemaker, I take that as a serious responsibility.

It is fascinating to consider how editing can be the primary means by which certain effects are created to impact the audience, both positively and negatively. I'm thinking of the shocking dream sequences in The Jacket *where Jack Starks is locked in a drawer after the doctor of the mental asylum has drugged him, and Jack begins receiving flash images of his past* and *future. Those sequences almost visually assault the senses in trying to pinpoint where Jack was in time.*

But that was always the question the film asked: where is he? It was meant to be a mishmash of his memories or his imagined memories all falling on top of each other. Definitely it was an experiment and a risk. That's why previewing is so important, to get an audience's reaction to what's working and what isn't working, and to help me stay objective to my own film. I tend to know I'm being objective when my palms start sweating in a preview because I sense from even one person in the audience that something isn't working! *(Laughs.)* My objectivity also applies to whether I'm doing English cutting as opposed to American cutting, depending on where the film is released. For *The Jacket*, we previewed in England with good results on our cut. We went over to America, and within five minutes I knew the same cut was too slow and I sweated for the rest of the preview.

People were looking at their watches?

Yes, or always going to the loo! They were fidgeting and not hooking in, or I could feel them hook in and then lose them again. And sure enough, we did not get good results. Exactly the same film, but I started in England and cut it with a very European rhythm.

Which is?

Slower. If *The Jacket* had been set in England with English actors in an English environment, we could have kept the same slower pacing. But because it was set in America, Americans expected it to be a faster film. As I told you earlier, I had watched *The Jacket* recently for the first time in a long time, and I was really quite shocked because I had completely forgotten that we had cut it so short and quick. In an early scene when the police officer gets killed, the original intent was to show that Jack Starks was innocent of the crime, but after the American preview, we moved faster into the movie and skipped over that revelation so that you don't know he's innocent until the end. In general, the European flavor of a film is not to speed through everything.

More like savoring the experience?

More savoring, slightly more languid, slightly more landscape. A more haunting feeling, rather than frenetic, harried, and rushing through to the point of feeling discombobulated. When we previewed the faster version in America, the numbers went from low to high. I know the audience liked it. Even so, the film was not successful and it may well have had to do with what followed in marketing and publicity. There was nothing more I could do about it by that time. As long as we got mid to high eighties in preview, we told a story that the audience enjoyed. Then it goes out of our hands.

In the life of the film, then, certain things can fall beyond your control, but within the editing room, you can make the most of your position to control what the film conveys emotionally. The Jacket's dream sequences involved many editorial techniques that made a visceral impact. Can you comment on that?

I did a lot of superimposing images on top of each other. I use super-impositions more than some cutters because I have this theory that people experience things with their personal emotions superimposed over them. For example, a shot of a train moving across a landscape for one person will be a terrible thing because someone they loved died being run down by a train. But to another person, the same train will bring a feeling of joy because he met his wife on a train. I try to apply this "theory" to my storytelling when I superimpose images in montages or scenes. I take the emotions of the characters and superimpose their emotions onto that "train," so to speak, onto the particular images. For example, in *The Jacket*, Jack Starks is sitting in a chair being fed drugs through a drip in his arm, and Dr. Becker (played by Kris Kristoffersen) confronts Jack and tells him the horrible story about another inmate-prisoner, Ted Casey, who had killed a nine-year-old girl. During that scene, I used superimposition of sound as much as superimposition of images—layers and layers of story—to get the feeling that Jack was becoming more and more stoned. We're hearing and seeing the distortions through his ears and eyes. I also superimposed images of trees, near where Casey was supposed to have buried the girl, and you hear his laughter and the voice of the girl and the continuous whisper of the doctor telling the terrible story, all of which gave a feeling of Jack's disorientation that we wouldn't have if we were watching the scene more straight-on. I had gotten a sense that the director, John Maybury, didn't want it to be conventionally edited because he shot these massive close-ups of mouths and eyes, so I presumed he wanted a dreamlike perspective. But he admitted, "Oh, I did that because it was such a crap scene and I thought I'd shoot some odd things and then just cut the whole scene out of the movie!" *(Laughs.)* In fact, I think I am right in saying that this scene became one of his favorites.

In Kinky Boots, *you also superimposed at some pivotal memory moments for the character of Lola.*

Yes, there is an important scene when Lola, the transvestite played by Chiwetel Ejiofor, revisits the seaside pier which was so important to him as a child, where he danced on the boardwalk in red high heels and experienced a liberating sense of freedom about who he was—until his father stopped him with a sharp rap on a café window and a look of disdain. It is the opening of the film. It was not scripted to have the "memory" of Lola as a boy dancing supered over his walk along the pier *later* in the film when he is a grown man. But I decided to do that in the assembly, along with echoing the original music, as if to get inside Lola's head and heart and let the audience feel it as he does. That then became like his father's ghost still haunting him.

I assume again that most of these decisions are made right in your room.

Yes, such sequences will usually not be scripted and it will be my choice to do it a certain way. Of course, initially, in my first cut, it is important to be more faithful to the original intention: I don't take lines or scenes out or swap scenes around, although as you're cutting, you start to be aware that you probably want to. I have been wrong, of course. I've thought, oh, there's no way this line is staying, yet it does remain in the final version! But an editor's job is to follow the original line-up at the beginning out of necessity because sometimes five scenes could be dispersed throughout the whole movie that all take place in one room and they will all be shot in that room at the same time. When I get the dailies, it might be the opening scene, three scenes in the middle, and then one for the end, and I'll have to cut everything out of sequence. So it will not be possible to make decisions about deleting or swapping scenes at that point. However, I try to make every scene as perfect as it can be in its own little capsule, with a strong beginning, middle, and end—a little story unto itself. When you put the whole movie together, then, you've got all these perfect little stories together, and then your job is to make that one big story. That usually involves chopping! I tend to chop off the first and last few lines of a scene. You need to save those lines because they filled in what was happening in that particular scene, but when the whole is together, some of those lines become absorbed by what comes before or after, so you can lose them. Within the little scenes, that's when I like to start trying something that the director perhaps hasn't thought about, knowing I can always do it more conventionally if he doesn't like it, but still have fun with it. There's such an example from *Worried about the Boy.* In one scene, Boy George is waiting for his boyfriend to visit and he's cooking him his favorite onion rings and then sitting and waiting—the boyfriend never shows up. How do you convey that waiting for hours without boring an audience? In addition, Julian Jarrold had shot that scene at the very end of the day in only a wide shot and a close shot. He had run out of time and two shots were all he could do—and he hadn't yet arrived at a concept of the scene! So I decided to play with the timing. I sped up the wide shot where Boy George is moving around, but then cut into the close-ups when he is doing something significant like lighting a candle or putting a rose in a vase, and slowed those down to real time. Then I'd switch back to speeding up the bits of him rushing around the kitchen and so on. Luckily, Julian loved it. You always take a risk when you play around with a director's dailies! I made the scene shorter, maybe fifteen seconds, but it still suggested the hours that Boy George waited for his boyfriend.

So again, when you make leaps of faith, so to speak, looking at fragments of scenes and turning them into reflections of someone's inner mind, are you in your head or in your heart?

In the heart. In that middle part I mentioned before. It happens not in the watching of dailies as much as in the cutting process itself. I don't think about my cuts, and I don't look at my cuts. I just cut because I *want* that close-up or that wide shot. I *want* that look from the actor as he hears something because it makes sense emotionally. And then I'll leave it—what I call my "line cut"—and don't even overlap the sound at that point. It's just all cut. If you look at my Avid line, it would just be straight cuts across sound and picture. Then the next day, I'll sit down and watch that version of the scene, and I'll know whether or not my structure's right. It will be clear suddenly that even though I liked the wide shot, I should actually be in a close-up. That's when I'll tidy it up and look at the cuts a bit more. However, it's not till much later when we're getting to the "fine cut," when I'll ask, "Right now, is every cut perfect? Is every cut the best it can be?" Unfortunately, schedules are getting so tight now, I hope I will still have the luxury of double-checking every single cut.

It almost seems as if crunched schedules and increased footage are a contradiction in terms for an editor.

Yeah. Look at the amount of footage I got from *Blue Crush*, especially from the water team, and I sometimes still didn't have the piece I needed to put the puzzle together. How could I possibly have this much footage of surfboards and still have a missing piece? *(Laughs.)* Sometimes I had to bring the water team in, show them a sequence, and say, "I'm missing this, this, and this." What was happening was that they were just going off and shooting this incredibly beautiful water footage, but it was not all directed to the *story.* The surfing stories were essentially created from the footage we had. After all, you can't direct a wave to do what you want! Nor can you make a surfer on a wave do what you want because sometimes he's just happy to be on the wave and not get killed. So it was my responsibility to tell the water team, "Hey, I've got the beginning of the wave and I've got So-and-so crashing on the other side of the wave, but I need the actor in the middle and then going over the lip of the wave." And they would go out to shoot something that specific.

So then the poor actor or stunt person had to keep hitting the waves, hoping to give you the shot you needed.

And also be in the right costume, on the right surfboard, doubling up with the right actor. There were so many different things to consider. Usually the script descriptions of those surfing stories were general, something like: "She went for the wave but then she chickens out." I had to take footage from different shoots, sometimes months apart, and decide how to crash-and-burn one of the surfers, for example. When we began to time-grade the film, we were lucky to be doing it digitally, which was very cutting-edge at the time, so we could change costume colors, surfboard colors, even sea and sky colors to match what I needed. Sometimes the poor girls, Kate Bosworth and Michelle Rodriguez, were so cold, their lips were blue and we had to change them back to pink! Kate was even taken to hospital one day with hypothermia!

Were any water effects simulated in a tank or on a computer?

No, no, everything you see there is real. There was an amazing cameraman on the water unit, and I told him I needed a few specific wave shots. And he said, "What!?" And I said, "Well, basically, you need to go with your camera into a wave and just let it take you and crash you." He said, "Oh, thanks!" *(Laughs.)* "Sorry," I said, "I really want to have a POV of what it is to be taken into the washing machine." And he went off on a boogie board with his camera and got it for me. It would have been such a joy to just watch the footage if I hadn't been so terrified at how much there was and how to use it all! That's when I said to my editorial crew,

"Don't worry about continuity 'cause if you do, you limit yourself so much." On *Blue Crush*, if I'd worried about continuity, I couldn't have cut it. I also would have left a lot of the best footage on the floor. As I was watching the film again last night with more of a continuity eye, I mean, it was all over the house! Almost every other shot, cutting left, cutting right! But when you watch it with your emotional eye and go with the story, you don't notice.

So you're asking people—literally—"Ride the wave with me and go with it."
Absolutely. Go with the flow, go with the emotion, go with the story.

Sometimes having music over the scene helps to push the flow along, doesn't it?
Yes, it probably wouldn't be as impactful without the music. Music is definitely part of our tool bag as moviemakers. To not use it just to be different or make a point that we shouldn't have music in a scene is only depriving yourself of a tool that may help the audience get the most out of the experience. Before I lock a film, I always ask the director to sit down with me and watch the film stripped of all temp music. It is a totally different experience. As for other techniques, I think the effective use of silence is so underrated and underused in a movie—but I think that's because audiences are quite noisy these days! If you have complete silence, all you hear is the person next to you crunch-crunch-crunching on the popcorn. *(Laughs.)* Likewise the technique of pitch-blackness. When I was cutting *The Jacket*, we would always screen it in private cinemas to ourselves, so the scenes with Jack Starks in the drawer were literally pitch-black. When we previewed it, of course, the auditorium had all the emergency lights and aisle lights and you can never have pitch-black in the cinema because it's a fire hazard. So I had to cut those scenes differently because pitch-black with sound alone did not work.

Do you ever argue with your director about how to recut something like that?
If you have to argue with your director, then your head gets in the way. I'm not a big arguer in the cutting room because I think there's no right or wrong, as I said before. You've got to try it and trust that the director will turn around and say, "You're right," once they've seen it. Or

you turn around and say, "You're right, that's so much better." It becomes
an instinct after a while of knowing what works. **p.195**

*Can everyone achieve that level of knowing now that editing is much
more readily available through software?*

People have asked me, "Are you worried that everyone can edit now?"
as if that clutters the playing field or something. And I say, "No, I think
it's brilliant that everyone can edit." In the same way that everyone's
always been able to draw or paint or do any of the arts, the true artist will
rise to the top. I'm not saying that I'm a true artist, but certain people will
be phenomenal and have an instinct that is one step ahead creatively of
anyone else doing the same thing. It may be something you're born with
or maybe your life experiences have given it to you, but you just have it.

*Do you remember that moment in your work when you first tapped into
the middle and knew you "had it"?*

I don't think I became aware of it until I started being asked about the
"middle" bit. I never was a "thinking" editor. I never studied film because
I did theater. I've never been cerebral about film. When I worked with
John Maybury, he had really studied film and loved Cocteau especially,
and I was like, "Ooo, I better probably watch a few of these movies." So
I saw *Orpheus*, which had sequences when Orpheus passes through the
mirror into Hades and goes backward. Like he's putting on gloves, but
they ran the film backward so he's seen taking them off. In *The Jacket*,
there's a big close-up of Jack's open eyes after he's terribly wounded in
the first Iraq War, and he starts to cry, with one tear going down the side
of his face as he realizes he is going to die. At the very end, I replayed the
same shot when he's dying and ran it backward so that the tear goes back
into his eye. And that was just me giving a respectful nod to John and the
fact that he loves Cocteau so much. Of course, I wouldn't have done that
if it didn't suit the dreamlike quality of the movie, but it did. It's a subtlety
I like, and it also gave John great pleasure. It is my job, after all, to make
directors as happy in the cutting room as they can be!

*Okay. I have to ask the inevitable question: do you ever discuss editing
with your mother?*

When I was a child, my dad was a director, my mom was an editor, so
what did we talk about around the table? Filmmaking! Since then, though,
I think it's become osmosis as opposed to specifically talking. In the same

way, if your parents are bankers, I don't think you necessarily sit around and talk banking with them, but it's a form of osmosis. Everyone's talking about banking so you pick it up. My mother and I talk about editing a bit or about movies we like or don't like, or if she's having a hard or an easy time on a picture. But we don't ever talk specific cutting. I don't think we can be specific because her experience of a scene will be different from my experience of a scene.

And she hasn't seen your footage and vice versa.
Exactly. We don't know each other's daily challenges or what our producers or directors are saying. I also think we purposely keep our two work lives separate from each other. When I was starting out, it would have been terrible to think people were employing me to get my mother in. But joyfully, I have a different last name so people didn't know she was my mother—they would find out later!

Is she happy that you entered editing?
Definitely, yeah.

And perhaps Matilda will follow in your footsteps? It seems to be in the genes.
(Talking to daughter:) Matilda, are you going to edit as well?
(No response.)
Well, I see she already understands the effective use of silence!

9. Honoring Lives

KATE AMEND

1984   *Women of Iron,* dir. Scott J. T. Frank

1988   *Homesick,* dir. Johanna Demetrakas

1989   *Metamorphosis: Man into Woman,* dir. Lisa Leeman

1990   *Legends,* dir. Ilana Bar-Din

1991   *Danger: Kids at Work,* TV, dir. Lyn Goldfarb

1992   *Asylum,* TV, dir. Joan Churchill

1992   *The Southern Sex* (short), dir. Christine Fugate

1992   *Innocence and Experience: The Making of* The Age of Innocence, TV, dir. Laura Davis

1993   *Come the Morning,* dir. Michael O. Sajbel

1993   *Skinheads USA: Soldiers of the Race War,* TV, dir. Shari Cookson

1996   *Mother Love,* TV, dir. Christine Fugate

1997   *The Long Way Home,* dir. Mark Jonathan Harris

1998   *Some Nudity Required,* dir. Johanna Demetrakas and Odette Springer

1998   *Tobacco Blues,* dir. Christine Fugate

1999   *Free a Man to Fight: Women Soldiers of WWII,* dir. Mindy Pomper Johnson

1999   *The Girl Next Door,* dir. Christine Fugate

2000   *Into the Arms of Strangers: Stories of the Kindertransport,* dir. Mark Jonathan Harris

2000   *Ladysmith Black Mambazo: On Tiptoe,* dir. Eric Simonson

2001   *Out of Line,* dir. Johanna Demetrakas

2002   *Dylan's Run,* dir. Steven Johnson and David M. Rosenthal

2003   *Pandemic: Facing AIDS,* TV miniseries, dir. Rory Kennedy

2003   *Beah: A Black Woman Speaks,* dir. LisaGay Hamilton

2005   *Cowboy del Amor,* dir. Michèle Ohayon

2005   *Grief Becomes Me,* dir. Christine Fugate

2003–5 *The American Experience,* TV:
- *The Great Transatlantic Cable,* dir. Peter Jones
- *Bataan Rescue,* dir. Peter Jones

2004   *Peace by Peace: Women on the Frontlines,* dir. Lisa Hepner

2005   *Pretty Things,* TV, dir. Liz Goldwyn

2006   *The World According to Sesame Street,* dir. Linda Goldstein Knowles and Linda Hawkins Costigan

2006   *Thin,* dir. Lauren Greenfield

2007   *Sisters of Selma: Bearing Witness to Change* (consulting editor), dir. Jayasri Hart

2007   *Steal a Pencil for Me,* dir. Michèle Ohayon

2007   *Jimmy Carter, Man from Plains,* dir. Jonathan Demme

2008   *The Brothers Warner,* dir. Cass Warner

2009   *The Girls in the Band* (consulting editor), dir. Judy Chaikin

2009   *American Harmony,* dir. Aengus James

2010   *One Lucky Elephant,* dir. Lisa Leeman

2011   *Crazy Wisdom: The Life and Times of Chogyam Trungpa Rinpoche,* dir. Johanna Demetrakas

2011   *There Was Once . . . ,* dir. Gabor Kalman

2011   *First Position,* dir. Bess Kargman

2012   *Birth Story: Ina May Gaskin and the Farm Midwives,* dir. Sara Lamm and Mary Wigmore

AWARDS

2001 Eddie (ACE) Award, Best Edited Documentary Film, *Into the Arms of Strangers: Stories of the Kindertransport*

2004 CINE Golden Eagle Award, Professional Telecast Nonfiction Division: People and Places, for *Peace by Peace: Women on the Frontlines*

2004 Peabody Award (shared with Patricia Smith Melton, executive producer; Lisa Hepner, director-producer; and Nisma Zaman, producer), *Beah: A Black Woman Speaks*

2005 International Documentary Association Award, Outstanding Documentary Editing

2010 Woodstock Film Festival, Best Editing, Documentary, *One Lucky Elephant*

Kate Amend's professional life has been primarily dedicated to portraying the conditions of women in a number of powerful documentary films. From a raw and gripping look at bulimic women, to tracking families ravaged by AIDS around the world, to entering the mind of black actress and activist Beah Richards, to documenting women on the frontlines of war, and even to chronicling the adventures of a cowboy matchmaker, Amend "conducts" the footage that her gifted directors provide to construct riveting stories of women who might otherwise be forgotten and women's issues that are critical to remember. Amend discusses the power of imagery to create mood and emotional response. Citing many examples from her award-winning film *Into the Arms of Strangers,* Amend speaks of how digital editing helped her create visual metaphors and suggest a world of memories through the respectful manipulation of sound and image. Calling documentary editors both scriptwriters and filmmakers, as Oppenheim, Corrao, and Bini did previously, Amend relates her experience on *Strangers* of finding crucial props to help her compensate for sparse material and inadvertently triggering a global response that ultimately led to some of the most heart-wrenching montages in the film.

In considering films with multiple characters and storylines—and usually no preliminary structure in place to guide their development, Amend offers practical advice for weighing the impact and dramatic qualities of the stories being told and the lives being captured. Again echoing other documentary editors' concern for responsibility to the truth, Amend identifies the need to be authentic to the subjects of the films, especially when they reveal their polarizing, shocking, and graphically disturbing life choices. By being unafraid to look at these realities, Amend feels that open-minded, compassionate audiences can become one with those who willingly share their vulnerabilities.

How did you first get into documentary editing?

The shorthand version of that story is that feminism and the women's movement got me into editing. But let me back up a little and say that I went to Berkeley and San Francisco State and received my master's in humanities in the midseventies, and then realized there wasn't anything much I could do with that degree. I had no concept of the career I wanted anyway because when I was brought up, basically a woman either became a teacher or got married. That was a woman's career path at the time. So I became a teacher. I taught humanities at City College of San Francisco and, given the emerging women's movement, I became more involved in teaching women's studies and reading feminist literature. I also started watching every documentary made by a woman filmmaker and showed them to my classes, even English classes, and assigned essays on the films. I'm sure you're familiar with Barbara Kopple's *Harlan County, USA* and Lynne Littman's *Number Our Days*. In 1976, their documentary films had won Academy Awards, which were presented by Lillian Hellman.

A great feminist author herself.

Yes. She presented both the short and feature documentary awards that year. Everything for women was coming together at that moment. I was also very interested in women artists and was a big fan of Judy Chicago. Johanna Demetrakas had made the film *Womanhouse*, which was very influential to me. I simply became fascinated with the idea of making feminist films. Luckily, the college I was teaching at had a little film department, and I enrolled in some film classes.

So you were both student and teacher.

Exactly. Sometimes I would be in a film class and my own students would be in the same class! I started making little Super 8 films.

Any particular topic?

They always had a feminist slant to them. I did a black-and-white short that was a sort of neo-Italian Lina Wertmüller-style feminist fairy tale. Basically *Snow White and the Seven Dwarfs* Italian style! *(Laughs.)* And the gist of it was that Snow White went from being oppressed by the dwarfs to being oppressed by the prince!

Makes sense to me! Did you have seven people playing the dwarfs?

Well, if you didn't count, you didn't know. Basically a crowd of my friends really got into it. It was hilarious. I think it was when I was cutting that little film together in my apartment, like three o'clock in the morning, I realized that time had just flown by and I was having the most fun. It was a moment when I thought, wow, this is something I would love to do for the rest of my life. Also at that time, I was feeling ready to leave San Francisco and I met a friend through a friend at a dinner party. His name was Jack Leber, an assistant editor working on the TV show, *Dallas,* at Lorimar. I mentioned to him, "Oh, I want to be an editor." He said, "Well, you should just come to Los Angeles. You can get a job." And I did.

Other than the seven dwarfs film and other films you made for class, did you have any professional training?

No, but I felt I knew enough to at least be an apprentice or I could sync dailies, which is what I did. I got a job fairly quickly, but unfortunately, it was at a postproduction house that did really horrible low-budget exploitation films that went against every feminist scruple I had?

It must have been an education in itself that reinforced your beliefs.

It sure was. I worked mostly with sound editors, I became a sound effects librarian, and then an assistant editor. I got a little taste of Hollywood, and I also got a sense of what I *didn't* want to do.

Which was?

These low-budget exploitation films!

How about high-budget exploitation films? (Laughs.)

Those too! I left that job the day they asked me to do ADR cue sheets on this horribly violent film with a rape scene. I couldn't even watch the film, it made me furious. I said I couldn't do this anymore because in the evenings, I was also working with Judy Chicago on *The Dinner Party,* which was a major feminist artwork telling the history of women in Western civilization through china painting and needlework. I knew the exploitation business contradicted everything I believed in. After leaving, I worked as an apprentice with Johanna Demetrakas on her film *Right out of History: The Making of Judy Chicago's* Dinner Party, and entered documentary that way.

Why did you gravitate toward editing of all the things you could do as a filmmaker?

Well, I didn't enjoy shooting or producing. And you know how there's always a class artist in school? Unfortunately, I was always the worst. A teacher once even told me, "You shouldn't bother to try drawing. You're not good enough."

How not encouraging—

I know. But I always loved art and wanted to do something in the arts. I played violin and piano, but I kept searching for something creative to excel at. There was a side of me that always wanted to be a writer and a storyteller, making something dramatic. It just clicked with editing. Telling a story through images.

Are you equating film editing with the writing process?

Absolutely. Especially in documentaries, the editor makes a major contribution to the writing of the film. A couple of directors have given me a writing credit or costory credit on their films. I have cut fiction and it is fun, but to me, the real challenge is finding the story in a documentary.

Can you describe how you find a story, or at least the spine of a storyline, from the mix of footage you get when first starting a documentary?

One of my early documentaries was called *Metamorphosis: Man into Woman*, directed by Lisa Leeman, about a man undergoing a sex change. Shot over a four-year period, that film had a clear, obvious linear progression and had to be structured chronologically—that is, in shooting order—because the main character Gary/Gabi was changing physically. Her looks would be different from month to month and the film reflected that evolution. But one film where I really felt like the director and I had to find the structure to tell the story was *Beah: A Black Woman Speaks*. The director, LisaGay Hamilton, shot twenty interviews over a year's time with Beah Richards, this incredible African-American poet, political activist, and actress who most people would recognize for her role as Sidney Poitier's mother in *Guess Who's Coming to Dinner*. LisaGay wanted to do something with this footage as a film, but it was basically straightforward interviews with one talking head. The only real vérité scene she had with

Beah was her packing up and moving out of her house. When LisaGay and I started working on the film, we knew that we didn't want to do a linear life story. Instead, LisaGay's intention was to share Beah's *mind* with the audience.

That must have required a very different, even abstract approach to working with the material.
    Definitely.

What did you think when the director said she wanted to get into Beah's mind, not her linear life?
    I knew it was a great idea. This was a conversation over the phone so I had not seen any footage yet. But it was a very wonderful conversation about not wanting to do a traditional biography. However, it was still just a talking head. So I asked LisaGay, "Well, do you have scenes?" And she said, "Not really!" *(Laughs.)* Then she added, "It's just that I would go over and sit with Beah and I would tape her talking and she just blew my mind. Every time I'd come out of her house, my head was spinning and I was just so energized and inspired by her words." So LisaGay simply said, "I don't want it to be about acting or an actor's life." When I began to look at the footage, I had no idea what to do. The first tape I saw was Beah on an oxygen machine! She had become very ill and in fact had died before I began working on the film, but I didn't know any of that at first. When I saw the tape, all I could think of was, wow, this is going to be off-putting to the audience. But within five minutes, I completely forgot about the oxygen machine. Beah was an incredible speaker and an incredible woman. LisaGay also had a few of Beah's photographs, so we started basically with footage and photographs. Eventually, we gathered a great deal of archival footage, home movies, and film clips to tell the story. We started to build a story that went into Beah's past, but came back to her present condition. So the film did become the story of her life, but also the story of the end of her life and how she was coping with that.

Is there a written or even unwritten editing rule that if you capture a person's life in a documentary, you must treat it chronologically?
    I think that as long as you set up a particular convention for the film, and the audience feels you are guiding them through the story with a clear vision and goal, it can work. You want people to feel comfortable with whatever you set up from the outset so that they will go where you want

to take them. You don't want to throw in anything that will confuse them during the presentation and essentially take them out of the story. Basically, in *Beah*, I found that the interviews had been conducted in a thematic order, like, "Let's talk about your childhood," "Let's talk about moving to Los Angeles," or, "How did you get to Broadway?" Conducted in that way, the interviews had a natural progression we could follow which became the spine of the film. But in between those sequences, we would present scenes from Beah's present-day life, clips from her films, and excerpts from a 1973 broadcast of Beah's one-woman show in which she performed her poetry.

Another film you edited, Cowboy del Amor, *told the life of Ivan Thompson, a real cowboy in New Mexico who ran a matchmaking business to bring men to Mexico and meet women for possible marriage. There, you told his life story within the larger context of how he helped three men meet the "women of their dreams."*

That film was a very different challenge. The director, Michèle Ohayon, heard Ivan speaking on the radio—NPR, I think—and then had a conversation with him and thought he was a great character for a documentary. When he told her, "I'm going down to Mexico, if you want to come to see what I do," Michèle just went off by herself—not even with a crew—to do scouting, and she ended up shooting Ivan introducing his client, Rick, to prospective brides. And she actually caught Rick meeting Frances—love at first sight!—right on camera. It was incredible how that happened. Michèle hadn't planned to get the heart of the film in her first shoot, but she did and it was a phenomenal job. She filmed that first story on her own. The other two couples were filmed on later trips with a small crew.

Yes, three matched-up couples appear in the film. Were there other couples you chose not to include?

No. That was it. Michèle saw three couples, filmed three couples, and the three couples appear in the film! One man and woman met, fell in love, and got married. Another man and woman went on a couple of dates but didn't click. And another much older man and woman married—they were both friends of Ivan's who he felt might hit it off, and they did. Being a feminist, of course, I never felt comfortable with films about matchmakers or mail-order brides. I always felt those people were sleazy. But Michèle is a wonderful director who knows how to pull a lot out of her subjects for their very human side. We also set up the story in a humorous way because Ivan himself was very funny. He had even written a book about his business called *Cowboy Cupid!* Once we established his business, we went into the more poignant side of the story, about the search for love. We eventually told Ivan's personal story midway through the film, how he got into this business, his own shaky marriage and his children, and eventually we wrapped up with what happened to him and the three couples.

In one scene, you kept in the voice of the director talking with Ivan in his hotel room in Mexico. Isn't the preference in documentary to omit the offscreen voice of the interviewer and let the subject talk to the camera/ audience?

It depends on the film. In this case, I think it was appropriate to keep Michèle's voice in because she begins to address issues that I'm sure many in the audience were eager to hear about. She asked Ivan, "Do you get criticized for your work?" I think that was a skillful way to raise objections to what he's doing without challenging him head-on. And since Ivan could be perceived as exploiting women, it was important to hear a woman ask that question. So we left the question in. What ensued was a very funny scene in which Ivan talks about the criticism he receives. He defended himself hilariously by reading his hate mail! We also kept in scenes where Ivan was obviously addressing Michèle directly. For example, Michèle was filming Ivan and Rick in the hotel late one night after a very long day. He looked at the camera and said, "Do you want to see me get undressed? Because I sure am tired. And if you do, can you put on some music?" At that point, we cut. That scene always gets a big laugh. We kept it in because it added humor and brought the audience into a different space, like breaking the fourth wall. But back to the question—yes, in other films we make every effort to take the director's questions out. And directors will often ask interviewees to incorporate the question into their answer, to speak in complete sentences and so forth. Certainly, if the tone or convention of the film isn't set up properly for what an audience can expect and an outside voice suddenly pops in, it can be jarring and call attention to itself. The danger is always doing anything that may take the audience "out of the film." However, one of the most successful examples of hearing the director speak off-camera occurs in *Harlan County, USA*, when Barbara Kopple has a brilliant exchange with the villain of the film. It comes at a moment of great tension and beautifully cuts through it. It always evokes laughter and applause and is one of the highlights of the film. And may I add that *Harlan County,*

USA, edited by Nancy Baker and Mary Lampson, should be required viewing for everyone who cares about filmmaking.

Thank you for pointing that out.
    Just another thought on the subject. In documentaries, so many exchanges with subjects are on-the-fly that we refer to those interviews as OTF. A subject could be commenting to the director or cinematographer and some of that can be very effective to keep in the film. For example, in *Beah,* the personal exchange between the director, LisaGay, and this incredible woman was important. We wanted LisaGay to have a presence in the film, so that even though she was behind the camera, we often kept in both sides of the conversation. The whole idea was to make the audience feel they were in the room with Beah and that she was directly engaging LisaGay—and the audience—in a dialogue.

You said some key words there—"make the audience feel." It seems easier to touch audiences when you deal with subjects who are alive to share their stories. What about more fact-based documentaries, like Transatlantic Cable *and* Bataan Rescue, *which rely on photographs and archival footage?*
    Both of those films for *American Experience* on television were scripted and involved actors and re-creations. *Transatlantic Cable* was one of the few films I've done where the storytellers were authors and historians rather than participants in a particular event. But even there, you are looking for the best storytelling moments, when to bring that person on camera, when to let the talking play as voiceover, and how to introduce the speaker. Of those two films, *Transatlantic Cable* most strictly dealt with science, engineering, and colorful historical characters, so the film had a different personality, if you will, and a different feeling. *Bataan* was more like *Into the Arms of Strangers,* where we had actual witnesses and participants from a historic event. As you know, for *Into the Arms of Strangers,* we found the actual children—now elderly adults—who went through the experience of the Kindertransport during World War II.

Even though you had witnesses to those events, wouldn't most audiences consider Strangers *far more emotional than, say,* Bataan, *despite both being war documentaries?*
    Into the Arms of Strangers was different from *Bataan,* or even *The Long Way Home,* which dealt with the resettlement of Jewish survivors of the Holocaust in Israel, because *Strangers* was a children's memory

film. From the beginning of working on it, we knew that music and sound design were going to be very important to create this sense of memory— even though the music and sound work came much later in the editing process—and we also knew we didn't want to use realistic sound effects. In *The Long Way Home*, by contrast, the sound effects were completely realistic over the archival footage, and the sound design there was more realistic. But for *Strangers*, the director, Mark Jonathan Harris, knew that we didn't want to hear Nazis marching realistically, for example. We wanted to keep everything very "memory" and evocative of a time and place. One reason for that was practical: we could find no actual footage that depicted the story of the Kindertransport, no footage of the children leaving on the trains. So we had to re-create and manipulate the archival footage we found from the time period. I did not want people to think that the train we were showing in an old film clip was *the train* the children had actually taken. So I slowed down the train clip and stylized it with slow motion and reverberating sound effects. It was all about evoking a memory rather than seeing the actual scenes. In some cases, we did have photographs of the children, which they had carried with them when they moved to England and other places afterward. We definitely relied on these personal family photos to tell the story. When the adults who had been the Kindertransport children were interviewed, you could see in their faces and hear in their tone of voice that they were all still haunted by their experience, even fifty years later. When our crew returned from shooting in England and New York, we watched all the dailies together over a week, and we would just pass boxes of Kleenex around! The interview footage was incredibly moving. Mark was such a good questioner, but also such a sympathetic listener, that the participants gave him everything they could, even though some of them had not talked much about their war experience until then. Because the film was about children, we tried to get as many shots as possible of kids from the period or of images that felt like they could be seen from a child's point of view. You know, low-angle, child POV shots—looking up at Nazi flags, ground-level angles of menacing boots marching or a bunch of balloons decorated with swastikas floating by, which is one of the most chilling images in the film.

Is this manipulation of archival images a risky license to take in a documentary?

We were careful to respect that we were capturing real people's lives and stories, and we didn't want it to feel exploitative at all. But by slowing down and manipulating the footage, it was clear that we were creating visual metaphors and not documenting actual reality. The intention was always to have the film feel stylized for that reason. Even for the idea of how the children had to pack their suitcases to take the train— all we had to represent that event was a *packing list*. That was the only piece of original material I had to work with. I found it so moving to read what the kids chose to take with them and what their parents sent them along with. I thought this had to be a big moment in the film because it was so poignant. But, again, all I had was this one shot of a piece of paper, the packing list, and the interviews in which the people talked about what they took. So I had an idea: I went out in my garage and found an old suitcase, an old teddy bear, and other childhood objects I had. Then I asked my assistant, Alicia Dwyer, who had a camera, to shoot them for temp shots to mock up the sequence. Then we slowed the film down, made it black-and-white, added music with it, and cut that "packing list" sequence. Everybody liked it, but Deborah Oppenheimer, the producer, said, "Well, we can't really do that. The objects have to be authentic." Because she was in touch with the whole Kindertransport community, she began to ask if people still had any of the objects they brought with them. And they did! Deborah gave them her Fedex number and all of these wonderful artifacts started arriving at her house. Including a suitcase and a teddy bear!

So the toys that comprise the opening montage of the film had really traveled in the Kindertransport. What a beautiful miracle for the film to include them.

It was an amazing response. Although that was not the original opening planned for the film, we knew once we received all these rich visual artifacts that we could create both the opening sequence and the "packing list" sequence with them.

It's also interesting that you felt prompted to visit your garage and create shots with your own props. As a result, you launched a response which so enriched the film.

I guess I could kind of take credit for that! *(Laughs.)* At times, yes, I will suggest pickup shots that could be useful. The point is, in the archival footage, I didn't have anything like a teddy bear or a suitcase to go with the shot of the packing list. Perhaps we could have had our researcher, Corrinne Collett, find something equivalent. She was phenomenal in what she found. For example, I would say, "I need a British nurse, 1945," and she'd come up with an image of a British nurse from

1945! Her first assignment was to find shots of European children from the late thirties and early forties. But we didn't have material to fit the packing list.

From what you've just described, it seems that an important skill for working with footage is making spontaneous connections. How does one develop that skill?

It starts with watching the material. I watch all material—or I try to. I will say it gets more and more difficult with directors shooting three hundred and four hundred hours of film, but I do try to watch all of it. In some cases, I've had directors go through and make their own selects. Then we can always go back and look at what they left out if we feel we're missing something. You know, a director whittling the footage down to a hundred hours is very helpful! *(Laughs.)* But if you watch a forty-minute tape of dailies—actually now they're digital cards—but, say, you watch forty minutes of dailies, you *have* to watch the whole thing because you don't know where the gem is going to be. If you fast-forward, you might miss it. So I do sit and watch the footage and check my first reaction to what I see. If I laugh, I make a note of it. If I cry—and I do cry watching dailies—then I know that if it resonates with me, it's going to resonate with an audience. That's what I do to begin, and then I start to build the story or scene and make those connections.

Even though you might have no idea while watching dailies where you could use a particular shot in the film?

Exactly. So first is a gut reaction, and I make a note of it, although I usually like to watch and not stop-and-start. But if I've got a transcript or a log, I will underline or make a star next to the shot. I don't like to take a lot of notes. I just want to make sure I know where that spot is in the footage. Also, if there is repetition when you're going through the material, you can see who says something best or which character illustrates an aspect of the story best. That way, you start defining the story and the characters. Here's an example from *The Long Way Home*. In editing that film, I looked at vast amounts of footage shot by the Allies of the liberation of the concentration camps. That was a profoundly disturbing and life-changing experience for me. I searched through this footage many, many times looking for the right images to illustrate the particular stories being told. Mark Jonathan Harris's vision for the opening of the film was not only to convey the incomprehensible shock and horror the soldiers felt, but more importantly, the recognition on the part of the prisoners that they were being perceived as "inhuman" by their liberators. We were almost ready to lock picture when I went back through the archives one last time, and found one shot that I couldn't believe I had missed—an image that seemed to embody completely the point of the opening sequence. It was a slow tilt up the body of a naked, emaciated man being sprayed with DDT by one GI while others look on with expressions of disgust and horror. The look on that man's face is something that still haunts me.

Knowing the best shots must be especially helpful in building montages.
Yes. I do try to build a montage by figuring out what's the beginning image and what's the final image of a montage. A sequence like a montage can be used to advance the story, so you want to start one place and end up some place else. Montages may also serve as transitions, but they are part of the storytelling, to bridge scenes as well as to punctuate what you just saw and set up what you're about to see. A montage gives the audience time to reflect and experience a transition, like a chapter or page-turning that says we're moving on to something else now. Every shot should have a purpose and hopefully every shot is beautiful. I can spend an hour sometimes looking for just the right shot and I won't know what that is until I see it. Sometimes I will remember, "Oh, there was this shot of whatever that would work over there." So I'll comb through the footage until I find one that I think will work. I look for composition, I look for color sometimes. You want to keep things visually cohesive. I really love shots that reveal something *within* them that I can connect to, such as a move starting in one shot that I can carry over to the next. You know, beautiful camera moves. When I was working in film, there was nothing like beautiful camera moves. Sometimes in video . . . well, if it is a good camera person and high-quality video—it's high-def now—it can be beautiful, but camera moves on video really have to be perfectly shot to hold up on the big screen.

That's one challenge of the new technology. Any other challenges?
In one sense, there's more democratization because of the technology. It's not as difficult, expensive, or prohibitive to make a film, so more people can do it—and not everybody is as good at it as others are, so there is definitely that aspect. Also the shooting ratio has definitely changed. When I was cutting film, I would be given maybe forty or fifty hours of material and I thought that was a lot. But I could pretty much memorize the footage and readily access something I was looking for. Now editing

on Avid, for example, you're much more reliant on a good assistant and the technology to organize all the footage properly so it's easy to search and access. If a project with four hundred hours is not organized well from the outset, it's a recipe for disaster.

But just because there's ten times the footage doesn't mean there's ten times better material, does it?
No, that's the trouble. You had to be much more disciplined shooting film because it was so expensive.

Has the new technology impacted other aspects of editing for you?
Well, I'm talking about the "dark ages" now, when I used to cut in film. *(Laughs.)* Back then, I never made a dissolve. It was almost like a badge of honor, you know?

Why?
We had this expression: "If you can't solve it, dissolve it." *(Laughs.)* So we always wanted to solve a problem editorially *without* using a dissolve.

Don't you sometimes need dissolves for transitions?
Many of us just didn't use them. It was sort of a purist vérité approach. I only wanted to make cuts that worked, and if I needed transitions in the story, I'd make a transition visually, like to a wide shot or an establishing shot or some poetic shot that would signify the end of one scene or the beginning of the next. But I tried to do it all without the "crutch" of the dissolve.

How about fade-outs?
I don't like to use a lot of them, only when it's extremely crucial to the story. Otherwise, they can take you out of the story. If you use a fade-out, there has to be a need for a definite pause—it's a statement that something has just ended. Back in the "dark ages," to indicate that's what you wanted, you'd mark the film with a grease pencil because you couldn't see the effect while you were editing. You had to send it to the lab. Then if you didn't like it, it was expensive to change, so not using fades or dissolves was also certainly a practical decision. For a long time, even when I was cutting nonlinear, I wouldn't use dissolves. It wasn't until I got into the historical or memory films that used a lot of archival footage that I began manipulating and slowing the film down, dissolving one image into

another. The technology finally allowed that, you could see it. You could try it out, design it yourself, play around with it.

What about "the rule" of dissolves?

Well, that rule sort of went away! *(Laughs.)* Although I know some people who still adhere to it! Now, though, I just think of a dissolve as another color in your palette, another tool for visual storytelling. And sometimes even necessary.

Does the new technology facilitate working with music while editing?

Yes, that's an evolution too because you didn't have the range of possibilities of trying music. Now you can just put in a CD and try it. When working in film, it was more cumbersome and expensive to transfer music. But still, the real work is in searching for the right feeling, so I listen to a lot of music to find what resonates with the film I'm cutting. I have worked with some composers whose work I love, such as Lee Holdridge, Miriam Cutler, and Joseph Julian Gonzalez, so I will often use their scores from other films to temp with. Also, I'm always happy when I can cut with jazz or classical music. In *Into the Arms of Strangers*, I temped with Berg, Webern, and even a Viennese waltz.

Is it tricky to watch a film with music that you cut to but that will not be in the final film?

Yes, it's dangerous to fall in love with your temp score. In *Beah*, I used a Bessie Smith song to underscore the sequence of Beah packing up her house to move back to Mississippi. It worked perfectly, we loved it, and we wanted to keep it. We learned that it would be very expensive to license that song. But we were blessed because our angel, Dr. Bernice Johnson Reagon, who scored the entire film, performed a song for that sequence that not only transcended the temp track, but also elevated and deepened the moment. I have to say that the two days of working with Bernice in the music recording sessions is one of the highlights of my professional life. I felt privileged to be a witness to her brilliance and I was so grateful that our film had inspired her to create such powerful music. But again, in terms of cutting to music, I find that it helps to temp with the music of a composer we think we may ultimately work with, although obviously you can't always do that. Basically I'm searching for a mood or vibe—I never want to use anything too familiar or recognizable, but something that has the emotion, feeling, and pacing that I want—music that will underscore the story I'm trying to impart. Then I have to trust that the composers will do something even better. Sometimes they will compose a score so completely different from what I have temped with, and if it works, I'm thrilled.

And if it doesn't work?

The best composers are very open to working with you and the director to achieve the best sound for the film.

When you screen a film before it gets scored, do you remove the temp music and let everyone see the silent cut?

No. When I screen for feedback, it's with filmmakers and colleagues who understand how to look at a rough cut. They know it's temp track and they know how to give feedback accordingly. There was a time when *everyone* I knew was using the soundtrack of *Babel* as temp music! *(Laughs.)*

Is there an inner musical rhythm to your cutting?

There is. Sort of like one-two-three, one-two-three.

Do you always waltz through a film? (Laughs.)

Well . . . it depends on what beat you're going for. Sometimes you cut all the shots the same length and sometimes you don't. Sometimes you cut to music on the beat, but even when there is no music, all the shots seem to follow a certain rhythm.

Almost as if each shot turns out to be, say, three seconds long in a montage?

Yes, but it also depends on the visual. If you have a nice slow pan, that one shot might be enough. You might not even need any more shots. Or maybe like one slow pan and three short shots, if that's what the scene needs. You feel like you're conducting the film in a way because you're balancing so many elements: sight, sound, story, emotion, information. You want everything to resonate at the same time and contribute to the audience's understanding and experience.

The act of conducting must really come into play when you work on films with multiple storylines such as Thin, Pandemic: Facing AIDS, *and* The

World According to Sesame Street. *How do you keep the various strands straight?*

Each of those films was a little different. In *Pandemic,* for example, we cut the individual stories first, so I started country by country on five continents.

Was that because the footage was coming in from different countries at different times?

No, it was just the most sensible approach because each story was like a portrait of the AIDS crisis in each country. In fact, HBO ended up screening that film as five half-hours. So after we did the feature, we broke the film down into each story and it worked very well as a series. That was the only multiple-story film I've worked on that didn't have a lot of intercutting between stories. We stayed with one story for a good chunk of time and we all came up with that structure in the editing room. Rory Kennedy, the producer, had been in the field capturing these five stories, and then we worked with writer Mark Bailey to develop the structure of the feature film. Each of the individual stories had a three-act structure and could actually exist as a short film. In assembling the feature film, we intercut the five stories accordingly—exposition, conflict, and resolution. In the feature version, we naturally shortened, tightened, and eliminated some scenes, but the essence and integrity of each story remained intact.

You also had stories in different countries in the Sesame Street *film.*

In that case, we used the Bangladesh story as the spine or through-line of the film, and intercut it with sequences such as the origins of *Sesame Street,* the introduction of an HIV-positive Muppet in South Africa's *Sesame Street,* and the effort to bring Serbs and Albanians together in a coproduction, among others. By contrast, with *Thin,* which is about women struggling with eating disorders, we focused on four characters: Shelley, Alisa, Polly, and Brittany. The idea was to have one character come in and hopefully complete the treatment program and exit. The director, Lauren Greenfield, wasn't exactly sure who else she was going to find who would complete the program, so she had filmed more characters who we dropped. It is tricky to do a film with multiple characters since both major and minor characters emerge and evolve during the course of the film, and you know the audience will connect with some more than others, so you structure the film as major and minor as well. For example, in *Thin,* we followed four major young women who became the story's focus. However, other people who recurred throughout the film—particularly staff members, therapists, and a couple of other patients—played minor roles.

How does editing help an audience keep track of multiple characters?

I always look for a diversity of characters and make sure each one is clearly differentiated from the other. In films with multiple characters, you don't want the audience to become confused and mix them up, so I try to introduce each character with a memorable scene that has personal significance for that character. A couple of examples come to mind. In *Into the Arms of Strangers,* Lory Cahn was a vivid storyteller and related many significant childhood experiences. But we chose to introduce her with the story she told about how at seven years old, she was window-shopping with her father who bought her a very expensive suit that she admired. The gist of the story was that she was her father's pride and joy and he could deny her nothing. We learn later that when her father put her on the Kindertransport and was saying goodbye to her, his impending loss was so unbearable that he pulled her out of the window of the moving train. Consequently, she was sent with her family to six concentration camps. The core of Lory's story is her relationship with her father, which becomes memorable for the audience. A good example from *Thin* was Polly, who we introduced immediately as the rebel who explains how to "bend" the rules; later, she's the person who was kicked out for her behavior. Brittany is introduced through her relationship with her mother, whose behavior has clearly contributed to her eating disorder. Sometimes in a documentary, it might not be easy to like all the characters, but they still should be people the audience can engage with.

I imagine that some characters drop out along the way based on the strength of their storylines—not only through editorial decisions, but sometimes because of circumstances during the shooting.

That does happen. The strongest characters and storylines in *Thin* emerged over the course of shooting, and some characters were dropped during filming while another couple of characters were dropped after our first rough cut—which was four hours. The friendship that developed between Polly and another patient, Shelley, was crucial to the first two acts. When Polly left at the end of act 2, there was a big void to fill—both in the film and in the lives of the women in the clinic. Although filming continued on and off for several months, and a lot more happened at the clinic after Polly left, we ultimately collapsed the months with a "time passing" sequence and then resolved each of the other three characters' stories in act 3. Shelley was the only one who successfully completed the program and was discharged. Brittany and Alisa left because their health insurance coverage ran out. It always makes me sad to talk about Polly because, although she did have some professional success as a photographer, and through the film became active in helping other women with eating disorders, she continued to struggle with her demons and committed suicide a couple of years after the film was released.

It must be very difficult to present the problem of bulimia in film because of these tragic outcomes. But the presentation seemed even more intense by actually filming two of the women purging in the bathroom. What is the impact on an audience when you compel them to see such emotionally raw moments?

Hopefully, they have new awareness, understanding, compassion.

I suppose some audience members are curious about it, while others are extremely uncomfortable seeing such a private act depicted so graphically.

The women allowed it to be filmed. I don't know if it was a cry for help, but all the women who agreed to be in the film wanted people to understand that this is an illness which they are powerless against. We had an earlier scene with Polly purging. Then toward the end, we saw Alisa, who had gone through treatment—we thought successfully—and was at home with her kids, go into her bathroom and purge. But it was important to see. This graphic aspect reminds me of another film I cut, *The Girl Next Door*. It's a feminist film of a woman who starts out in the porn industry. Although she is actually enthusiastic about it at first, she gets completely beaten down by it. We had a graphic scene of her going in for breast implants and having liposuction, and the audience freaked out when they saw it, it was so horrible. But Christine Fugate and I wanted it in the film because we were making a statement about this form of self-mutilation. It made a point. It was a choice to include that scene and let it play as realistically as possible. In both cases, the graphic scenes not only contributed to the story, but they underscored important themes we were exploring. Both scenes are similar in that they involve women's body images and are related to identity, self-loathing, and self-worth. So I think it was legitimate to present this reality.

One could say the same about images of war.

Definitely. *The Long Way Home* contained many terrible images from the Nazi concentration camps. Those images are always shocking and horrific, but there is a danger that audiences who have seen them before can become desensitized. We tried to look for images that were not familiar, and we were told by many knowledgeable viewers that they had never seen some of the archival footage we used. Also, an important direction of Mark's was to find close-ups of faces—both still images and live action footage. We lingered on these intense close-ups as a powerful exploration and reminder of the humanity of the victims—people who had endured an unimaginable dehumanizing ordeal.

Given the harsh realities that documentaries often capture, I understand the need to "see" representations of those realities, however painful. In some way, though, that potential to "cut to the quick" reminds me, stream-of-consciously, of a line in the film Jimmy Carter: Man from Plains, *in which Carter comments on his experience of being interviewed by a Middle Eastern journalist and worrying that he will be misrepresented in the final cut of that interview. He bluntly said, "The editing always hurts." Did that comment strike a chord with you as an editor?*

(*Laughs.*) In a way. I think I left that in because I thought it was a touch of humor and irony.

But he has a point.

He definitely does. In editing a documentary, you are given a real trust and you should not violate that trust. It is easy to do cheap shots in editing, where someone says something but then you choose to cut to an image that contradicts or misinterprets it. That is exploitative and offensive. I think of the film I did about skinheads and a band of kids who hung out with this obnoxious, loathsome human being, who was the *hero* of the film, so to speak, the main character. Of course, when he saw the film, he really liked it! Sometimes we think people are not going to like their portrayal on the screen and then they do. I remember cutting the film at my house when a furnace man came by to do some repairs and he said, "What's that you're cutting? A Ku Klux Klan rally?" All this noise was blaring out of my house for a few months! But the film was about how this man was manipulating these young boys and we tried to portray the boys as sympathetic and how kids can fall under the spell of such a person. That was the point of the story and we had to present it in an honest and truthful way.

Interestingly, you said you tried to portray the boys as sympathetic. In a way, weren't you actually slanting the film toward that side? Or did you feel you were still being impartial to both sides, even though the main character was probably reprehensible to most of the audience?

We didn't censor him at all. We just let him say everything that came out of his mouth that contributed to the story. The purpose of the film was to take a look at this subculture and how it developed and was promoted. I suppose if one already embraced this man's doctrine, the film would not change that perspective. But the audience saw the film for our purpose and point of view. It was clear in how we presented the material. But the film really looked at issues of class and race. The boys were mostly disenfranchised, impoverished white youth who came from dysfunctional and/or abusive family situations. They found a home of sorts with this father figure who was able to exert his influence over them and indoctrinate them with his hateful views. Fortunately, the film ended with his arrest. We were quite pleased. *(Laughs.)*

With such polarizing characters and controversial subjects, editing a documentary is clearly a huge responsibility.

It is a responsibility to be honest and truthful. I believe in the integrity of documentaries and in the editorial process, and I want to maintain the integrity of the characters and their situations and not manipulate them. Of course, we have to condense the stories, but we still have to maintain and present their true essence. You owe it to the audiences because they know when they are being manipulated. And you owe it to the people who have entrusted you with the stories of their lives.

10. Weighing the Gold

RICHARD CHEW

1967 *The Redwoods,* dir. Trevor Greenwood

1969 *The Medium Is the Massage, You Know,* dir. Trevor Greenwood

1974 *The Music School,* TV (short), dir. John Korty

1974 *The Conversation* (coeditor), dir. Francis Ford Coppola

1976 *One Flew over the Cuckoo's Nest* (coeditor), dir. Miloš Forman

1977 *Star Wars* (coeditor), dir. George Lucas

1978 *Goin' South,* dir. Jack Nicholson

1979 *When You Comin' Back, Red Ryder?,* dir. Milton Katselas

1982 *My Favorite Year,* dir. Richard Benjamin

1983 *Risky Business,* dir. Paul Brickman

1985 *Real Genius,* dir. Martha Coolidge

1985 *Creator,* dir. Ivan Passer

1986 *Where the River Runs Black,* dir. Christopher Cain

1986 *Streets of Gold,* dir. Joe Roth

1988 *Clean and Sober,* dir. Glenn Gordon Caron

1990 *Men Don't Leave,* dir. Paul Brickman

1991 *Late for Dinner,* dir. W. D. Richter

1992 *Singles,* dir. Cameron Crowe

1993 *Mi Vida Loca,* dir. Allison Anders

1993 *My Life,* dir. Bruce Joel Rubin

1995 *Tall Tale*, dir. Jeremiah S. Chechik

1995 *Waiting to Exhale*, dir. Forest Whitaker

1996 *That Thing You Do!* dir. Tom Hanks

1998 *Hope Floats*, dir. Forest Whitaker

2000 *Shanghai Noon*, dir. Tom Dey

2001 *I Am Sam*, dir. Jessie Nelson

2004 *First Daughter*, dir. Forest Whitaker

2005 *The New World* (coeditor), dir. Terrence Malick

2006 *Bobby*, dir. Emilio Estevez

2009 *The Great Observer* (coeditor), dir. Dan Pritzker

2010 *The Runaways*, dir. Floria Sigismondi

2011 *The Way* (coeditor), dir. Emilio Estevez

AWARDS

1975 BAFTA Film Award, Best Film Editing, *The Conversation* (shared with Walter Murch)

1976 Oscar Award (AA) nomination, Best Film Editing, *One Flew over the Cuckoo's Nest* (shared with Sheldon Kahn and Lynzee Klingman)

1976 Eddie Award (ACE) nomination, Best Edited Feature Film, *One Flew over the Cuckoo's Nest* (shared with Sheldon Kahn and Lynzee Klingman)

1977 BAFTA Film Award, Best Film Editing, *One Flew over the Cuckoo's Nest* (shared with Sheldon Kahn and Lynzee Klingman)

1978 Oscar Award (AA), Best Film Editing, *Star Wars* (shared with Paul Hirsch and Marcia Lucas)

1978 Eddie Award (ACE) nomination, Best Edited Feature Film, *Star Wars* (shared with Paul Hirsch and Marcia Lucas)

1978 USA Award, Outstanding Editing, Academy of Science Fiction, Fantasy and Horror Films, *Star Wars* (shared with Paul Hirsch and Marcia Lucas)

1979 BAFTA Film nomination, Best Film Editing, *Star Wars* (shared with Paul Hirsch and Marcia Lucas)

2001 Eddie Award (ACE) nomination, Best Edited Feature Film— Comedy or Musical, *Shanghai Noon*

When reminded of the "chemical reactions" that editing symbolically produces from the powerful images and sounds that make up a story, Richard Chew did not hesitate to mention yet another metaphor that editors often use to describe themselves and are described by. As an "alchemist," an editor can "create" gold where only its potential seemed to shine. But lacking spells or magic wands or Bunsen burners, Chew discusses the many practical aspects of creating this illusion with examples from his now-classic fiction films spanning more than forty years. His anecdotes provide rich comparisons and contrasts between directors' approaches to storytelling and the challenges of entering the mindset of a "style" that may not immediately make much sense to an editor. In particular, Chew details the demands of working with multiple-character films such as *One Flew over the Cuckoo's Nest* and *Bobby*, including principles governing action-reaction and constructing the arcs of each little story. Having worked briefly in documentaries before turning to fiction features, Chew weighs in on the similarities and differences of these two film worlds. The principles of seamless storytelling—although the meaning of seamless is debatable—are pillars of good editing for Chew, as are films with heart and social consciousness. As a member of the Foreign Language Films Committee at the Academy, Chew is increasingly aware of how international filmmakers are faced with the similar goal of telling good human stories, while transcending cultural boundaries in a shrinking, technologically dominated world.

Although starting in the industry when celluloid reigned supreme, Chew has adapted well to the digital revolution, and he enumerates some of its inevitable pros and cons. Never discounting the possibility of a pendulum swinging back to an earlier way of filmmaking, Chew nevertheless believes that rising above all the fancy technology is still an old-fashioned concern for content over form. The flash that dazzles like gold can sometimes be derived from a single solid performance, and not from the more commonplace cacophony of squealing tires and exploding cars.

Let's start off with your background and how you moved into the film business.

Sure. My path may be a little different from others because I come from a bicultural background. My parents were immigrants from China. My dad learned English through an English-speaking family who raised him when he came as a boy to Los Angeles. As in traditional Chinese ways, he later married my mom through a matchmaker in China, and brought her to L.A., where she ended up stranded not knowing the language or culture, then having to raise a family. I came at the tail end of a brood of five, some ten years after my sister. I grew up in a bilingual household— English is not even my first language.

Flash forward for a moment: do you think your background has enhanced your work in film at all?

Coming from a bicultural background and growing up in the inner-city public schools of Los Angeles with racially diverse groups has helped me to be open to experiences of different cultures coming together. I've always been drawn to the kind of films that deal with outsiders, to topics that give voice to the underrepresented.

I've read that you also earned a degree in philosophy and attended Harvard Law School. How did you move into those areas but then switch over to film?

When I was thirteen or fourteen, I became spiritually curious, so I joined other young people in my community church, learning its teachings about the big questions of life. Eventually I soured on religion while in college at UCLA and moved on to study philosophy. It was, at least in a secular setting, an expanded opportunity to ask those questions and search for answers. And of course, I didn't find any answers! In a university setting, philosophy basically is just asking more questions, or learning to reframe those questions, and all so-called answers are merely provisional. So it didn't really help me other than with developing my analysis of questions and problems, in an academic way, and force me to write essays about it. Maybe intuitively, some of the problem solving that I have to do in editing films might relate to analytical techniques I picked up in philosophy. Then, going to law school—that was to forestall going into the adult world! I didn't really know what direction in life to take after I got my degree, but because of my dad's insistence and law school friends' encouragement, I applied for law school. To my surprise, I got accepted into Harvard Law. So I went, not knowing any lawyers personally, not knowing what the profession was about, not having even spent time in a law office. I went essentially because I was drawn to the prestige of the school. When I got there, it was a huge culture shock. I felt assaulted right away with hypercompetitive, driven, type-A personalities. Some of my fellow students were already accomplished individuals—former Air Force officers, guys with PhDs, ex–Peace Corps volunteers. I felt, wow, this isn't like the laid-back philosophy department at UCLA!

From law school to film editing—how did that happen?

Well, what lit a flame within me was a film I saw while in law school. It was the midsixties, and the film was *Nothing But a Man,* starring Ivan Dixon and Abbey Lincoln. It was directed by two guys out of Harvard named Mike Roemer and Robert Young. Because it was filmed in black-and-white, it seemed like a documentary about this young African-American couple in rural, racist Alabama. Ivan Dixon played a gas-station attendant and Abbey Lincoln played the daughter of a preacher, who was very strict, very class-conscious, and did not approve of her relationship with this blue-collar guy. To me, growing up during that era and seeing a film like *Nothing But a Man* made me realize that film could be a mirror of society and teach us about the human condition. It blew me away that it could be so real and also so moving. I decided that making films like this would be something I wanted to learn to do.

Did you ever meet Roemer and Young?

I looked them up in New York, and even though I had no background in film, Bob Young took the time to counsel me over coffee in midtown Manhattan. A few months later he helped me find a job in Seattle at a television company, King TV. This company was under a politically progressive leadership at the time, and it was looking for motivated young film graduates. Though I had no training, they took me into the news department initially as a go-fer. Within a month or two, I was moved up to covering small news stories with a Bell and Howell Eyemo camera. It was a hand-held, spring-wound 16mm camera with a three-lens turret. It held a hundred-foot load, which is about two and a half minutes of film. News stories at that time were shot on 16mm black and white negative. I would cover a story, drop off the film—usually two or three rolls—at the lab, then run off to shoot another story, maybe one with sound recording, then dash back to the lab to pick up the film of the first story, and return to the newsroom to edit it. When I was done with that, I was off again to pick up film of second or third stories to edit back at the studio—all in time for the newscast at six o'clock sharp. This was my film school, without costing me a dime of tuition! They were paying me to learn. The downside were some weird news assignments I got sent to.

Breaking-news types of stories?

No, fluff stuff, like a birthday party at the zoo for the gorilla! Or they would fly me to central Washington to cover the crowning of the Apple Blossom Queen. The toughest story to shoot was a murder crime scene—the most grisly, horrific sight I ever experienced. I'll never forget it. But after six months of begging, I got transferred to the documentary division of King Broadcasting. Those guys were making exciting documentaries. A film about César Chávez organizing farm workers in California. A film about antinapalm demonstrations against Dow Chemical during the Vietnam War. Stuff I was interested in. I fell in with this group of tuned-in, ambitious, young film school graduates. Luckily they tutored me. My film education continued.

Did you work on any films we would recognize today?

Yeah, one early film was *The Redwoods*. It was commissioned by the Sierra Club to save an extensive grove of virgin redwood trees in northern California. The director, Trevor Greenwood, who later became a professor at USC Film School, taught me how to correctly set up a tripod *(laughs)*, and how to use different 16mm cameras like an Arriflex, a Bolex, and an Éclair. Then he brought me onboard as the cameraman to go out with him to shoot this film about the redwoods, which he had been researching. These virgin trees were many hundreds, if not a thousand, years old. Later, I watched how he edited and asked if I could learn that too. Previously in the newsroom we slapped together the footage. Editing was determined by the length of the story to be aired. The news editor would say, "We need thirty seconds for Bobo the Gorilla's birthday party." Or "Give me forty seconds on that hotel fire." So I rolled out the film from rewinds through a Moviscope—which is a viewer—and a timer. I'd take three seconds of this, five seconds of that, and so on. But on *The Redwoods*, Trevor would explain to me the storytelling and atmosphere-building techniques of editing, like using juxtaposition, or parallel editing, or alternating points of view, or adding sound effects. The more I edited, the more excited I got about arranging images and structuring stories. As a cameraman in cinéma-vérité documentaries, you're recording images—there's no structure in terms of dialogue or characters. You're trying to capture the real life in front of you. But when it came time to tell the story, you needed to dramatize and structure it through editing. I came to realize that editing was a more deliberate process. Rather than being reactive—which I was as a cinéma-vérité cameraman—I preferred weighing the value of a particular moment or composition. Also I was learning how to use sound. To create atmosphere, I began to use very simple background sounds to fill out what you don't see. That was something I learned early in documentaries—not even to mention the use of music— to use sound effects and backgrounds to help define or expand the visual image. The more I did this, the more I appreciated that whole canvas I had to work with. In *The Redwoods*, our visual subjects were inanimate characters, although we did have some loggers at work. What we had were trees, ferns, water, sunlight, fog. How do we make these come alive? Our writer-producer Mark Jonathan Harris created a moving voiceover to wrap around these images. When all was woven together, the final tapestry made for an effective film, which the Sierra Club used to lobby members of Congress.

In essence, you were creating a portrait or poem about the trees.

Right. *The Redwoods* won an Oscar for Best Short Documentary of 1967. It was really amazing and completely unexpected that within a year or so after I left law school, a film I helped to create won an Oscar!

So going to law school was good for something anyway! It got you into film.

For sure it was a crooked path. First, it got me to the East Coast, where I had an awakening to the power of film. Then, a chance meeting with a New York film director who noted I went to Harvard Law. That led me to a job in Seattle where I started learning my craft. Seattle led to San Francisco, which led me back to L.A., though it was Hollywood actually. But having that documentary background enabled me to look at film differently from many of those I met in Hollywood, who were following their parents into the film industry or who had ambitions to make popular, big-tent movies. I came in with different sensibilities.

But your career took a trajectory into the Hollywood type of film—or should I say fictional film versus documentary. How did you feel about working on films that were not documentaries?

The first two features I worked on, *The Conversation* and *One Flew over the Cuckoo's Nest*, are actually very documentary-like, so I didn't feel like I was moving away from documentaries as such. Those films portrayed characters in real-life dramas, in the same way that I loved in

Nothing But a Man. In the case of *The Conversation,* the protagonist has a moral crisis, and I loved that! Coeditor Walter Murch and myself were given the freedom by Francis Ford Coppola to constantly rework the structure of the film—the sequential order of the scenes. On the one hand, it was documentary in terms of the setting and issues it posed, but it also made me aware that dramatic filmmaking, narrative filmmaking, doesn't require editing to adhere rigidly to a script. Since I had never worked on feature films before, I had the naïve idea that the director shoots what's on the page and the editor strings everything together. So luckily for me, my first feature film was really fluid, constantly changing. We only had to adhere to the basic ideas, to the intention of the script, but we were always switching and playing with how the characters went from place to place internally.

Was Cuckoo's Nest *similar?*

As far as its issues, yes, but not as far as structure was concerned. This film had a linear storyline. *Cuckoo's Nest* was interesting because we filmed on a first-floor wing of the Oregon State Hospital. Adjoining the set were production offices and a cafeteria. Up on the second floor were our editing rooms and make-shift theater, which had a wooden box built around the noisy projector to buffer its sound. The third floor was the maximum security ward for women mental patients. Some male patients worked on the crew as carpenters, painters. We were surrounded by the reality of the story! Our superb actors, except for Jack Nicholson, were basically unknown previously. And it was winter in Salem, Oregon—really wet, cold, and gray. It was bound to make anyone depressed! Like I said, editing *Cuckoo's Nest* was different from *The Conversation.* While *The Conversation* was just so fluid and open, the script of *Cuckoo's Nest* required that it be sequential. But I didn't have an issue with that. The problem was more of choosing performance, and the one thing I learned from director Miloš Forman was how to use reaction shots. In documentaries, for instance, when you don't have footage on the person speaking, you use what is called a cutaway—you cut to some other image to avoid a jump cut. We were very old school at the time—you did not use jump cuts unless it was absolutely necessary! So in documentaries, you just cut to somebody else looking or nodding. But on *Cuckoo's Nest,* I learned how to use other characters' reactions to further the emotion or narrative of a scene. For example, during group therapy sessions, if Nicholson's character was holding the floor, then the other characters like Cheswick, Billy Bibbit, or Nurse Ratched were all reacting to Nicholson. Forman had multiple cameras on them. And it was much more interesting sometimes to see how they were responding *to* Nicholson than to be *on* Nicholson. You know they had to be good if we would cut away from Jack! So I learned how to use reaction shots in a different way.

Cuckoo's Nest was such an intense film because of all those close-up reaction shots. How did you know when enough was enough as you cut from reaction to reaction in a group-talk scene?

It was fashioned in the editing room. The choices really were Miloš Forman's in terms of how long we should be on something and whether it worked or not. The producers, Saul Zaentz and Michael Douglas, completely trusted Miloš, so it was really Miloš working with me and the other editors, Lynzee Klingman and Shelley Kahn. Once in a while, Miloš would have some of his friends screen it, like Buck Henry and Werner Herzog, but I don't remember if they saw the whole film or just parts—after all, it *was* over thirty years ago! Contrary to common practice today, we never previewed *Cuckoo's Nest* in front of test audiences. The point is that Miloš is very painstaking. His sensibility ruled. We would argue over two frames, and if the two frames were not right, he would have me redo it. After Lynzee and Shelley came and left, I went back through the film in the last month of editing with Miloš to make all these adjustments to replace or trim or extend something before our sound mix.

With three editors working at different times on the same film, were there conflicts in working style or editing style—if there is such a thing as editing style?

Both in the case of *Cuckoo's Nest* and later in *Star Wars*, we were submerged in the director's vision. There were no conflicts because we're just helping Forman or George Lucas execute their singular ideas, and we were their tools. Editing styles reflect directors' storytelling styles. In these films, one is documentary-like, the other action-adventure. As such, these projects were formidable learning experiences for me.

Did you learn about editing or was it more about dealing with personalities?

Both. Learning about editing, we've been talking about. But just as hard is learning how to work with others. Learning not to be protective of the preciousness of what I've done. It was a mistake I made early on to think like, "I got the answer." Like, "I worked so hard on this and thought about it *so* much, this is the *only* way to go!" The more experience I've gotten, I've learned to let go. I don't have the exclusive view of one thing, and I've come to enjoy more the exchanging of ideas and passing things back and forth.

How do you exchange ideas about "two frames" then? Is it really about two frames, or is it just a director's strong personality rising to the surface?

It depends on where those two frames are. For instance, I learned from Miloš, say when you're cutting a dialogue scene and you're at the end of the line, where do you make a cut? Do you make the cut at the *end* of the word before you cut to someone else, as in a reaction to another line? Or do you cut *before* the end of the word and let the last syllable or last two syllables—the sound of those syllables—drift into your next visual cut? It makes a difference to the momentum of the scene. That's what I learned. It's like if you wait till the very last frame, to the end of a word at the end of a line, then the momentum seems to stop and makes the line or scene more choppy. Whereas if you literally cut two frames sooner and let the end of a word drift into the next picture, the sound provides a momentum into your next cut, making it a little more seamless—if that's what you want to do: make it more invisible.

The goal of editing was long considered to produce seamless cutting. Do you think that is still true or was that only "of a time" in editing history?

That period of invisible editing may be past because visible editing is the prevalent style today. Initially, visible editing was kind of refreshing, you know, how everything hit you in the gut or socked you between the eyes.

Which can be exhausting on the viewer too.

Yes, it can distract the viewer from a film's lack of narrative or clarity or character development. It appeals solely to the senses because the whole pacing is just so pushed, and the images are so pushed, that it exhausts you with its sensations. You don't have a chance to process anything or feel the emotion of the story. Ironically, in making the transition from documentaries to fiction films, I had to learn how to make something seamless because, to draw the viewer in, I had to learn to make cuts invisible and have a really light touch. I would develop a natural flow with a scene or the style of the picture. But then, of course, with *Star Wars*, because it's an action picture, I learned to make visible cuts because you needed that technique to enhance a sequence's impact when necessary.

And then with a film like The New World—*not quite action à la* Star Wars, *of course—you have very visible cutting in a straightforward historic narrative.*

Terry Malick is such an unusual talent. He is peculiar in what he wants and he wants you to be aware of the cut and where the cuts are and where they take place in the action. And in using voiceover, he uses a random technique to make internal monologue more indirect. In *The New World,* there's lots of surprising cuts or shots because they are not part of the narrative flow. Unexpected images are thrown in. One instance I think of—it really surprised me because of how well it worked when it didn't make any sense at all—was when Captain John Smith (Colin Farrell) was following the Princess through the woods. In the middle of the walk, there is a cut to the ground, a moving POV of the shadow of the Princess over a footprint. Of course, when I was looking at the dailies, I just thought it was a bad camera move! But Terry—

Planned it that way?

No, not planned. You see, Terry never says, "Cut!" when he shoots. "Cut!" occurs when the film runs out. All his takes are about four minutes long because on the Steadicam cameras, the magazine holds four hundred feet of film—a little more than four minutes. So Terry would turn on the camera, sometimes surreptitiously, and let the actors walk through a scene, or occasionally direct the actors with his voice offscreen, and the take only ended when the film ran out! *(Laughs.)* There's a naturalness to the action because the actors don't know when the camera's on them or not. Some actors love working this way, but some others, those more classically trained, go nuts!

Are you obligated to use the whole scene?

No, that's the thing. He's looking for those off-moments that are on someone's back! Literally. I mean, it's almost like he would never, ever want to cut to the actor saying a line *facing* the screen. *(Laughs.)*

Yes, I noticed many shots of the backs of actors' heads, or the close-up of a face not speaking, yet a voice is heard.

Right. I went through countless sequences with Terry where I would choose shots that were too "right on" and he would instead choose the shot that would be on, say, the Princess's shoulder! Or on Smith's back, where you're looking at his earring! As the camera drifts around, he prefers moments that seem accidental. He looks for randomness in the image because he doesn't want to appear to be posing his actors or composing for the camera. He wants to find a telling moment where the camera just drifts past someone or catches a shadow crossing a corner of the frame. And because he likes that, it obligates us as editors to choose a moment that would juxtapose to it something that is completely discontinuous from that—because he doesn't look for continuity either! It's like continuity is for pussies. *(Laughs.)* So you, the viewer, become aware of the editing.

In numerous sequences—you could call them montages—you cut, say, from one angle on the Princess to another angle of her, followed by a shot of her lips, a shot of John Smith, a shot of her forehead, then to someone swimming, a fragment of a mirror, a fish, and so on—a veritable chain bracelet of images. Or like you've gone on a trip, but you don't quite know where you've been!

For sure. Another example of this randomness is Terry's use of voiceover, which is a favored technique. He wrote a beautiful script for *The New World,* but once we started editing, he threw out much of the dialogue! Thinking it was too literary, he didn't want to use it as written and performed by the actors. He rewrote reams of voiceover, but unlike other directors, he would send sixty pages, say, to Colin Farrell, and have Colin show up at his agent's offices in Beverly Hills, where a sound recordist would record him reading those pages without rehearsal, and even without Terry being there. Of course, Terry would have a brief phone conversation with Colin prior to the recording session, but not show him any scenes. Colin would just be reading off the page, blah-blah-blah, blah-blah-blah, as unaffected and understated as he could. Then the hard drive of the recording would be sent to us with a couple hours of Colin reading those sixty pages, and Terry would say to me, "Why don't you use a section of this? And on this other page, I like this." He would pick forty minutes out of those couple of hours. And then, of course, me being an ex–philosophy, ex–law student, I would try to impose some logic on it, right? Oh, I thought, I can use this paragraph mixed with that paragraph, and put them over these images. I was proud that I found a parallel between the words and images, thinking it was kind of cool because they all went together, right? Well, Terry would look at it and say, "Well, that's kind of interesting. . ."

But?

But then he'd say, "Throw everything to the right." What he meant was on the Avid, which is our editing software, there's a timeline which runs from left to right. The left end of the timeline is the beginning of the scene, and the right end is the end of the scene, and you can slide your soundtrack along it. So when he said, "Throw everything to the right," it meant he wanted me to slide, or retard the soundtrack. Wherever I had placed a couple of lines or a paragraph, he wanted me to *move* it *away* from where I had it. *Let's not put it in an obvious place! (Laughs.)* He also had me assemble a bunch of the Princess's voiceovers as well, but didn't want me to place them anywhere logical.

Because of that, the film seems to have a deep internalization even within the voiceovers, with different voices speaking together. An inner thought within an inner thought within—or am I imagining that?

It does have that feel because it's poetic, not just in the words and what they suggest, but in the depth of visual imagery, which is stitched together in a way that leaves the film very specific for you as the viewer. Each viewer, I think, will come away with a very different experience. Terry's a little like James Joyce, creating a stream-of-consciousness through the use of random, indirect thoughts. To accomplish that, he needed the time in the editing room to uncover the richness of what he recorded, and in a certain way, when it's all laid out, not everyone can appreciate it.

That could be challenging for an audience.

Yes, for some, but I remember going to some screenings out in L.A., where many in the audience thought it was brilliant.

The DVD of the film included an additional twenty minutes—the extended cut—so could you comment on what specifically was added? But perhaps it doesn't matter because it was all random anyway. (Laughs.)

What was added were nonnarrative, character moments. Typically, a studio wants a theatrical version which is narrative-driven. The DVD allows the director to restore the stuff he had to drop under duress. *(Laughs.)* Terry liked the unpolished moments. For example, after I did a lot of the careful work in constructing a scene, Terry preferred the more ragged assembly of that scene. As you know, there's different stages an editor goes through in putting together a scene: you look at dailies, start pulling out sections you like, and string these together. You end up with ragged tails or heads to them because, at that point, you are not looking to cut them together as much as assembling the most telling moments. So I would show Terry a scene that I actually cut together, but he would ask to see the *assembly* of that scene instead and frequently would like that more, with all the ragged heads and tails that included the bad camera bump or the back of an actor before the camera corrected into the proper frame.

Did you finally follow his mindset after a while or did you just let him redo whatever he wanted?

In trying to understand his sensibility, I changed my cutting style. I drank his Kool-Aid, so to speak. His work is unlike any other filmmaker's, so that's an inducement for me to adapt. I might even become a more complete editor. That's why I mentioned that example about the shot of the ground with the shadow, footprints, and feet. Nothing about that ever struck me as usable, yet when he chose that and had me put it into the sequence, I immediately thought: "That's brilliant." I didn't even understand how he picked that moment, but it worked.

Now in a more structured film like Bobby, *what freedom did you have in that editing process? It must have been challenging to weave together so many characters' lives along a narrative continuum, leading to the climactic moment of Robert F. Kennedy's assassination, when all those stories come together.*

I feel I have lived such a charmed life to be able to work on films that matter to me. Yes, *Bobby* offered several challenges that required me to draw on my thirty years of working in movies. A big challenge was interweaving the characters and sorting out which characters were weak. Which ones should we trim? Which ones should be extended? Luckily we had enough characters that when we trimmed weaker ones, we still had a story outside of Bobby Kennedy.

Did you remove entire characters?

No, every character in the script makes an appearance. It's just that we didn't follow his or her through-line. In some cases, we may have dropped only the middle of their stories.

I did feel some characters didn't get "equal time," like the Martin Sheen–Helen Hunt socialite story. I wanted to know more about them but it wasn't there. Did you cut the stories separately as units and then intercut them?

Initially, the stories were intercut as written. But as we cut the picture, the momentum of the main narrative took over. We had to shorten or rearrange the placement of other stories to get to Kennedy. Enter Harvey Weinstein, the renowned producer, whose involvement came late in the picture. He wanted to introduce Bobby Kennedy earlier in the film. In the original script, Emilio Estevez, the director, was trying to be subtle by weighting the movie toward the characters and not make it about Kennedy until the last act. For example, Kennedy doesn't appear in person until the end of the second act, when he gets out of the limo and, walking into the hotel, is greeted by Anthony Hopkins. But Harvey thought, hey, the audiences today are too young to know who Bobby Kennedy is. So he wanted us to establish Bobby and why we should care about the guy. That whole beginning, the prologue to establish the volatile time of 1968 and Bobby's candidacy, was something that came about at Harvey's urging. Throughout the film, all those cuts to Bobby during his campaign— whether on TV screens in the hotel rooms or at different locations in the country—all that was added. I agreed with Emilio initially, but you know, Harvey wielded a big stick and we eventually gave into him. But I think he's right, really, that we had to establish the time and build up Bobby's character for the younger audience to understand why he was so inspirational.

It does make sense, but when you first heard that, did you feel it would ruin the film?

Yes, I thought it would turn it into a bio-pic, especially with that opening. I thought, oh, now people are going to expect a film about Robert Kennedy. I always liked the original script because it was about all these people living their lives, dealing with their issues, and they had no idea that their lives were going to be united at this historical juncture. I always liked that notion in Emilio's script. I feared that people would get disappointed or mad at the picture for not being all about Bobby Kennedy.

I also thought it would have been difficult for you to tell the story of "a day in these people's lives"—from the morning to the evening's tragedy— while also inserting footage of Kennedy's events that happened months or even years before. It challenges the continuity of the characters' day.

That was a tough thing to weigh. Were we helping emotionality more by doing that? Or was it a kind of narrative background of the immediate story? Which then leads to the issue of balancing all the characters. Scripts, of course, should flesh out the story and characters, and you have the actors perform it all out. But once you start editing, you begin to see what is really going on. You say, oh, I understand now what this character is about and I actually don't *have* to play the rest of the scene. We reached that point with certain characters, and that understanding informed us about making deletions.

What is an example of something you deleted?

In one scene, we join William Macy's character, the hotel manager, who is married, and Heather Graham, who's one of his workers. They have just met again in a hotel room for their usual afternoon liaison.

Yes, and they are totally silent with each other.

Right, but in the original script, there was a long dialogue scene between them. She was saying something like, "I can't do this anymore," and he was saying, "Don't you know how much I care about you?" It was a little soap-ish.

The silence did seem to interrupt something tense, yet it made such an impact that you wanted to know what had been going on before we actually see them.

Yes, and that happened because we cut all the dialogue. For one thing, the talking was taking too long. Once you start getting into dialogue, you got to let it play out. And that was an example of, wait, do we understand what they have going on? I mean, what is *this* scene really about? It's about them breaking up. It's not about how he feels and how she feels and so on, which you can just tell from their expressions. So out with the dialogue. Then for me, it was important that, okay, if we're going to have only this much showing, let's not play any music. Let me try a sound effect. So I put in a police helicopter hovering outside, which made sense because there were Secret Service agents and L.A. cops all around that hotel since Bobby was coming that day. Instead of using a music cue, I thought a cold, hard city sound behind the couple would enhance the emotionality of *that* particular scene, and Emilio agreed.

That certainly contrasted with the many long dialogue scenes in the films. You recreated a fictional reality with the sound of the helicopter, but how was the rest of the film going to work when intercutting Kennedy's archival footage with the fictional-story footage?

That was the other interesting aspect of editing this film. At first, Emilio had screened different documentaries and made tape recordings of that footage and gave it to me, saying, "Use what you can." He also screened that material with our DP, Michael Barrett, because they had to figure out how to move the camera when they staged the scenes with the actors to intercut with the archival footage. The camera style for the scenes Emilio was going to stage had to fit in with the camera style of the documentary material. Much of the archival material was pretty degraded because it was so old, or they were dupes of dupes of original sources, or scratched film negative, you know. Sometimes we couldn't even get the original stuff because the footage had been passed from library to library. For instance, CBS footage was actually owned by the BBC, or the University of Oklahoma would have material that the John F. Kennedy Library didn't have. Once a researcher found it all, then we looked at it and it was like, oh my God, this stuff looks awful, can we really restore it enough to use it? But that was only one difficulty. The tricky part was to marry the camera movement and jerkiness of the staged film to fit in with the archival material. To help with that, I used the chanting that the extras did in the staged scenes, like "Bob-by! Bob-by!" or "R-F-K! R-F-K!" or "I wanna see Bobby! I wanna see Bobby!" When I layered in the crowd chanting, even in the temp track, and married it with some of the actual sounds from the assassination, it all came together. I was like, wow! I realized how sound can hide discontinuity or jumpiness in the visuals.

The sounds also built up to the climactic moment of the assassination. But once chaos breaks out in the ballroom, you sublimate the sounds and run music and images against Kennedy's speech, even though he is no longer in the picture. Didn't that risk overwhelming the audience and prevent them from concentrating on the speech?

We did think it could be too much, but we did not want to pull back on this emotion either. We wanted to have everything going at once. I remembered when I had read the screenplay, what really grabbed me was Bobby's speech, which in the script read as one page. Tears came to me because I realized what a vision this man had, how articulate he was, and how we miss leaders like this. So I knew that speech, not his assassination, was the climax. I suppose we had the choice of lowering this or that sound, but I think we also discovered that depending on what venue you see the film in, certain elements are louder than others anyway. As I've discovered in many films I see in theaters or at home, the sound plays out of balance and what sounded great to us in the mixing studio can change depending on the screening venue. I don't know if we ever found a solution for that. But even so, the music, rather than just the words, added an element of universality to the scene, kind of like spreading the hurt that everyone was feeling, uniting all the people, all the victims, all the witnesses to this terrible event. The words bring a different content to the scene. Now, in the ballroom, the actual speech Bobby had made that night after winning the primary was one of mainly thanking his supporters, and not one which was very inspirational. It included some predictable lines like, "Let's bring our boys home from Vietnam and bring justice to America," and he was cracking jokes. We didn't want to get into those particulars.

It would have almost trivialized the drama about to happen.

Exactly. Emilio also wanted the last speech in the film to be his most powerful, which was one he had given only two months before in Indianapolis, in the aftermath of Dr. King's assassination. So in a way, by putting that speech at the end, Robert Kennedy was reaching out from the grave. But to do that, I tried dropping his words from the ballroom speech. I cut to archival footage, suggesting that this was what he was really talking about: the destruction in Vietnam, the disenfranchised in America. Emilio's first reaction was, "What are you doing? You're not going to play his actual speech?" I argued, "Let's show the content of the speech through images and throw some music over it." After some thought, Emilio played Simon and Garfunkel's "The Sounds of Silence" over the scene. The result was so powerful for me the first time I saw it, I had to leave the room. I was overwhelmed. That's the thing I love about editing—having the luxury of discovery. As you may imagine, making those discoveries involves a lot of give-and-take with a director. We each had our own thresholds about how much time to spend recutting a scene and when to move on. Ultimately, I had a really good collaboration with Emilio. Our sensibilities aligned.

Speaking of discovery, some editors have said that they often unleashed many creative connections in film through the hands-on, physical cutting of film. Since you've worked both before and after the "digital revolution," can you say how the more "hands-off" technology has altered that creative process?

No doubt the step-by-step process has been accelerated. In question are the benefits. Certainly it's easier to access and retrieve material. You can move around footage so much quicker. Also I think it has contributed to the use of multilayer, nonlinear narratives we see so often today. Digital programs have enabled that because the process was so cumbersome before. When you were working with film, you had to think things through more because it was so time-consuming to undo something. Back then, if you wanted to move shots around, you had to make a black-and-white dupe of a sequence before you started breaking it apart, and it would take you a half a day to do that. You had to unpeel the tape splices, or if something broke or if some emulsion peeled off the print, you had to get it reprinted. If you had filed anything away that you had used the day before, you had to view the dailies reel to find it again. You would have to thread up the reel on a Steenbeck or KEM, which were the flat-bed editing machines of choice, and roll down to the footage you need to retrieve. And as you were fast-forwarding—or even rewinding—the images ran through the KEM picture head. As you looked at them going by, you got a feel for it again—"Oh, I forgot about that!" Even though it's slower to work with film, when you do, editing is a more deliberate process and not as scattershot as some work is now.

Can the story suffer because of that? Or are storytelling principles the same, regardless of editing format?

Storytelling may follow the same principles, but then the question is: in whose hands, you know? It depends on whose hands the film ends up in. The technology allows many more people to participate in the process because anyone can jump in and recut a movie on his laptop, but does it lead to better storytelling? It merely admits more cooks into the kitchen.

Plus instant gratification! Do you think some directors go a little wild with overshooting because of that?

Yes. It used to be . . . *(Pause.)* Now I'm beginning to sound like an old guy! "Well, sonny, let me tell you about how I used to drive downtown in my Model T!" *(Laughs.)*

And I'm still recording interviews with tape cassettes! (Laughs.)

There you go, different strokes for different folks. As I was saying, it *used* to be that a director might shoot thirteen or fifteen takes, but he would print only three or four of the best takes from the negative and that's what you basically worked with in the editing room. Later, if you felt like you were missing something, you could pull out what they call "B-negative" and print up some of the other takes you neglected earlier.

But basically the director on the set would decide after that series of shots which ones to print. In the editing room, you further refined it by saying, "Okay, I liked take three because she did such-and-such here" or "I liked take seven because he did this over here." Then we put that all together. However, now with digital technology, everything is printed, so to speak. Every take is digitized, put into the computer hard drive, and so you might have all thirteen or fifteen takes. Used to be when you looked at dailies, with the three or four printed takes of each scene, you could watch dailies in a half-hour or forty minutes, and that's the material you'd work with from the previous day's shooting. Now, you might have to sit through three hours of dailies because you're looking at every take that was shot! You know you're not going to use it all, but you don't have notes from the director because he's on the set still shooting or too tired at the end of the day to screen dailies with the crew. We don't watch dailies together anymore because the practice is to put dailies on DVDs for all concerned, and they watch it in their trailers between camera set-ups or at lunch. Meanwhile, I'm back in the editing room screening it with my staff. The director and I don't even have a conversation about it anymore. So after I watch my three hours of dailies, it's like, okay, what am I going to do with this now?

Kind of takes the fun out of it.

Certainly it hinders any initial collaboration. I mean, I still have to put together a first cut anyway, but it's usually without the director's input. Whereas before when I watched dailies with him or her, I got an indication of what the director liked, either generally or specifically. I got a hint of where to go with the scene.

So, is this the future and it's here to stay? Or might a pendulum ever swing back to an earlier time?

I'm a believer of pendulums. *(Laughs.)* But I'm a content guy, basically. I believe that content should be of prime importance, and unfortunately, I think that films today are giving much more emphasis to style and form. Form over content. If we examine art history, we see that over the centuries, painting, for example, has swung between content and form. Baroque styles transitioned to more realistic styles, or what in one century focused on the backs of women's necks became in another century a realistic depiction of political events. Of course, we still see films today that emphasize performance and take their time doing it, and they don't try to dazzle you or feed you with eye candy. There are still audiences out there who seek that and are more interested in character and story than to be thrilled for two hours.

Perfect segue for asking you about I Am Sam, *a lovely character story. Yet the form of it was rather fragmented at times—harking back to our chat about seamless and visible editing.*

Yes, early on, the director, Jessie Nelson, in a pact with the DP, Elliot Davis—whose style is to use a constantly moving camera—wanted to give the film a subjective feel. She wanted to show a kind of unsteadiness for Sean Penn's character, Sam, his unpredictability, his discombobulated view of the world.

As in the opening, where you only see jump cuts connecting shots of Sam's hands arranging sugar packets, without ever seeing him or the café where he works.

They shot those scenes with a moving camera and no two takes had similar moves, which made it difficult to cut because you just couldn't say, "Well, this moment didn't work in take one, let me go to take two or take three." You couldn't do that because in take two *and* take three, the camera would be at different places in the action. So because of how it was shot, I had to jump cut from take to take. But we do eventually widen out to an objective view revealing Sam and the context of his job.

Do you think the jump cuts clashed with the sentimental nature of the film?

They could, but Jessie in fact said to me, "I know it's sentimental already and could be really schmaltzy, so how about if we kind of go against this?" Since another one of her films had a sentimental story and was cut more conventionally, for *I Am Sam* she encouraged me to go against that. I have to say that even though there were jump cuts, we developed the emotionality of the characters. The growing relationship between Sean Penn's character, Sam Dawson, and Michelle Pfeiffer's character, the high-powered lawyer Rita Williams, was well illustrated, particularly in the scene when he goes to her home for the first time, and he's overwhelmed because he's never been in any home like that. He sees how she treats her son, but when she begins to coach Sam on how to behave in the courtroom, he slowly responds to her coaching. Then the scene culminates in her tying his necktie for him because he can't do it by himself. At first, the jump cuts were jarring, but Sean Penn's character was also disoriented. Yet all the shots lead up to the moment when he realizes how nurturing she is and how much she cares for him. Even though it was full of jump cuts, it still had an emotional through-line. That film also illustrates, now that I think about it, how freeing it was for me as an editor not to have to observe rules about matching. The more conventional rules require match cutting, staying on the same side of the 180-degree line, or motivating a cut. This film was liberating because in all my previous films I had more or less observed the rules. So in a way, I can see why that style of discontinuous editing is used—or overused— today because so many editors must feel like, "Hey, that's great! I don't have to follow no stinking rules!" And the trend has spread to other countries and cultures. I'm a member of the Foreign Language Films Committee at the Academy, and every year I watch a bevy of films from all over the world. Recently I saw a film from Lithuania, and God! It was just full of dizzying camera moves and jumpy cutting. I kept thinking, okay, I'm over this now, you know? In contrast, there was a film from Luxembourg and the camera was either locked down or the moves were done on a dolly. This countertechnique allowed the story to develop slowly, but seductively. The point I'm making is that you can see films from Kazakhstan to Thailand, with cameras moving every which way and shots joined in jump cuts, all very modern but a little alienating. Yet a small film from Luxembourg reacted against the modern style and drew us into its own reality. So getting back to the pendulum metaphor, it may swing back one day to where there's *no* cuts at all, like in *Russian Ark,* or having very few like in Hitchcock's *Rope* or Yasujirō Ozu's films!

You certainly have seen both sides of the pendulum in your career—from documentaries to Hollywood narratives, from hands-on film to digital, from seamless to visible editing. If you had to choose one particular scene or sequence as representative of your best work, what would that be?

Like for my memorial service? *(Laughs.)*

Well, no, I was thinking more of an awards ceremony—of which you have won many, in fact. Is there one sequence you consider your exemplar of editing?

There's the climactic sequence in *Bobby* when Kennedy leaves the ballroom. Then there's the sequence in *I Am Sam* with the necktie I told you about. Oh, but there's one I didn't talk about yet. The "love-on-the-train" sequence in *Risky Business.* That was created purely in the editing room. The way Paul Brickman, the director, had shot it based on his original script wasn't quite working. It had been too general on the page anyway, something like: "Joel and Lana pass through the turnstile. A series of shots of unrestrained passion against a window of romantic imagery. (To be devised.)" Really loose, but open. Paul tried something the first time around that looked like it was from Antonioni's *Blow-Up*. Most of it was shot against a blue screen, with the train stationary. Paul had hoped to superimpose the moving train POVs on the blue screen as background. When he saw my assembly, his face fell. So I suggested, "Let's give the scene the visual equivalent of a sexual climax." To do so, I cut together his second unit shots of all these trains crossing, left to right, right to left, and left to right, so that it ended with a train shooting off a little spark at the end!

Good metaphor. (Laughs.)

Paul liked that idea and said, "Well, let's keep that and I'll go back and shoot more with Tom Cruise and Rebecca DeMornay." Both the producer Jon Avnet and I said, "You need more buildup to it. You can't have those two just all of a sudden doing it on the train." So he went back and wrote some other scenes to add tension to Joel and Lana getting on the train and comfortable with each other while people exited, before getting to the moment of their encounter. When I cut together this new footage, Paul especially liked a profile two-shot where Lana is facing Joel while sitting on his lap. But connecting all these moments would have required jump cuts, which we didn't want to do. To circumvent this, I had to come up with some kind of editing trick. I saw that whenever elevated trains in Chicago cross tracks or whatever, the lights in the cars blink off and on. So I came up with this device of using short fades to black between all these two-shots to conceal the jump cuts. The fades to black work even better than jump cuts because they added to the dreaminess of the love scene. Everything up to that moment was shot at the normal twenty-four frames per second, but as the couple warmed up to each other, I altered the speed of each cut by step-printing them, to highlight this dreamy, sexy quality. On top of all that, the music from Tangerine Dream augmented everything going on between them. So I would say that sequence is probably my favorite!

And it certainly shows how the power of editing images together in just the right way can create a chemical reaction between people.

Yes, we editors are alchemists. *(Laughs.)*

11. **Making It Work**

VICTOR LIVINGSTON

2006   *The Defector*, dir. Mark Jonathan Harris

2008   *Greensburg*, TV Reality, nine episodes

2008   *The Dungeon Masters*, dir. Keven McAlester

2010   *Wreckage of My Past: The Story of Ozzy Osbourne*, dir.
          Mike Piscitelli

2009, 2010 *Craft in America: Origins*, TV, dir. Dan Seeger and Carol
          Sauvignon

2011   *Corman's World: Exploits of a Hollywood Rebel*, dir.
          Alex Stapleton

AWARD

1996 Eddie Award (ACE) nomination, Best Edited Documentary,
    Crumb

Fresh off his success at the Sundance Film Festival premiering his latest documentary on Roger Corman, Victor Livingston admitted how rewarding editing can be when both the subject and the audience are happy with a story he labored to construct as the "truth." While truth is his responsibility, Livingston has also discovered inventive techniques to unpack a larger essence that encapsulates this truth while heightening the cinematic experience for the audience. Intrigued by the idea of film as mimicking the processes of the brain, Livingston, much like Zucchetti and Corrao, relishes atypical ways to cut typical scenes. As Livolsi noted in his discussion of montage for fiction films, Livingston considers montages as a mirror of mental processes, in which the brain makes connections that transcend words, images, or music and creates a deeper engagement with the film. Livingston openly describes the difficulties he faced in re-creating a historic time period for *The Defector*, for which little source material was available, and discovering an inventive way to design atmospheric sequences as a sophisticated pastiche of fiction and reality.

When asked how far one can be "creative" in a documentary before the "truth" feels distorted, Livingston reflected, much as Corrao did in his earlier conversation, on the phenomenon of reality TV. The idea of "everyone" finding their fifteen minutes of celebrity with their own show has tended to oversaturate the media and carve a new subgenre into the documentary form. On the flip side, the phenomenon has challenged filmmakers to avoid clichés and become more inventive in satisfying audiences who are no longer as "shocked" as they used to be. To address this challenge, Livingston relies on his valuable experiences in both fiction films and documentaries, where the search for what is true in a story hinges on the characters' emotional connections to their particular "realities."

Before we begin, I'd like to say congratulations on the premiere of your latest film at Sundance Film Festival. How was that experience of seeing Corman's World: Exploits of a Hollywood Rebel *for the first time with a large audience?*

It was just a thrill. I had never seen the film with an audience because we hadn't had an opportunity to screen it before it went to Sundance. Other editors had been working on the film before I started, but the director and producers weren't satisfied with its progress. I started on the film about three months before we submitted it to Sundance. It wasn't much time to get familiar with the material and rework it into a coherent piece. When we did get accepted, we had to figure out how to finish it in time. There was no chance to show an audience, so I was basically playing on all my past experience and hoping it would work. It was a lot of pressure, but for me, it was one of the most entertaining pieces I've done, which is appropriate to the film subject itself because Roger Corman is a great entertainer. Of course, for five months, we saw the film over and over and over and over, playing it through, listening to the sound, watching the picture, making sure they're in sync. A film begins to feel stale after a while and you start to wonder if any of it will work with an audience. And it did! It was fantastic to see that it really did work. The audience laughed where we had humor and were engaged in the dramatic parts.

Was Corman there?

Yes, he came for the first two or three screenings, but I have not met him yet. Alex Stapleton, the director, had screened the film for Corman and his wife probably a week and a half before we had finished, but it was very close to what we took to Sundance. You can see from his interviews in the film that he's not at all the image you would have of a person who has made hundreds of exploitation films, some of them very violent and even offensive but always entertaining. He's Stanford-educated, very gentlemanly and soft-spoken. Apparently when the private screening ended, Corman stood up and said to the director,

"Alex, you did a wonderful job!" He was effusive about how wonderful the film was.

That must have made you feel great as the editor to hear about his reaction. Is that what editors live for?

Yes! I mean, if the subject and the audience are happy with the film and you feel you've told the true story as honestly and compellingly as you can, then being an editor is truly rewarding. But it depends on the subject. Sometimes people don't like what is depicted about themselves in a film and one needs to carefully examine their objections to sort out what their problems with it are. It might be objections to choices in the editing, but it can also be many other things the editor has no control over, sometimes very personal and private issues.

The Corman film is the latest of several biographical documentaries you've edited, including films on artist-cartoonist Robert Crumb, writer Charles Bukowski, and rock-and-roll musician "Roky" Erickson. Did you have a sense at the outset of your career that you wanted to work on these types of films?

Well, actually, I thought I wanted to be a scientist! I started out at Cornell University in the late sixties as a physics major, but very quickly I realized I wasn't cut out for it—I didn't like going home to do math problems! I was always drawn to writing and pursued that for a while. But I really was not sure where I wanted to go. I was drifting, and at the same time, I was experimenting with some drugs—it was the sixties, as I said! And either the first or second time I was tripping *(laughs)*, I went to see a movie by Joseph Strick called *Ulysses,* based on the James Joyce novel, and it really, *really* impressed me! The next time I took a "trip," I saw a bunch of experimental films, short abstract films made by students, and that's when I decided that I wanted to make films. I had never been a big film watcher or devotee at all. In fact, when I considered film as a possible major, I thought it would ruin movies for me. I didn't understand that studying film would actually deepen my appreciation for it. But that's how it began—watching experimental films and realizing that's what I wanted to do.

What was so attractive about what you saw?

It was in the way film mimics the processes of the brain, the processes of consciousness, I would say to be more accurate. Film can be as abstract as thought is, or it can be very concrete and explicit, but it can also move instantly between abstract and concrete without drawing any lines. I guess that's what has interested me the most about film, and editing particularly engages that magic.

How did you move into the business, then, after your enlightened discovery?

In very clumsy fits and starts *(laughs)*. Because so much of film is taught as revolving around the mind of the director, I thought, "Well, then I'll be a director." But I've come to realize that while some of my abilities are very much directorial, the politics and self-promotion a director has to deal with are not my skills at all. I think I'd be very good on a set, and from my experiences on film sets, I usually know what should be done. But I don't like trying to convince people to come along with me and launch into a project, it's really an awkward effort for me. A director is a different personality type. I am in awe of the people skills of the many successful directors I've worked with. I may yet direct something, but I'm at peace with not becoming a director. I find that I can bring a lot to a film as an editor, particularly in documentaries. An editor has much more control of what is going on in a film moment to moment and cut to cut than the director has.

You've actually bridged both worlds of fiction and documentary film.

Yes. So much of commercial film is fiction, and in studying film, I learned about the split between documentary films and fiction films, the sort of Lumière versus Méliès dichotomy. You know, Lumière set up his camera and recorded reality while Méliès made a fantasy trip to the moon in 1902! So I was drawn to the fiction side and thought that was where I would go. But this is really odd—I'd grown up in Los Angeles on a lemon grove and became resistant to staying in L.A. and Hollywood. At Cornell, I took every film class they had—which weren't very many—but the best class was film history as it was up to that point in time. I became intrigued by the San Francisco art film movement with Maya Deren, Kenneth Anger, and Stan Brakhage. So I moved to San Francisco in 1972, but the movement by then had dissipated—in fact, it had died out entirely! It wasn't a happening movement anymore. *(Laughs.)* I stayed in San Francisco and for a while went to San Francisco State, but the film department there at the time wasn't happening either! Instead, most of the professors taught structuralism and were fascinated with theories of Lévi-Strauss, and students weren't encouraged to *make* films. I did manage to shoot and edit a little film called *A Disease*, which I was proud of—very Kafkaesque! The story is narrated by a man who is too sick to leave his bed—he is the only character in the film. To occupy his mind, he starts recording everything he can observe about his room. He charts the process of an apple on his table gradually decaying, light moving across his walls, dust collecting, everything he can record about his limited environment. He eventually accumulates many notebooks of data. He creates formulas and tables to predict the various changes occurring in the room around him. One day as he is examining his data, he realizes he can express any of his formulas and predict its outcome through a single formula which he names "the Unimeter." The film ends with the man still studying, still looking for further connections and insights to his research.

Sounds like a very thoughtful film that reflects what editors go through in looking for connections and insights.

Never thought of it that way, but it does! Anyway, I had to quit film school because I needed an income and I worked in a film lab in San Francisco and later drove a cab. Eventually, through an acquaintance, I was hired as an apprentice editor on *The Wanderers*, directed by Philip Kaufman. That was made at Francis Ford Coppola's American Zoetrope, so I finally got a foothold in that little community of film and sound editors. At the time, Coppola was making *Apocalypse Now*, so dozens of people were around doing the same things I did—apprentice, assistant editor, sound editor. And Saul Zaentz, who had produced *One Flew over the Cuckoo's Nest*, had a film and mixing postproduction facility as well in Berkeley. My career was launched with those jobs. It took quite a number of years. Of course, it was all done on film then. Computer editing had not been developed yet, though some intriguing rumblings were going on.

So you had made a little film of your own and began to work officially in several aspects of film. Did you find editing most suited for your interests and personality?

Yes, but it did take me a while. There were some hard lessons because I still wasn't sure I wanted to do editing. I understood its power, but I was also very interested in cinematography and worked as a camera assistant— or tried to! I found cinematography more difficult than editing because I guess an apprentice editor has more opportunity to learn on the job. As part of an editing crew, assistants and editors could stop and show you how to do things. On a camera crew, you are there to get the shots and get out, and there is not much time to teach on the job. You had to know how to load a camera and fix it if the film isn't running right through the magazine.

I would imagine if you didn't operate the camera properly, you could make some costly mistakes.

Yes, you better get that shot and it better be exposed right because it's all *film*. One time I loaded a magazine in a bag—which you had to do, you know, totally blind—and I handed it to the cameraman, and the film wouldn't run through the camera. Oh my God! *(Laughs.)* I also learned that editing jobs, once you've landed one, tend to last longer than the kind of production jobs I could find in the Bay Area.

Did you find yourself starting to analyze the art of editing, or was it all just very mechanical, worrying about how to make cuts?

I didn't have enough experience yet to understand the depth of it. I mean, I watched the editors work and I was mostly absorbing the logistics because there's a *huge* amount of logistics in feature filmmaking: logging footage, keeping track of camera rolls, printing lights, shots, scenes, take numbers, and descriptions. It was library work basically, but it was interesting, complex, and all new to me. The challenge was to keep that library at your fingertips so that when an editor wanted something, you could find it quickly. Now the library is on a computer and the organization is just as critical, but when I started, the library could fill an entire room or several rooms with reels of film and sound.

Did you identify connections between shots as the editors put them together? Or, as you mentioned before, did you see connections reflecting how the mind works?

No, I wasn't seeing those connections anymore. In fact, I actually became aware of a disconnect and I didn't know why. I mean, I had a little glimmer of what connections were possible when I was experimenting with film as a student, but I still didn't know very much about the process—and I wasn't taught it either. When I first walked into an editing room, they started talking about edge coding—putting inked edge numbers on the film and soundtrack so you could keep them in sync. There would be numbers printed every foot, or every sixteen frames of 35 millimeter. But I didn't know what they were talking about! I'd spent a year and half in film school and had never even heard of it! Everything seemed very cultish and mysterious, and editors seemed to work very hard to make it even more mysterious. I think they still do!

Do you prefer editing to be mysterious to others?

Oh, no, I don't. Well, not usually—maybe when there's a personality conflict going on! *(Laughs.)* And if whoever I'm working with believes in the mystery of editing, then I might play to that! But usually no, I don't want it to be mysterious. However, I agree that it is mysterious on a really deep level. Why do cuts work? Why can we make connections between images? Many theories have been proposed, some very tantalizing, like those of Walter Murch, who is a brilliant film editor, writer, and thinker. However, as much as there's a theoretical aspect to editing that can be endlessly dissected and examined, at the same time it is not mysterious at all. It's just putting things together and seeing if they work, if the images and sounds are compelling and evocative. My best work has been simply putting things together that I maybe didn't even think would work, but I thought I'd give it a try. Even then, I'm not sure they work until I watch them with somebody else. I need to watch a scene or section of film I've cut with someone who hasn't seen it before to know if it is resonating. It's important to try things and be in an experimental zone, that creative zone that writers, painters, musicians, and others get to, trying things with no assurance that it will work but feeling free to try.

In one sense, the film then works for you when you're trying to put it together by yourself, but then your choices are affirmed when you are with others.

That's right, because sometimes I think I've made something that plays well and resonates but I'm too close to my own work, I'm not seeing it objectively enough. When I've cut something together successfully, I find that other people are reacting in a similar way as I am to the material. They're getting a depth that I'm also getting, although they may actually be making different connections than I am. But it's resonating for all of us. Sometimes I realize that a part I designed is working pretty well because people comment on it or point it out. But I would also say that a good part of what I do is to discover things serendipitously as I grope my way through a story.

There's a striking example of a possible "experiment" in You're Gonna Miss Me. *The mother of the musician "Roky" Erickson speaks at times in a way that is contrary to what we expect of a "talking head." You hear her voice, but in her image, her mouth is not moving at all.*

I love that technique! At the same time, I wasn't sure it worked until I watched it a few times with Keven McAlester, the director, and Lauren Hollingsworth, the producer.

It's unexpected, not logical, not traditional, yet riveting.

That technique goes directly to what I was talking about with the cinema having such strong parallels to stream of consciousness. To hear the voice of Roky's mother, yet see that her lips are not moving is really like the way we think. We're all teeming with voices in our heads, whether we're talking out loud or thinking silently. Sometimes it's other people's voices, sometimes our own, chattering, complaining, criticizing, mocking, arguing, agreeing. Voices overlap in our heads as thoughts, even if we're not speaking.

That scene resonated for me in terms of the person you were depicting in the film—a successful rock musician who suffered terrible mental problems because of drug and alcohol addiction. The technique almost sets the stage for understanding a broken or split mind. Do you try to find techniques that capture the essence of your subjects?

That is certainly what you're trying to achieve in the end product, but I've learned to not get too intellectual or theoretical when I'm editing a scene, to keep things on a simple and emotional level for myself. I'm more interested in the subjects expressing their own essence than in me imposing a clever technique. It's better to trust the subjects and let them evoke their own "essence." The first pass in cutting is to get the chaff out, the slow, boring stuff, the moments that aren't compelling or that are repetitive or not well said. The editor wants to get down to the essentials—the most direct and clear statements, the most emotional and moving moments. When you do this, then you in a sense have captured the subject's essence or, rather, you've allowed the subject to express that essence. Most editors, including myself, do this in stages, in repeated passes through the same material. You may leave something in that had already been expressed, but once you see one shot after the other, side by side, so to speak, you can choose which bit you want to use. I have found that if I think more about technique or devices and less about content—that is, the emotional or entertainment factor of what I'm working with—then more often than not, I am not doing useful work. Of course, this is a constant question I ask myself: "Am I being too conscious of how I'm putting this together and not conscious enough of what's playing on the screen?" If the answer is "yes," it probably won't end up in the final piece, so I might as well just stop and move to something else.

That is one way to avoid wear and tear on yourself as an editor, which is a common problem for those obsessing about making the shots "fit."

Now, I might try something that doesn't seem logical or sensible, but I'm going for emotional truth, not logical truth. I must say the great majority of the unusual "techniques" or "devices" I use are more out of desperation than actually consciously figuring out a cool trick. In documentary editing, it is very common for editors to find they don't have proper coverage. Coverage in this sense means other shots that were taken at approximately the same time in the same setting of the scene which seem to cover the same action in the scene. "Coverage" is desirable because if it is shot properly, it allows the editor to cut between shots without jarring the audience or drawing attention to the act of cutting between shots. It allows the audience to maintain focus on what is being said in the scene visually and aurally, and not be distracted by the jump between shots which have most likely been shot at different times. In *Shakespeare behind Bars*, there was a scene with a prisoner who was being held in solitary confinement. He was brought into a holding area, but both time and access to him were very limited. His interview had to be shot with great efficiency and there was no time to pick up alternate angles of him or his surroundings. He was quite emotional as well, though he wasn't crying. Of course, I didn't want to use everything he said as it was filmed. I wanted to use very carefully selected bits of what he was saying to compress it into something compelling. Because there were long pauses between the phrases and statements he was making, I needed to cut those pauses and stammers out. I was able to overlap the picture and the audio so that sometimes his lips were moving and matching what he said, while sometimes he would pause and seem to be thinking but his words would continue. I felt that technique worked in this instance because he was talking about very deep emotional issues and he was, after all, a prisoner who spent most of his time alone with himself and his thoughts. When I first cut the scene, of course, I just cut picture and sound at the same place. When I rough out a scene, I cut it first for the audio, for what is being said on the soundtrack, and then I worry about making the picture work later. This is how most editors I know work, and certainly most documentary editors. This is referred to as a "radio cut," cutting to the sound and what is being said first, then figuring out how to make the images work later. Now, more and more you find editors and filmmakers willing to make jump cuts and demanding the audience to maintain focus on what is happening in the scene. I'm thinking in particular of a film like *The Fog of War* by Errol Morris. In many of the interviews, they cut to make the words make sense or to take out unwanted words or pauses, but they didn't cut away from the subject or change to another camera angle, and so the image of the interviewee seems to jump. This jump-cutting technique is becoming more and more common and is quite liberating for the editor. It allows you to use things that might have been set aside because they couldn't be "covered." That said, I still insist in my work that jump cuts mean something and are not there just out of editorial expediency. So it is incumbent on filmmakers, directors, editors, whoever is involved in putting a film together, to employ techniques they feel fit a subject or character and reinforce the emotional and contextual thrust of the film.

It does seem that jump cuts can be both very evocative of what occurs in the scene, while at other times they can intrude on the audience's concentration.

They can be both, interestingly. But you can see that in fixing problems in the shooting or sound recording, a fair amount of the documentary editor's work does boil down to repair or reconstructive work. The time pressures on the shoot are enormous. The crew has to move incredibly quickly and shots don't get done—or they get done improperly and editors have to make do with what they got. The most important sound you have in a documentary is the voice of your subjects, and it's not always possible to record it in what would be ideal studio situations. You may also have to replace a word here or there that is garbled, fumbled, or muffled with the same word or even a different word. If you know they meant one thing and they're saying another, you might have to fix it for them. If someone says, "It's not easy," but you know by the context that they meant, "It's easy," then you take the "not" out so that they say what they really meant, not what they misspoke. Or you might need to take out stammers and ums and ahs. People say "um" a lot, which I take out, even if they're on camera saying it.

Doesn't that cause a jump cut?

No, I don't cut the picture down. I just fill it with ambience if it's on camera because it makes what's being said easier to follow. Sometimes people talk with partial words or phrases or stumbled syllables and it's better to take those out and have ambient sound there, as long as the person's lips aren't flapping wildly! Sometimes if someone says "um" in the middle of a pause, it often looks like a swallow or a breath so I take those out.

That is such a split-second consideration.

Yes, but it's enough to be distracting, and it can make your subject seem to be wandering or stammering when you don't want them to.

Even though they really are wandering.

Yes, yes, yes, they are! *(Laughs.)* If your subject seems to be wandering or disengaged, even for a split second, the audience will start to wander too and you don't want that. In the course of a feature film, say ninety minutes or thereabouts, those split seconds really add up and the audience feels their weight—if not consciously, then unconsciously, which is just as bad.

Another technique that affected me very strongly was when the prisoners in Shakespeare behind Bars *were all telling the same story, yet clearly each man had been filmed separately. To make the story flow, you let one man start a sentence, then cut to a second man who picks up the next word, then to a third who continues the sentence and so on—as if they were completing each other's thoughts.*

Yes, that's not an uncommon technique. It's another way to compress the material entertainingly. You don't stay on any one subject very long. Changing the subjects rapidly stimulates the eyes and ears of the audience and gives them more information to digest as the inmate-actors move through the passage. You also contrast the inevitable varieties of deliveries by different people. Since this was an acting class, in which each of the inmates was presenting the same passage from the play, they were all taking a crack at the same material. It's not uncommon for editors to use two or more people to tell a story. In this way, editors can find cut points so, again, pauses and fumbles can be eliminated and move the story along. I remember trying that technique in the Bukowski film, where Bukowski and his friend Neely told the same story at different times. What I was trying to show in that instance was that each man had very different recollections of the particular facts in the story. But I never thought that came across clearly. For some reason, every audience seemed to want to overlook the discrepancies between the two stories and tried to meld them into one coherent story. That was an interesting lesson to me. So I ended up moving the contradictions and discrepancies since they only seemed to be confusing or seen as the filmmakers' mistakes.

Doesn't Crumb *have something similar?*

Yes. The film, as you know, is about Robert Crumb, or R. Crumb as he signed his artwork, but his brother Charles, who was essential to the film, also did comics that then degenerated as his mind degenerated. He started out drawing comics, but his characters began to have longer and longer speeches in these huge cartoon speech bubbles. Eventually Charles began filling page after page of his notebooks instead with nothing but words. Then even the words disappeared and he filled more notebooks with lines that appeared to be letters and words but were just scribbles. We had a scene of Robert, who had collected all his brother's notebooks, talking about how that process happened to Charles, and suddenly we cut to Charles in *his* bedroom in another place altogether who begins talking about the notebooks as if continuing his brother's thoughts. Yes, the subject was covered at two different times in the shooting. One time, Robert was alone explaining the evolution of his brother's madness and illustrating it with the gradual devolution of his comics into nonsense writing. The second time, Robert talked about it and Charles was there as well and he joined the conversation. When I first saw the dailies of those scenes, I thought, wow, there's a way to blend the two scenes together because the topic was essentially about the writing in these notebooks, and we had footage of both Robert and Charles talking about it. But what made it work was the wonderful close-up shooting by Marise Alberti of the notebooks. You couldn't tell that you were in different locations in the extreme close-ups of the writing. So I used close-up shots of the writing to bridge the two locations and introduce Charles to the discussion. Charles was even talking and laughing about it as matter-of-factly as Robert was. It just struck me to switch between the settings with a cut because of that connection, even though the scene with Charles and Robert was in a completely different city than the scene with Robert alone. Audiences seem to enjoy the surprise of having Charles suddenly appear and speak matter-of-factly about his own writing, although Robert's scene began with his talking about Charles to reveal something rather private and secret, something you wouldn't expect him to be openly discussing. I also think it was a great opportunity to illustrate Robert's exceptional honesty. If he says something about someone when they're not around, he's probably going to say the same thing in front of them. Finally, there is something to be said for changing the location of a scene or beat in a story in unexpected places. It stimulates an audience—if it's not confusing—and gives them more to digest in the course of the scene. Of course, those opportunities don't offer themselves very often.

Do you think such creative liberties call into question whether you are being true to the situation or time in which things happen in a documentary? Wouldn't they jar an audience?

I hope they do jar an audience! There's nothing more documentary than a technique that helps you *illustrate* your subject and shed light on it in a nonconventional and intriguing way. As I recall, at the time I felt it was also a nice surprise that would keep the audience entertained and engaged. I am far more concerned about keeping a film entertaining than I am about showing things strictly as they happened. In any case, as soon as you put two shots together in the editing room, you are manipulating the "reality" of what happened. There's simply no way to avoid it, so I'd rather embrace that fact and use it to my advantage. I use this technique to make the subject and its presentation more interesting to the audience and to myself. That's the bottom line, keep things interesting and keep the story moving. If you don't do that, you lose your audience and you might as well not make a film!

If a "bio-pic" were to be made based on the life of Crumb with an actor playing the artist, do you think the filmmaker would have greater freedom to tell the story without blurring lines that might confuse an audience?

I think to make a compelling, interesting, "fictional" yet "true" film about Crumb would actually be very difficult. Some of it would just not be believable. For example, some of Crumb's little quirks that come through in the documentary footage, like the way he laughs nervously at things that are not even funny, things that clearly pain him. I don't think that would work in a fiction film very well because it would probably come across as irritating and contrived. But in a documentary, you understand it's not phony. This *is* Crumb being who he is. Certainly some gifted actors can portray nervous habits like a false laugh successfully, but usually that kind of thing doesn't work for an audience for very long. That said, the most important thing in both a documentary and a fiction film is story, and to tell a story that is coherent and flows, you have to take liberties. You can't get bogged down in every detail of how something happened and everything that led up to it. It's too tedious. Good documentaries and good narrative films both propel an audience from heightened moment to heightened moment. We don't go to movies to see ordinary everyday things, real "reality." That's boring. Documentary *and* fiction films have to connect with the audience and touch the emotions. With a fiction film, the story is carefully constructed in a way to touch those emotional points at key stages in the script. In a documentary, the story is written in the editing room, so the editor has to find the emotional points in the film and then find a way to tell that story, to move as it were from point to point. In documentaries, we don't always have footage on the most important points, so something else, like a creative technique, has to stand in for it.

That reminds me of The Defector. *The film was about Victor Kravchenko, who exposed the crimes of Josef Stalin, but that story was framed by his son's efforts to solve the mystery of his father's death. You had little to re-create Kravchenko's life and times except photos and archival footage, yet you used intriguing techniques to replicate the time period.*

Yes, the source material was obviously very sparse. We were making a film about events that had disappeared in history and probably wouldn't have been documented even then because of social circumstances. Instead, the director, Mark Jonathan Harris, had the idea to use scenes out of feature films from the time period that had a narrative and tonal parallel to the actual events. In this way, the manners, as illustrated by Hollywood, would resonate with the actual situations which were described in the narration. For example, in illustrating Kravchenko's American wife, her privileged background, her fashion sense, her affairs, we "rhymed" her story with clips from *Humoresque* with Joan Crawford. While such a film was not a direct translation of what happened, of course, it was the same era and the same manners. The way Hollywood chose to portray that time period would also allow people to connect with it in a broader way and help them become more familiar with an unfamiliar story. Those clips also helped us move between the more traditional talking heads or voiceovers we used to tell the rest of the story and to give some variety to the narrative line. Victor Kravchenko defected to the U.S. during World War II when the U.S. and the Soviet Union were allies. The paranoia and desperation he must have endured must have been insufferable, not knowing who might be following him or intending to capture or kidnap or kill him. Stalin certainly did all that and I don't know that our side was above any of it either. We used a scene from an old 1951 Warner Brothers film called *I Was a Communist for the FBI*, in which a man is being followed by agents peering around corners, and then is chased and shot at. The scene is full of paranoia and furtive peeking around corners and then a shooting, all that fun spy stuff. We hear an actor, Liev Schreiber, reading lines from Kravchenko's book *I Chose Freedom*. He describes his fear and paranoia, which the scene helps to show how it might have been. Then we learn from a scholar of Russian history that although Kravchenko was certain that he was being followed by Russian agents, it was actually the FBI following him. Now I don't even remember what was actually happening in the story of the spy movie we used, but it isn't important. We were using a piece of this Hollywood fiction fraught with paranoia and noir spy atmosphere to evoke a time and situation which was never recorded and which would have been very expensive to stage. By identifying the films and the dates they were made, I think the audience understood that this was not literal documentary imagery, but was standing in for what was never recorded. I thought it was a very inventive and interesting solution that Mark came up with to tell this story.

Would montages also have served the same purpose?

We did use montages in places where we thought we had the right imagery to tell the story, for example, when we hear Liev Schreiber reading Kravchenko's description of his defection to the U.S. during World War II. We used archival footage of Russian trains and New York City from the mid-1940s. I suppose that could be called a "montage," although I thought of it more as a way to illustrate the story we are hearing. We did use archival footage of the Russian slave labor camps, of Lenin's funeral, and a little of Stalin as well. Montages again go back to what we were discussing about mental processes. Montages have meaning that you don't get from words or people talking, and the brain makes connections by a series or flow of images that works on a level other than the verbal. It can be a purely nonverbal level that is often more compelling, easier to understand, and less tedious. Sometimes a director or producer or I will come out and say, "We need a montage here." We mean then that the film needs to break from its narrative line or linear explanation. It's a way to stop the talking and engage the eye and the brain more directly to entertain the audience in a different way for a while.

But montages can contain words.

They certainly can. In fact, some montages can be purely verbal and equally effective. There is something about the succession of sounds or images, about the juxtaposition of images and/or sounds that build a greater statement that is not explicitly stated. Or perhaps it is pretty explicit in a series of images, but not said verbally. For the editor, it's all about compressing what you're saying into an idea the audience will not get bored with. By telling something linearly, you risk boredom. If you take the time you really need to convey something in detail, you can slow the film down too much for the audience. Or the audience might actually be leaping ahead of you because they already know what you're trying to say. So you want to maintain the emotional level that connects with the audience very quickly in a sort of shorthand. A montage is hard to beat if you want to compress information or ideas and put them together very tightly. It's well known that our eyes and brains are always working to find patterns in our environment. Montages play to that particular predilection.

Sounds have subliminal effects on people, especially when they are multilayered and seemingly blurred. Yet if heard separately, you might discern unexpected sounds that were mixed together, like thunder with heartbeats with footsteps, and so on. Why do so much layering when one sound might convey the same point?

That is definitely always a choice. Very often a simple sound is more eloquent than a whole mess of sounds. But other times, the layers of many sounds together create a dense, rich atmosphere that is evocative and emotionally powerful. To me, film is so much more about emotion and atmospherics than meaning—it's more than real meaning—because it's hard to get very deep with a film and keep the audience engaged. Changing the atmospherics and surprising an audience help to keep their attention and hopefully reinforce the mood you want to create. I often layer sounds for that reason. When I do, it becomes more of a sketch for the sound editor to work from, but sometimes what I design ends up being in the film because documentaries just don't have time or money for elaborate sound work. The Corman film has a great example of a sound montage. A very important element of Corman's career occurred at the time *Jaws* and *Star Wars* came along, two films that were directly taken from what Corman had been doing for thirty years—exploitation films. Both subjects—hungry sharks and space battles—were absolutely the very thing he had done many, many times very effectively years before. But *Jaws* and *Star Wars* had much bigger budgets and were cultural sensations that had never occurred in the same way with Corman's films. The audiences had also changed. They had discovered how much fun it could be to sit with others and go through that experience of watching blockbuster films.

So I built a montage of archival sounds and images from the hysteria around *Jaws*. I used bits from the *Jaws* trailer and TV newsmen and shots of people lining up to see the movie. The TV newsmen are all on top of each other and we hear snatches of them chattering about this summer blockbuster. We also hear crowds screaming and see them running from the beach, while the trailer's narrator says, "See it . . . before you go swimming." The sequence lasts probably less than thirty seconds, but it evoked the cultural frenzy of the media and of the film itself. Interestingly, the director, Alex Stapleton, wasn't even born when that happened, but she certainly got the point.

The effect of the montage can no doubt evoke different opinions from different people because not only does it play so quickly, but it also impacts the brain in emotional ways.

It can sometimes also challenge an editor's work with a director. *Crumb* had a montage when Robert talks about his old record collection and his love of old music, and it's set to a blues piece by Geechi Wiley, "Last Kind Words Blues." Terry Zwigoff, the director, is extremely conversant with early recorded American music, and I think there are only two copies of that record known to exist with collectors. We had planned that Robert's talking about his records would launch the film into a montage of Crumb drawings against that kind of music. Terry had selected the blues song, had all the drawings he wanted to use in the montage, and had a template in mind for it. We couldn't afford a good animation stand or a fancy animation camera to shoot the images with, so Terry went off and shot it live one afternoon with a cameraman who was very good at that kind of close, tight, and steady work. Then I took the film of the images and music and tried to fit it into Terry's template, but to me it just didn't work. So I cut my own response to the music and images, and it really flowed for me. I was very happy with the montage, the producer loved it, and I thought it played very well at screenings. Then, about a month later, Terry said he wanted to recut the montage because it didn't fit his idea of what he was trying to do with the images. It was very disappointing to me, but I recut it the way he wanted it.

What was the difference?

Terry thought the images should follow a particular order. But I thought the order was less important than the way each image flowed into the next.

My version was less literal because the images did not connect literally, but viscerally. I felt the visual rhythm from one image to the next was more important in this case than which particular image followed another. Terry wanted something more literal. It is still a good montage, but in my heart, I ache for that old montage. The producer even told me that the montage I had done brought tears to her eyes every time she saw it. That was my first documentary and I didn't want to fight Terry for it. Now I think I might fight more, but back then I couldn't. I am proud of what's in the film and when people see it, they have said to me, "Wow, that's a good montage." But I thought the first version was better. *(Pause.)* Unfortunately, it's also impossible to retrieve that old montage now and put it side by side with the final version because it was all on film. I had to take it all apart. It's just lost to the editing floor. *(Pause.)* That is an example of those inevitable disagreements between two individuals trying to make the best movie they can. Terry's version certainly plays well for audiences, so there you are.

I want to revisit a phrase you used earlier that's been nagging at me. You said that it's hard to get "deep" with a film. I'm not sure I understand what you mean as your documentaries seem to be very deep and profound in both content and execution.

I mean that because the nature of the film medium is immediate and visceral, it's hard to get "deep" ideas or concepts. In the course of film history, we have trained audiences to want to be entertained. Roger Corman maybe understood better than anyone in the history of film that that is why lots of people go to see films and that's how you get the money to pay for the films you've made in order to make another film. You have to give audiences what they want.

By "deep," are you also suggesting a "thinking" film?

I do mean a thinking film. But I don't think—

That audiences think anymore? (Laughs.)

I think two things are going on. Audiences still think as much as they ever did. But audiences are also used to filmmakers trying to top themselves with more and more sensational elements, surprises, effects. The medium itself is not given to going very deep and I think that is why film has evolved the way it has—into a medium where audiences expect and demand to be entertained. If filmmakers fail to entertain at a significant level, audiences won't go to see their films. As Corman puts it, "The audience is the ultimate arbiter of your film." His solution was to think of films as having both a text and a subtext. The text is what is happening on the surface of a film, and the subtext is what is being said underneath, beneath the surface. The subtext may be very different from the text, it may even contradict it. Corman took this concept from Method acting, which was just coming into vogue as he started his own career. When I heard Corman say this, I realized he was articulating what all of us working in the film medium have internalized to a large degree. Most of us haven't managed to articulate it as simply and clearly as he. Now, all filmmakers will come to their own balance between text and subtext and, yes, the audience will be the arbiter of how successful they are. But that does explain why it seems like films are always getting more sensational and more trashy, if you will. Filmmakers feel enormous pressures to come up with bigger and better sensations and surprises to satisfy the audience, and I don't think documentaries are immune to this at all. Only a certain segment of audiences will sit still for any documentary, but those who do still have the same hunger for a lively and entertaining text, regardless of how delicious the subtext may be. I have to agree with Corman that this is a reality every filmmaker must come to terms with. It does seem to me that there are different levels of expectation and demand for entertainment among the current subgroups of film media—that is, feature films, documentary feature films, episodic television, television documentaries, and so on. For example, I've found that montages in reality TV can be difficult to cut because of different expectations.

How so?

When I began working in reality TV, I brought along my feature documentary experience and I cut these long lingering montages that savored the images and the music—and then the producers came in. They would get irritated because my montages would go on for ten or fifteen seconds and all they wanted was a five-second blip of really fast images as a transition to the next scene. They didn't want what *I* called a montage, as I knew it. I had to learn that the hard way. My skills as an editor came under scrutiny when really I just didn't understand what they were going for because of the difference in medium.

Might that be because in reality TV, you need to show events unfolding as they happen and there's no time to be too artistic as in a film?

Well, yes and no because, first of all, TV people would never agree that it's less artistic *(pause)*, although I agree! *(Laughs.)* It's more a matter of they want to stick with showing the subject and the conflict, and not take the time to illustrate it in other ways. There's an intolerance for it, actually. And they are probably right because their audience isn't usually looking for or expecting that kind of license.

Do you consider reality TV a subgenre of documentary film?

Yes, I think so. It can be in the realm of a documentary film, absolutely. It can be a very powerful medium. I think it is an interesting development of our times, but it is also too often subject to commercial parameters and commercial tastes. That said, however, I showed a piece I worked on from a reality show to a friend of mine and she said, "That's the best piece I've ever seen of yours!" *(Laughs.)*

How could that be? (Laughs.)

It was an episode for an HBO program called *Sexual Healing* with Dr. Laura Berman, a brilliant Chicago sex therapist. My show dealt with two couples in sex therapy with her and the discussion became very deep and profound. I thought it was art, definitely the documentary form at its best, because she was so good and the subjects were so willing to be intimate and reveal their conflicts. You just saw raw humanity there. Both couples did a week of therapy and we followed them in their therapy sessions. My job was to find a story arc for each couple that laid out the problem and showed them working on it with Dr. Berman's guidance and then seeing what further problems arose. A story arc, of course, is built from lots of smaller arcs, so it becomes a matter of placing things where they work dramatically, creating a big dramatic arc. Sometimes we had to rearrange meetings or days and put them a little out of order—not much because there was definitely an evolution in the couples' behavior as they went through the week. But sometimes you have to move things out of order because they fit the arc you are trying to delineate more neatly.

That wouldn't be distorting the truth?

It's distorting the chronology, the surface events in order to get at the deeper truth. The literal order in which things happened, the chronology, is the least important truth. Novelists discovered this a long time ago. But of course, you do have to follow certain conventions in reality TV. All TV shows with commercials are constructed to build to a suspenseful moment in order to keep the audience watching so they don't go away during the commercial break. This may be irritating to the viewer, but it is quite logical to the commercial sponsor as well as to the people constructing the show. I did several episodes of *The Real World,* which I believe is considered the first reality TV show, in which seven young people in their late teens or early twenties live together in one house in one city and are filmed for what they do every day. It's now in its twenty-fifth season. Some years they had more than one season, and I occasionally worked on three or four shows in a series. I do like moving back and forth between different kinds of projects. I would say reality TV is much more informal than a feature documentary that intends to play in a theater or on PBS. There's usually less time to polish a reality TV show and it tends to be more assembly line, in the sense that more than one editor may work on the piece as it gets passed around. The point is to get the shows finished on the deadline. That's much more important than making it exactly "the film" that somebody wants it to be. Also, at least in the case of *The Real World,* each episode had to fit within a larger arc for the season because you may be building a character up for a fall or revelation later on.

Is all the material shot first and then subdivided into episodes?

Yes, on *The Real World,* they would shoot as constantly as was practical. Fixed cameras set up in the resident house can be turned on and off, including in the bedrooms. Then the producer can send crews to cover whatever gets interesting. There are almost always cameras on the young people and a whole team of story people trying to sift stories out of what happened and set up the arcs for each character and the conflicts that arise. The first episodes are airing well before the shooting has wrapped and well before all of the conflicts have developed between the participants. The story and editing teams are as much in the dark as the audience on what's going to happen by the end of the season.

So much of reality TV now is celebrity-studded or sensational, like following the Kardashians around on their latest family squabbles or business ventures or shopping sprees. Certainly documentaries show similar arguments or mundane events, such as Robert Crumb sitting in a café drawing passers-by on the street, or Roky's fights with his mother that erupted while the camera was running. Is reality TV somehow diluting the impact of a documentary film or just rehashing the same expectations in a different form?

That's a good question and I think my answer would be the latter. I don't feel that reality TV is diluting what documentary filmmakers are doing, and I certainly don't feel threatened by reality TV. It's just another way to make TV entertainment and it happens to have a connection to documentary techniques. As an editor, I like dipping into the reality TV world because it's fun to work with a collection of editors all making the same kinds of shows. I learn a lot from the other editors. But if anything, it's begun to change the way some documentary filmmakers work.

In what way?

For one thing, it's harder to provoke or tantalize an audience now that they've seen the *Jersey Shore* people batting each other around! After all those shocking revelations that pop out all the time or seeing such uninhibited behavior, it seems harder to surprise audiences. And I've certainly been in cutting-room discussions where one of us says something like, "That feels too much like reality TV." We try to avoid that tone where it feels like one sensation is piled on to the next simply to titillate the audience rather than tell a real story. But that's the whole history of film. I remember hearing an interview with Alfred Hitchcock who was asked something like, "There are so many films now doing what you've been doing. Does it get harder to shock an audience?" And Hitchcock said, "Yes, it does get harder. There are so many more clichés now." That is always the filmmakers' dilemma, whether in documentary or fiction. How do you keep the audience entertained when they've already seen so many exceptional things? What do you do next?

Perhaps Corman was thinking along those lines when Jaws *came out.* (Laughs.) *Is that the best time then to come up with some nontraditional techniques in documentaries, as you've mentioned, and not fall back on clichés?*

Yes, or at least be inventive with the way you *do* fall back on clichés!

Maybe that was your intention when you let Roky's mother "talk" without moving her lips.

It worked for me at that time. It was the right solution.

"It worked," meaning?

That's an editorial term: "It works." Does a cut work or doesn't it work? And it usually is completely subjective. I remember when I was an apprentice or assistant editor putting a cut together, and the editor said to me, "It doesn't work." I asked, "Well, what do you mean it doesn't work?"

All she could say was, "It doesn't *work*." She couldn't tell me why it didn't work or why she didn't like the cut.

But you thought it did work.

I thought it worked and she said it didn't. I tried to get her to be more specific and I couldn't. "It doesn't *work*." That's all she said. Now, as a more senior editor, I find I can tell people that and I don't have to justify it! *(Laughs.)* I also find at times when I'm in the editing room with the director or producer and we are watching a scene, one of us will say, "It works!" or "It doesn't work." And we understand, even though it could mean a hundred different things. It could mean the cut has the wrong timing or there is some sort of mismatch in the action between cuts that doesn't look right or it's confusing and doesn't make sense.

Do you go down a checklist of what it could be?

Yeah, I usually have a roster in mind. Inevitably in an early stage of the assembly, I'm aware something's bothering me about a cut, and it stays in the film because I haven't found a solution or haven't yet figured out why it isn't working. My collaborators can often tell as well and sometimes someone will just come out and ask, "Why doesn't that cut work?" We all agree that it doesn't and we don't know why.

There's that mystery of editing again! If your assistant showed you a scene she worked on and you said, "It doesn't work," would you explain that or leave it vague, as one editor did to you?

No, I don't like to do that to people! But usually I don't give notes on specific cuts unless it really illustrates what I'm talking about. For example, because people are always trying to work faster and faster these days, an assistant may have clipped the first few frames off a person's word as they begin talking. Every editor does that now and then, but when it's consistently appearing through a cut and they're not noticing it, I'll point it out. Or maybe another angle is needed to give the eye a wide shot in order to understand the geography of the situation. I can pinpoint more concrete errors, but I don't tend to get into discussions with assistants on what is more emotional or subliminal. Hopefully, though, they get the opportunity to watch my adjustments and internalize them. At the frame level, it's really not right or wrong. It's so subjective and personal and involves one's pacing and style. You know, it's almost like trying to fix someone else's poem. Maybe you can find a different word than they had, but does that make it a better poem? Maybe it does, and maybe it doesn't.

Sometimes someone who has more power can demand a change to the cutting and so that person is "right." That said, I think it's fantastic that we happen to be living in a time when potentially millions of people can own relatively inexpensive cameras and computer software to make new films that will hopefully break new ground and upset conventions. Right now, however, it seems to be endemic in the film business that whoever has the power is the person who knows what's "right."

Does that "power" also manifest itself in the way awards are given to films?
I may not be the best one to answer that—or maybe I am!—because a colleague of mine, who was on the Academy screening committee for selecting documentaries when *Crumb* came out, told me how that committee started watching it, but after fifteen or twenty minutes, someone said, "Let's turn it off," and they did. They put it aside and never considered it again for an Oscar nomination.

What was that about?
I guess it had everything to do with the nature of the committee at the time, but my recollection is that the film critics Siskel and Ebert were just enraged that *Crumb* wasn't nominated. I don't know if they actually heard that story about the committee, but because *Crumb,* and the year before *Hoop Dreams,* were never nominated for Best Documentary, Siskel and Ebert devoted two or three of their shows in a row to talking about the outrage. In fact, the nature of the committee was changed after that. Look, I'm not a critic, I'm not a distributor, I've never been on an awards panel, nor have I ever been a judge at a festival, but I do know that horse trading and whatnot goes on. I'm just glad I don't have to be the one to do it. I simply try to make the best film I can. But I will say this business never ceases to amaze me *(pause)* . . . and disappoint me.

But then there are the high points, like seeing your film well received at Sundance.
Yes, now I can go to Sundance with a film I worked on for many months and watch it play for an audience. Many people working on that film gave me explicit credit for getting it there.

That's a great victory for an editor.
It's probably what makes a collaboration on a film so rewarding. When you come down to it, it's all about each of us—the director, the producer,

the editor—having moments of discovery, of seeing what wasn't seen or even understood the first time. And it's all about finding a way to string together a bunch of what are actually fragments into something that feels whole and coherent while striving to pique the interest of the audience. I think of the example in *You're Gonna Miss Me*, when Roky's mother is reminiscing, talking fondly about her son, whom we've seen both at his peak as a rock-and-roll legend in the 1960s and now as he is—a troubled man with mental problems living in poverty and chaos. But when she says, "My sweet little boy," instead of showing a baby photo—which I could have done—I showed an image of Roky in his current disheveled, almost tragic condition. That's a moment that is begging to upset the audience's expectations. The audience can't help but expect a sweet, innocent image to follow such a sentiment from a mother, but if you don't give them the obvious, you make it more interesting. Sometimes you can make that kind of discovery right away. Sometimes you have to keep trying things until you find a satisfying and surprising solution. But then it's also a matter of keeping the best accidents and happenstances in, just because "it works."

12. Striking the Balance

MICHAEL TRONICK

FILM EDITOR

1987 *Beverly Hills Cop II* (coeditor), dir. Tony Scott

1987 *Less Than Zero* (coeditor), dir. Marek Kanievska

1988 *Side by Side,* TV, dir. Jack Bender

1988 *Midnight Run* (coeditor), dir. Martin Brest

1989 *Mothers, Daughters, and Lovers,* TV, dir. Matthew Robbins

1990 *Revenge* (additional editor), dir. Tony Scott

1990 *Days of Thunder* (additional editor), dir. Tony Scott

1990 *The Adventures of Ford Fairlane,* dir. Renny Harlin

1991 *The Marrying Man* (additional editor), dir. Jerry Rees

1991 *The Last Boy Scout* (additional editor), dir. Tony Scott

1991 *Hudson Hawk* (coeditor), dir. Michael Lehmann

1992 *Straight Talk,* dir. Barnet Kellman

1992 *Scent of a Woman* (coeditor), dir. Martin Brest

1993 *True Romance* (coeditor), dir. Tony Scott

1994 *The Cowboy Way,* dir. Gregg Champion

1995 *Under Siege 2: Dark Territory,* dir. Geoff Murphy

1996 *Eraser,* dir. Chuck Russell

1997 *Volcano,* dir. Mick Jackson

1998 *Meet Joe Black* (coeditor), dir. Martin Brest

1999 *Blue Streak*, dir. Les Mayfield

2000 *Remember the Titans*, dir. Boaz Yakin

2001 *American Outlaws*, dir. Les Mayfield

2002 *The Scorpion King*, dir. Chuck Russell

2003 *S.W.A.T.*, dir. Clark Johnson

2005 *Mr. and Mrs. Smith*, dir. Doug Liman

2007 *Hairspray*, dir. Adam Shankman

2008 *Iron Man* (additional editor), dir. Jon Favreau

2008 *Hannah Montana / Miley Cyrus: Best of Both Worlds Concert Tour*, dir. Bruce Hendricks

2008 *Bedtime Stories*, dir. Adam Shankman

2009 *Jonas Brothers: The 3D Concert Experience*, dir. Bruce Hendricks

2010 *The Wolfman* (additional editor), dir. Joe Johnston

2011 *The Green Hornet*, dir. Michel Gondry

2011 *Battle: Los Angeles* (additional editor), dir. Jonathan Liebesman

2011 *Abduction* (additional editor), dir. John Singleton

2011 *New Year's Eve*, dir. Garry Marshall

2012 *Act of Valor* (coeditor), dir. Mike McCoy and Scott Waugh

MUSIC EDITOR

1977 *Semi-Tough*, dir. Michael Ritchie

1978 *Forever*, TV, dir. John Korty

1978 *Mean Dog Blues*, dir. Mel Stuart

1978 *The One Man Jury*, dir. Charles Martin

1978 *Movie Movie*, dir. Stanley Donen

1978 *Who'll Save Our Children?* TV, dir. George Schaefer

1979 *California Dreaming*, dir. John D. Hancock

1979 *Sunnyside*, dir. Timothy Galfas

1979 *All That Jazz*, dir. Bob Fosse

1980 *M Station: Hawaii*, TV, dir. Jack Lord

1980 *The Island*, dir. Michael Ritchie

1980 *Xanadu*, dir. Robert Greenwald

1981 *All Night Long*, dir. Jean-Claude Tramont

1981 *Death Hunt*, dir. Peter R. Hunt

1981 *Zoot Suit*, dir. Luis Valdez

1981 *Looker*, dir. Michael Crichton

1981 *Reds*, dir. Warren Beatty

1982 *Young Doctors in Love*, dir. Garry Marshall

1982 *Jekyll and Hyde . . . Together Again*, dir. Jerry Belson

1982 *48 Hours*, dir. Walter Hill

1983 *Let's Spend the Night Together*, dir. Hal Ashby

1983 *Star 80*, dir. Bob Fosse

1983 *Romantic Comedy*, dir. Arthur Hiller

1984 *Streets of Fire*, dir. Walter Hill

1984 *Body Rock*, dir. Marcel Epstein

1985 *A Chorus Line*, dir. Richard Attenborough

1986 *Off Beat*, dir. Michael Dinner

1986 *Ruthless People*, dir. Jim Abrahams, David Zucker, and Jerry Zucker

1986 *Tough Guys*, dir. Jeff Kanew

1986 *Nobody's Fool*, dir. Evelyn Purcell

1987 *Outrageous Fortune*, dir. Arthur Hiller

1987 *Predator*, dir. John McTierhan

AWARDS

1993 Eddie Award (ACE) nomination, Best Edited Feature Film, *Scent of a Woman*, shared with William Steinkamp and Harvey Rosenstock

2008 Eddie Award (ACE) nomination, Best Edited Feature Film— Comedy or Musical, *Hairspray*

Film may have diverted Michael Tronick from an intended career in law, but in hearing his excitement over numerous encounters with "film royalty" on both sides of the camera, one cannot imagine Tronick doing anything else. Moving from his early experiences with industrials into a music editing gig, Tronick quickly became a well-respected music editor on some of Hollywood's "greatest hits," and he provides an important consideration of this specialized postproduction field, which seems arcane and undefined to most outside the industry. He eventually switched to cutting film itself, and this joint perspective allows Tronick to articulate the complex interrelationship of music with image in editing musicals, rock concert films, and nonmusical films with soundtracks. Not afraid to ask questions about the highly technical processes that are involved in filmmaking today, Tronick elaborates on the complex nature of editing in 3D and with green screens and computer-generated effects in a gamut of films, from blockbuster actions to straightforward dramas. As someone who panics when his Internet crashes, Tronick admires those who speak computer-ese and create digital film magic. Yet as an editor concerned with what the "story" needs, Tronick is not beyond insisting that an expensive, elaborate, star-studded stunt be left on the cutting room floor because it simply does not work for the film.

Tronick's conversation fittingly caps off this collection of interviews by revisiting both the "old" and the "new" in film, and finding the balance between. Having worked in the industry when film meant celluloid with sprocket holes, Tronick expresses a nostalgia for a time before digital. Compressed schedules and monumental workloads have challenged the more contemplative aspects of the process, relegating the intimate "feel" of film to memory. Nevertheless, as Tronick's still starry-eyed reverence for films and filmmakers affirms, the "movies" continue to flicker on dark screens as they have done for a century, captivating both audiences and editors.

You started out in the business as a music editor. Was that what you set out to be?

Actually, when I was a student at UCLA, I was a political science major and I was on the fast track to law school or something predictable like that. But I had friends in the film department and I got derailed when I became exposed to film as a crew member on their student films. I also started taking film history classes, which I thought was a much more beneficial way to learn about a country or society. Rather than reading textbooks, seeing situations portrayed in films was much more compelling to me.

Were those documentary films?

Every kind of film. I specifically remember taking a class about Erich von Stroheim and prewar Germany while I was studying twentieth-century American poli sci and theory. But just something about how society or a particular country was portrayed filmically and how the characters reacted or behaved within those contexts really indicated to me much more vividly what was going on than those textbooks did. After I graduated, I took a year off from school, primarily focusing on trying to avoid getting drafted. When I got deferred, I started a six-month cross-country trip and one of my first stops was San Francisco State University, where I applied to graduate school. I met with the head of the film and television department, sat on a bench outside of his office for a couple of hours, and got accepted! I spent a year in grad school but reached a point where I maxed out on academia. I was losing patience with term papers and projects! *(Laughs.)* So I went back to L.A. and got a job with an industrial filmmaking company called Gene McCabe Productions.

Once again, textbooks weren't doing it for you!

No. I felt that for me to really grow in the field, I needed practical applications, and while academic work is phenomenal for what it provides, it still doesn't—

Pay the rent. Yes, I know.

I mean, as a graduate student, I was living on food stamps at the time! In a way, it was a real crisis: what am I going to do with my life? My older brother knew he was going to be a scientist ever since I can remember, and he turned out to be a terrific research scientist. But I didn't have a clear delineation of what I wanted to do, except I knew I needed to go to work. It was the first time that I hadn't completed something I started, and I had great pangs of guilt over not getting my Master's and disappointing myself and my parents, but I couldn't spend two more years in graduate school.

That was a brave decision, but you knew what you had to do for yourself. Did something about your film experience at UCLA keep tugging at you?

There was kind of a duality to that situation. First of all, I enjoyed the camaraderie of a film crew. I enjoyed working with other people of different skills and backgrounds, all of us working towards a common goal. Also, I didn't know what I was doing. *(Pause.)* I'll let you in on a secret: I still don't! *(Laughs.)*

You could've fooled me. I imagine your classmates may not have known what they were doing either.

No, but we all had some idea. "Okay, this cable goes in here, right? And then the other end goes into the microphone, right? Okay, and you're gonna put the camera *here?*" Everyone had a good time, but everyone also took the work seriously. We had a real sense of self-importance that what we were doing could possibly make a difference. And this leads me to the other part of that duality. The years I was an undergraduate at UCLA, from about '68 to '72, this was a very potent time. I was a freelance photographer for UCLA's newspaper, *Daily Bruin,* and got chased by police during student demonstrations—nothing as serious as Berkeley or Kent State, but still *(pause)* and it was a time when music and film really made a difference. I can remember when the Beatles' *White Album* came out, we'd wait on long lines at the student store to buy it because it really mattered. And when I took these film history classes, went to screenings every weekend, and discussed them with my colleagues, it started an insatiable desire in me to participate in something that felt so vibrant and could possibly make a difference.

Difference, meaning social change?

Listen, I didn't have any grandiose idea that I was going to run for Congress. Just *something* in my own way. It was ironic that I ended up working at McCabe because their primary client was the Chrysler Corporation—you know, the establishment! Glamorizing automobiles in the infancy of the environment movement! That kind of went against the grain of my feelings. But I wasn't an idealist. I was a pragmatist in terms of needing to work. I hadn't really had a dream about what I wanted to do, but the UCLA experience was like the beginning of my dream to work in the industry because I had so much respect for the films I was seeing. I remember too as a kid looking out the car window as my family drove along Sepulveda Boulevard and we'd pass MGM. I'd see this big blue background, the site they used for shoots, and the sound stage with the big rounded roof. Even then film had quite an allure for me and for my mom, who absolutely loved the movies and constantly talked about them. It's very nostalgic now for me to think about this. I'm fortunate to have grown up when I did, when there were still sprocket holes! *(Laughs.)*

Then, working at McCabe was the official start of your dream work.

Yes, and I did everything there because it was nonunion—I was grip, gaffer, assistant camera, camera operator on all these industrial films. Nothing exotic, except I was working in film, most of it in 16, but we also had 35 millimeter shoots which were very exciting. One cameraman I worked with was a gentleman by the name of Russ Alsobrook, who was very influential for me—he was as knowledgeable as any college professor about film history and taught me about lenses and lighting. And one of the production managers, a gentleman named Hal Bell, was Jerry Lewis's personal assistant, a real go-getter, gung-ho kind of guy. But I found myself gravitating towards the editing rooms, of which McCabe had a small suite. That's where I met Dan Carlin, Sr., and Jim Henrikson, who were both moonlighting as film editors, but their real gig was music editor. That was the door that opened for me as far as pursuing music editing. As I've said, it's not like the day I was born that I knew I wanted to be a music editor or anything else in film. It's all been fortuitous. I've had a tremendous amount of luck in the progression of my career and meeting extremely generous individuals who helped me and shared their knowledge with me. I've been very fortunate as far as mentorship.

Were the Chrysler industrials you worked on challenging from a film-making standpoint?

Well, it was about, okay, this is a car, but what's going to show this car in its best light? What is the angle of the camera going to be? Everything from making sure the bumper is spotless to how the reflector provides a little kick of a shine on it. I understood that I was really at the ground level of learning about film production, and it was all accessible to me because it was a small crew and I was working with very, very generous individuals. We had all these crazy 4 A.M. calls to be out at sunrise for film shoots, then wrapping up and having dinner at 7 P.M. and getting a few hours of sleep. We went on the airstrip at Hearst Castle to shoot running shots. We even went to the testing grounds in Chelsea, Michigan, where the Chrysler Corporation tests their cars. And we had shoots in Colorado with a hang-glider dropping in and landing right by a car. There was also a tiny bit of glamour to it—we got blue crew jackets, which was cool! So even though the content wasn't as rewarding as some of the films I was influenced by as an undergraduate, or even before then as a kid, I was part of *something*.

I assume music editing was the next step up the ladder to where you are today.

Yes. When I left McCabe Productions to work with Dan Carlin, Sr., as a music-editing schlep, the first film I was on was *The Killer Elite*. All of a sudden, I found myself on a dubbing stage with *Sam Peckinpah!* Oh my God! Again, that's like following paths that are so inexplicable in terms of the fortune that can be bestowed on an individual.

Let's segue into the music editing world, then. What specifically does a music editor do?

Well, like everything else, the job has changed. When I became a music editor, the primary job was servicing the composer.

Not the film editor?

No. I mean, sure, the editor was part of it and definitely is a great part of music editing today, but back then, 1977, when I became a music editor, it was helping the composer. In fact, I was always tremendously intimidated by film editors because they were like, I don't know, Greek gods who knew all about internegatives and CRIs and labs!

Even more intimidating than directors?

At times, yeah. I remember Dennis Virkler, who was one of the first film editors I worked with as a music editor. He was tall, always dressed in black, and had an aura about him and all this knowledge. I kept saying, "I could never do that!" But anyway, my first gig was on the picture *Semi-Tough*, with Michael Ritchie as director and Jerry Fielding as composer. So a music editor would sit down with the director, the editor, and the composer, and go through the film to decide where underscore would start and where it would go out—and now I'm talking specifically about a nonmusical movie. *Semi-Tough* used a lot of classical music during football games, and we would decide on the most effective way to start the music, what the music should say, and where it should go out. That was called spotting. Then I would take my spotting notes and go back to my IBM typewriter (no computers then), type up the notes, and send them to Jerry Fielding. I would break each scene down into tenths and hundredths of seconds, so Jerry knew from the start of the music that there was a cut to a close-up of Kris Kristoffersen, say, at 5.25 seconds. If he wanted to hit that with a musical flourish, he knew that he had to write something at a certain tempo and which note and which bar would hit that. These were called timing notes, which became a whole thick notebook, depending on how much there was. Then Jerry would finish writing the score. These were the days when we would go up to his house—not too far from where I'm living now—and he had only a piano to work with. There were no synthesizers, no sampling. Jerry would sit at the piano and play for me and Dan Carlin. Jerry would say, "Okay, here's what the strings are going to be doing," and with his right hand, he would do some trill or chord. Then, "And this is what the brass is going to be doing," and he would hit a certain melody or whatnot with his left hand. So he was describing what the orchestra would do, but on a piano. Things have certainly changed dramatically! Then we would prepare the black-and-white 35 dupe which was used on the scoring stage to record to, and we would put in streamers—these were three-foot diagonal lines that you would see going across the film. At the end of each streamer, there was a punch, an actual physical circle that you would punch with a hole punch. At that same time, you would hit a digital metronome which had the tempo assigned to that particular cue. We'd record that either straight to 35 mag or to a twenty-four track which had to be mixed-down for the dubbing stage. Then we would cut it into units so I knew that at two hundred feet, twelve frames, the music started. Then I would go down in a music unit, which was blank fill leader, and at two hundred feet, twelve frames on the synchronizer, for example, I would cut in the mag and then create a cue sheet for the mixer so he knew that was when the music came in. And that was pretty much music editing when I started!

Almost like a science.
At the time it was very mechanical, very technical. Once, I put a streamer in at the wrong place so that a cue ended one bar early, and it was one of those moments where I wanted to disappear. But luckily, I was able to edit a repeat in a certain phrase—I can still hear it in my head!—so that the four beats were added, and it could end where the music was supposed to end.

How have the responsibilities of a music editor changed?
As I said, music editing when I started was just working for the composer. There were no temp scores per se. That is, the film editor would cut in temp music himself. Then when previewing mushroomed, it became the music editor's responsibility to also provide a temp score for movies.

My first real successful temp score was for *48 Hours* with Nick Nolte, directed by Walter Hill. James Horner was the composer. I would go to a record store, pick out albums for soundtracks, and take them to the transfer department. They would transfer the music to a single stripe, which is like mono sound on film, and I would keep trying the music on a KEM, a flatbed, over and over until I got something I thought would work. It was gratifying and terrifying at the same time. When I was the music editor on *Young Doctors in Love*, the first feature that Garry Marshall directed, I remember having thousands and thousands of feet of mag with temp music on it, and just trying things, hoping I would find something that worked. Nowadays, every single soundtrack is digitized and music editors have instant access to it. The difference in the process is astounding. But even in those prehistoric days, we still got the job done. We worked within those limitations because that's all we knew and we did it.

Which stage of the film did you work on as a music editor in those pre-historic days?
It was often a film that was already locked. Composers would usually come on after the director had finished his cut. Now music editors come on during the first cut, which is great for me now that I am the film editor. I don't want to spend my time cutting temp music anymore. It's easy to get typecast in this business, like, "Oh, Tronick knows a lot about music. He'll cut the temp score." No. Now I want to concentrate on telling the story pictorially. The music editor can do the temp score.

Music editors must certainly have a deep understanding of how music works in a film that transcends the mechanics of laying in a musical track.
They do, and as I became a more experienced music editor, I slowly started pushing the envelope on what music editing did in a film. Bob Fosse, with whom I worked as music editor on two of his films, and composer Ralph Burns taught me how to *listen*. They taught me to focus in on a certain phrase within an orchestra and the importance of that phrase. For example, the subtlety of a French horn solo and what levels it should be. Even though I was a musician as a kid, I never had that gift of listening. I played trumpet and drums in college, and my quasi "I wanna be a rock star" fantasy never quite worked out. But I'm blessed to have had my experience as a music editor because now I feel like I know how to listen to music. Well, it's a blessing and a curse because I'm hypercritical of music in film in terms of levels and balances. If the composer wasn't on the dubbing stage, *I* started talking to the mixers and said, "Can we raise

the brass a touch here on this part?" Some mixers weren't used to input from a music editor, they only wanted to work with the composer. But those early days were the beginning of my creative involvement in the musical contributions of a movie.

What are those contributions? In other words, what does music do to an image and, therefore, to the audience?
   Well, let's think about music on its own terms. I'm sure there are doctoral theses on this!

But we can stay away from academia if you want. (Laughs.)
   I think it really goes back to the first days of man beating on drums. Every culture, every society has developed music. It's about something that goes straight to my heart. It's an emotional response to what I'm hearing. These men and women who can create original underscore for film have an overwhelming gift. I remember the first time I was on a scoring stage at the CBS Studios in Studio City—it was the stage where *Fantasia* was recorded, so it was like I walked into the room and could breathe in history. In front of me was a large orchestra and Fred Karlin had composed and was conducting a score for a television movie called *Minstrel Man*, a true story based on the minstrel acts that toured the South post–Civil War. Of course, I was too inexperienced to do anything in terms of working a clock or the digital metronome. I was just an observer. In those days, it was black-and-white film on a big screen, not on a monitor like you have now. The film started, Fred played the downbeat, and all of a sudden, the orchestra came to life. It was for a scene I had seen twenty times without music, but all of a sudden, this first rehearsal became so profound and magical. I have never forgotten that first experience of seeing a live recording put to film. So, what is music? It is a gift that composers have to thematically develop melodies that can be evocative emotionally, that can be suspenseful, terrifying, shocking, passionate, energetic, exciting. These remarkable virtuosos know how to effectively enhance what is being seen on the screen. Not everyone can do this. There are composers—who will go unnamed—that I would mute the music channel, if I could, because I find their music obtrusive, glossing over the emotions.

Almost canceling them out for the viewer.
   Exactly, and doing more harm to the movie than good. As a music editor, what I sometimes did on a dubbing stage was take a piece of existing score and edit it to fit a scene where there was no music. In *48 Hours,* there was

a quick little cue, I think an exterior shot of San Francisco that led to Nick Nolte visiting Eddie Murphy in prison, and there was no music for it. So Walter Hill, the director, asked me to come up with something.

That prompts another question of why a scene even needs music in the first place.

That's an excellent question because I'm all for "let's try it without music." I don't want to sound like the grizzled old veteran that I am, but I think directors need to trust what's on the screen without relying on music as an emotional crutch. I'm working on a film by John Singleton right now, and there's a lot of background songs going on in one scene while two kids are doing research for school on their computer. John hasn't seen the scene yet so I don't know if he's going to like it *(laughs)*, but I took out the source music. I found myself more involved with the dialogue between the kids, and *removing* the music enhanced the dramatic content of the scene because, suddenly, there wasn't this barrier of a song with lyrics playing in the background and distracting me. It's like when I'm having dinner with my family, we'll have music in the background, but rarely will we play music with lyrics because I don't want my ear to go off and say, "Oh, that's Thom Yorke singing." I want to hear *our* dialogue, so we'll play something instrumental instead.

That speaks to the subliminal pull music has on someone. In a movie, maybe half the time a viewer is not even aware of the music while watching what goes on.

And music in a film can be absolutely successful if you're *not* aware of it. As an editor, though, I'm always looking at scenes without music and sometimes realize how effective they are. Other times, I really miss the music because it contributes an emotional component that simply isn't there without music.

Reds is an interesting case of a very long film—nearly four hours—with relatively little music. It was very talk-heavy, in fact.

I came on *Reds* after the first music editor, Ted Whitfield, left. Remember, people were working on that movie for three or four years already. Warren Beatty, the director, had a pretty good idea of where music was going in. Because of the authenticity he wanted of following the journalist John Reed and all those phenomenal historic characters, music was used sparingly except for some of the actual music of the time. I had great adventures going downtown New York to a record store specializing in period music and saying, "I need music from 1922. It can't be '23 and it can't be '21. 1922!" And this guy—I wish I remembered his name—pulled out all these records of music from 1922! I would get them transferred, play them for Warren, and come up with what to use. But Stephen Sondheim wrote the love theme, which was very evocative and used sparingly throughout the film, and Dave Grusin did the orchestrations. We allowed ourselves one big moment—the emotional reunion between John Reed (Beatty) and Louise Bryant (Diane Keaton)—at the train station in Russia. But for all the political conferences like the Internationale, the music was inherent to the period. *(Pause.)* I can still hear that lilting piano melody that Sondheim wrote. Ironically, what ended up in the film was the demo that he recorded on a cassette. It was re-recorded, of course, in a movie studio by a goodly number of accomplished pianists, but Warren just went back to the original cassette and that's what is in the movie. But I don't think the sparing use of music diminished the dramatic impact of the film. And the sound job that Maurice Schell and about sixty sound editors did was absolutely miraculous and very textured, very rich. The movie was about the spoken word, pure and simple. Maybe in the scenes when John Reed was fleeing Russia and crossing the ice fields of Norway, there was plaintive Russian music, not quite a balalaika but a percussive instrument that very subtly played the emotion and atmosphere. But it was a very, very smart use of music. What an experience that film was! It's almost legendary now. The editor Dede Allen, almost like the General Patton of film, came into a room like a hurricane, with her assistants frantically following her. There were like eighty people in postproduction in an almost round-the-clock operation—not quite, but that's what it felt like. I felt remarkably fortunate to have had that exposure and meeting what was kind of the "Who's Who" of New York editorial at the time. Back then, music editors weren't prevalent and what we did seemed a little mysterious to most people. Sometimes it seemed like chaos, but everyone knew their roles and the work got done.

If that film had been done with today's technology, do you think it would have felt less chaotic?

No, I think it was the nature of the job and the nature of the director's personality. I mean, obviously it would be different in terms of accessing material and work flow. But if the *Reds* experience were transplanted to today's Hollywood? *(Pause.)* I think we'd still be working on it! You could try an infinite number of things and even shift your focus in a film. Sometimes the technology doesn't change a director's process of thinking about a film. For example, I've worked with Marty Brest on both the film side and the digital side. With film, we looked at every frame of every daily of every take, and Marty shot a ton of film. We did the same with the Avid, only it was a little quicker getting to the material. Instead of threading it up and hitting play, you just click and, boom, you play it. I know Marty adapted to the nonfilm visuals of looking at a digital image as opposed to an actual film image, but it didn't change his process. He let the process adapt to him. I think much in film editing is about "we are who we are and we work the way we work." Although I keep evolving, even I still come back to the fundamentals I established years ago in my methodology.

So the technology hasn't affected you much?

In what I do as an editor? No. I wasn't one of those film editors who could look at a take and know exactly where I was going to cut and what I was going to cut to. I would look at a take and formulate in my mind what I needed. But then deciding where to cut on what frame and/or play an overlap, and actually mark the film with a grease pencil, put it in the splicer, cut it, splice it—it was a task. In the process, I would generate so many trims because I kept trying different stuff. If one piece didn't work, I would hang it up. Then at the end of the day, I'd look at my trim bin and discover it was packed full! When I worked with Billy Weber and Chris Lebenzon, they had just a few pieces hanging up in their trim bins and I'd say, damn, these guys are good! They had this laser focus of knowing where the cut was and making it. But I'm not that kind of guy. If I make a cut—even on the Avid—and don't change a frame of it, that's rare! "Oh, what if I stayed on that for twelve frames longer and allowed the prelap of the dialogue? No, no, I liked it better the other way." I'm my own worst critic. Every now and then, I'll allow myself a modicum of, "Atta boy!" but as soon as I do, I'm like, "You stupid jerk! Why'd you do that?" I slap myself back to reality.

What eventually happens for you to finally say, "I know this is right"?

It's an intrinsic response to an edit, a gut reaction to what I feel works and doesn't work for me. Obviously I'm thinking about presenting it to the director and the audience, but I need to please myself first before showing it to anybody. I think it comes from being a music editor, when you're timing a three-minute scene and you have to describe *every* cut, *every* line of dialogue to a composer within a shot, so you have hundreds and hundreds of entries within a two-minute sequence. Somehow there was a bit of absorbing the rhythms of where you make the cut and how it flows. I remember on *Beverly Hills Cop II*—my first job solely as film editor—Billy and Chris asked me to come on to help out. Tony Scott, the director, shot the film in Scope, and I remember seeing this wide shot of Brigitte Nielsen driving up the street and being pulled over by a police officer. So I stayed in this wide shot of the car pulling up, with the camera looking at the front end of the car from a distance of about fifty feet—a big wide beautiful shot in Beverly Hills. Then, at that moment, I wanted to cut to a closer shot of her reacting to the approaching cop. I found the take, marked the cut, spliced it, played it through the KEM, and said to myself, "This looks like a movie!" It was exhilarating! I had cut something that *looked* like a movie. It resonated for me on a rhythmic level, like that was the exact beat I needed to be on in this other shot.

So the wider shot felt like it was hanging in space and you felt a need to move on from it.

Yes, there came a point in the wide shot where I lost interest. I said, "Okay, I need to be involved in what's going on and see a reaction on someone's face." After all, no one likes to be pulled over by a cop, so I wanted to see the reaction on the actress's face. That's when I decided where I wanted the cut. I will stay in a shot for as long as it holds up. This is something I learned from editor Joe Hutshing, who said, "Why cut out of the shot if the performances are good and it plays?" For example, if you play a two-shot with Anthony Hopkins and Brad Pitt in *Meet Joe Black*, when do you go to a close-up of Pitt? When do you go to a close-up of Hopkins? They are magnificent performers and I love being close because I want to see what's in their eyes. But sometimes you stay in the wide master because the full physicality of their bodies can be as impactful as going to close-up.

Speaking of physicality of bodies, a few song-and-dance musicals you cut involved editing a lot of movement while also being aware of musical beats and rhythms. Can you talk about the editing of a choreographed dance number, say from Hairspray?

That film was a blast! Adam Shankman did a spectacular job because the choreography was very well planned. Even so, the first challenge of cutting a musical number comes when dialogue is interspersed within it. Let's refer to the scene where Tracy Turnblad comes to the studio to audition for the rock-and-roll television show, and she and her friend are watching everyone doing their dance. We have to cut to the two girls talking, then cut back to the dancers still in tempo and doing the right choreography, then cut away again for *x* number of bars to capture the dialogue, then come back to the musical number again at a specific point to keep the tempo going. The second challenge is within the choreography itself. You are locked in to *movement* to the beat, and sometimes the dancers don't always do the same thing twice. Like someone's heel doesn't always come down on the downbeat when you want it to! The movement might be a little bit before, a little bit after the beat. But when you start shifting by frames here and frames there, the vocal relationship to the rhythm track is thrown out because they *are* singing on the beat. Then you have lip sync issues in terms of giving the songs a certain fluidity. Luckily, Adam shot several takes and I'd find the best one. That goes back to my tenet of always protecting the performers, whether it's in dialogue, dance, singing, or whatever. You want to protect your actors and actresses and put them on the screen in the best possible light. If there's an awkward movement, cutting to a different angle actually helps make it look less awkward instead of trying to keep the same angle.

I assume a musical number is shot several times and from different angles.
   Absolutely.

And you have to sift through a mound of footage for just one number.
   Definitely. The best examples of that are the Hannah Montana and Jonas Brothers concert films, which were shot over four nights. For any given song, eight cameras were going per song, and I would have four versions of each song. Four times eight is what? Thirty-two? So I'd have the equivalent of thirty-two cameras! And I had to cut a song a day on Hannah Montana because of the schedules. It was crazy! I devised a system of pulling selects from each performance and building them on different video tracks on the Avid. Then I would keep going through and figure out the best angle for each part of the verse, the chorus, the bridge, the dancing, until I had a song for each particular night. Then I'd do a "bake-off" between the songs. For example, I'd compare the first verse from each concert, decide which was the best, and start building a song using the best sections from each performance—a combo special. Luckily, Kenny Ortega was the choreographer and the dancers were very good, but they weren't always in the same position on the second phrase of the chorus, for example, from one night to the next, so sometimes I had to do some "cheating." Thank God I could cut away to the audience or band members. But I had to remember my core audience—teenage kids who were coming to see Miley Cyrus or the Jonas Brothers. They weren't

coming to see the drummer! *(Laughs.)* Although as an old drummer myself, I loved cutting to the drums, especially in 3D when he hits the stick and it flies up!

That was *pretty cool.*

I thought so. Dick Cook (at that time, chairman of Walt Disney Studios) wanted some big 3D moments in Hannah Montana and that flying drumstick was one of them. Same with the flying guitar pick. Bruce Hendricks who directed it was so wonderfully collaborative, yet so wonderfully hands-off. He trusted me and when I finished the song, he would come in, look at it, and have only a few changes. I'd do them and we'd ship it off to conform the mono image to stereo. We'd get it back on a drive, watch the sequence in 3D, and make modifications based on that screening. Now you can cut in 3D. Still, I'm not a big fan of 3D. I spoke at a 3D symposium at Fox not long ago, and these brilliant guys from labs were talking about stuff that goes right over my head. And I said, "Well, I'm here to tell the *story*. Can anyone tell me if comedy or drama plays better in 2D or 3D? Shoot a Harold Pinter play in 3D and let me see what that's like!" Yes, you can be right there with the performers, the immediacy, the reality of it. But I'm not sold on everything converting to 3D these days. The disadvantage of 2D to 3D conversion is that once the 2D version is done, it's a whole big technical process that affects even the shape of the characters on the screen. When they converted 2D to 3D in *The Green Hornet,* Seth Rogen at times looked a little like a mannerist painting which had to be corrected! Maybe it was just my eye. *(Laughs.)* But bottom line, what is the better format to tell the story?

3D seems to be yet another extension of making movies flashy these days. Even in musical numbers, it's almost like watching an action sequence with so much kinetic editing. By contrast, I think of Fred Astaire who insisted that his dance numbers always be shot in wide to show him and his partners from head to toe. Why the need for kinetic cutting today?

Well, I'm still schooled in the old-fashioned way, and I think I'm the least "action guy" you'll ever meet in the world. But because I've done action films, I've been typecast again: "Oh, Tronick cuts action sequences," so fine. Still, I would say for dance, action, even martial arts fight sequences which are like dance in terms of full-body movement, it always comes down to: when do you make a cut? If you're in a wide shot and you see full-body performers and sense their physicality, that can be as impactful as a close-up. I recently had an interview for a film with martial arts fight sequences and I told the director that I think seeing full body can be as impactful as a close-up of a punch across a guy's jaw. Maybe that's why I didn't get the job! But I do think a fight, or a dance for that matter, has to be conveyed for the most impact. I remember as a kid seeing Sean Connery as 007, and he was in a fight on a train with Robert Shaw, who played the bleach-blond bad guy. I can remember *feeling* those punches. You know, Connery kind of grimaces as he throws a punch in one shot, and you see the reaction shot of the bad guy, *boinnnng!* seeing stars or whatever as he gets hit. That kind of intimacy in the fight gets the audience involved in addition to the wide shot where you establish its geography. I'm a traditionalist because I don't want to lose an audience's sense of place. When I worked with Jerry Bruckheimer, he always asked "Where am I? Where am I?" about a scene, and I ask that very basic question too when I edit. But look at what Chris Rouse does with editing the Bourne movies. It's kinetic, it's energetic. Sometimes I get a little lost, but overall, my hands are clenched on the arms of my chair wondering if Matt Damon's going to get out in time. That style comes from the way movies are being shot today. Look at your proliferation of energetic camera moves, cameras that never stop moving. That lends itself to a certain style of editing to keep the energy going. Of course, I'm happy to try disorienting an audience too with kinetic cutting, and I guess my style has evolved into being a little more aggressive editorially, stylistically, where I'll take chances and be a little more nontraditional. But something simple and traditional can still have a tremendous impact. I recently saw on YouTube a video of an eight-year-old girl singing the national anthem at a hockey game. Someone was filming her with a hand-held camera, and as she's singing, her wireless microphone suddenly goes off. You could hear her tiny unamplified voice, but then the entire stadium started singing to accompany her. It was so sweet and so poignant. That was all filmed with a single hand-held consumer camera in one long shot, and it had as much or more impact as any flashy cut film. So yes, we are establishing new film traditions today, but hopefully we will still acknowledge where we have come from. I know tradition is a very large part of my editorial DNA.

Let's go a step further by talking about Mr. and Mrs. Smith *and* The Green Hornet, *which are action-packed films. Today's technology makes it possible to do fantastic things with even a traditional car chase sequence. Do you think computer tricks detract from the authenticity of a car chase for an audience?*

They can, but using this technology means more that there are no limits to what you can do to eliminate problems from a frame. For example, in *The Green Hornet*, five cameras were following a car chase for the beginning and end of the movie. Some shots were great, but crew members or cameras might have been standing in them. Because I really liked the action with the cars, I said, "Okay, we can paint those extras out and still use the shot." Usually my VFX editor will mock it up in the Avid or on Adobe After Effects to give the idea of what I want, and then I have the luxury of sending it to a VFX vendor who can clean it up and bring it back to me.

Do you get thrown off working with a green screen that has to be filled in later?

A lot of times, I have no idea what's going on when I see the actors in front of a green screen. What's the background going to be? What are they looking at and who are they talking to? You get some pretty rudimentary shots with a principal actor and nothing else. I remember the first time with Doug Liman on *Mr. and Mrs. Smith*, I'd show him a cut with the green screen and he said, "Well, what's that supposed to be?" And I said, "Well, that's meant to be the ravine." And he said, "Well, I need to see the ravine." And that was the first time I thought, "Holy crap. How do I do that?" I had never done much Avid compositing at that level of sophistication and didn't know where to get the elements for it. So I was ushered into grasping what the CG world was all about pretty quickly. Before that, like with *Under Siege 2*, for example, they shot a lot of interiors of a train on a green screen and you knew that plates were going to go into the windows that would show the passing wilderness or whatever. That was easy. But the ravine was way out of my league. I had to learn how to show Doug a sequence with a ravine in it, so we scanned the storyboards and did a composite that was a combination of live action and storyboards just so he could see it. I remember I used to think, well, I can't pull a rabbit out of a hat with this stuff. Now I can! Speaking of rabbits, I haven't done any movies with CG creatures, but I did work a little on *Wolfman*, where a CG deer gets attacked by the wolfman! But there's nothing like the real thing, though. As great as CG effects are, something in the weight and volume of the entity feels a *little* off and I think audiences perceive that.

Isn't that why suspension of disbelief is a prerequisite for watching action or science fiction films?

Yes. When I was a kid, I used to think *Invaders from Mars* was the scariest thing—until I saw the zipper on the back of the Martian. So much for suspension of disbelief!

Personally, I liked spotting the wires pulling the flying saucers. (Laughs.) *When it comes to special effects, then, it seems that many editors may do a lot of on-the-job learning.*

It can be challenging, but here's my secret: I hire people who know how to do it!

How do you think those people keep up with innovations?

You know kids and computers today! I learned to use personal computers when I was a music editor, in my late twenties, early thirties, and this is the analogy I've come up with for computers: it's like learning a foreign language. If you start speaking a foreign language when you're very young, by the time you're in high school, you're fluent. If you start a language in high school or later, you may never have that fluency—I think your brain hardens or something! Now kids who grow up with computers are fearless and speak computer-ese fluently, while for me, it's nerve-wracking. If my Internet goes down at home, I panic! But at work, what's important for me is to communicate to these wizards what I want and I have learned some of their language to do so. I don't want to sit there being Avid-visual-palette-challenged! *(Laughs.)* Just like I learned to listen to music, I have learned to use the language of visual effects. At this point in my career, I'm not afraid to ask stupid obvious questions—that's when I get the best answers! Now that I've gotten my feet more than wet with 3D, for instance, I want to understand it, so I ask questions, but sometimes I feel like I'm talking to a PhD candidate from MIT in interocular sciences! So I just say, "I don't understand. Please, tell me in layman's terms what this is about." Because if I don't understand the scene, I can't cut it.

Is that because something you can't see in one shot can affect what comes next?

Absolutely. So I approach cutting such a scene as if it's a regular 2D, non-CG sequence. I'm going for performance, I'm trying to tell the story. Let everything else fall into place. Once I learn what is going on in the scene, then I can modify or adapt to enhance what the CG payoff is going to be. Because of the expense of these sequences, the pre-viz artist will come up with little Quicktime movies of the sequences, like a cartoon of the scene or live-action storyboarding, so I can get an idea of what the sequence is all about. You can't be afraid to have a scene crash and burn because you don't understand it, but hopefully before I get to that point, I have enough input from everyone to understand what the visuals ultimately are going to be so I can be best informed on how to edit.

Once you cut the green-screen version of the film based on your understanding of it, then it goes to—

The visual effects editor, who does temporary composites for you right in the Avid. I realize the great potential of all this CG wizardry, so one of the first things I do on a movie is introduce myself to the visual-effects producer. I say, "I want to work with you and I'm not here to create problems. I don't want to choose a shot that's going to cost you a million dollars to composite because of its difficulty. If there's another shot you would prefer I use and I think the performances are good, let me know. But you need to understand too that, as the editor, I'm also going to make choices." So it's a continual collaboration. You know what's funny? It's still that same small film crew I started out with at UCLA, but instead of dealing with a budget of a thousand dollars, we're dealing with budgets of 140 million. Bottom line, I'm still dealing with the same fundamental problems and challenges as far as telling a story, which now tends to be told in such remarkably, miraculously sophisticated ways.

However, you could have all the CG effects in the world, but the movie could still bomb because it lacks compelling story or characters.

A huge bomb! You could have the most spectacular stunts, but unless you have an investment in the characters, who cares? You end up feeling, "I've seen this explosion before. I've seen them jump from this building to that building." So?

It becomes tedious, like effect for the sake of effect.

Within the context of contributing dramatically to a scene, then effect for the sake of effect is cool. But if it's an arbitrary effect, like a stand-alone for a "wow" factor, I think we have to go right past that. There was a scene in *Mrs. and Mrs. Smith* where Angelina Jolie is hidden in a shack in the desert waiting for a convoy and Brad Pitt shows up in a dune buggy. That was a completely reworked sequence for a big action scene that was supposed to take place in the Colorado Rockies, and it was the first scene shot for the film. They built an entire mountain façade on a Fox stage! We had a whole pre-viz sequence of what was going to happen. So we were into it for about two weeks and finally had a meeting. I started looking at the dailies and was becoming a little concerned. Everyone was there: Doug Liman, the director; Albert Cho, the first AD; Akiva Goldman and Lucas Foster, the producers; and Sanford Panitch, the head of Regency Productions. And Sanford turned to me and said, "So, Tronick, we're going to have a kick-ass action sequence here!" And I said, "No."

And the room fell silent. (Laughs.)

Well, I had to say it. What I saw was less than what this movie promised, even though the scene looked great. Doug had grandiose visuals for it, but from a fundamental level, something about this scene started going South. I want to be a cheerleader, a supporter, an enthusiastic ally to help everyone create their visions, but if something is not working, it's like the Emperor's new clothes: I have to speak honestly because that's what I'm paid to do.

Couldn't you have discussed that while reading the script to avoid creating an exorbitant shot that ended up being deleted?

In another scene in *Mr. and Mrs. Smith,* I did mention it after I read the script. When I interviewed with Doug, I said, "I have problems with the third act. Who are these bad guys suddenly showing up? Why are they all being killed here? It seems so arbitrary and needless." I mean, I don't like killing people on film at all, but there has to be a purpose to it—you vanquish bad guys because they are really bad and have to go. So I told Doug there was a problem with the third act and the problem never went away. That is why the scene at the end—which is now a deleted scene on the DVD—went out, and the big shootout at IKEA is a vestige of a larger scene. It was like gratuitous violence that didn't further the story and it was an obvious drop. They still spent the money and shot it, and then we dropped it.

No one screamed?

No one threw anything against the wall and said, "We've spent all this F-ing money, what the hell?" Regency was really enlightened and Sanford was such a wonderful man. They believed in the movie and did whatever it took, including pouring in additional funds to make it right. They said, "Okay, let's get Simon Kinberg in here to rewrite some stuff." We had to mock up things, do pre-viz for the new scenes, do new storyboards. Brad and Angelina both came back in and looked at them. We had to get their approval for these reshoots. Regency agreed to spend additional money, get the crew back together, add more days, and delay the release just to make it right. Obviously it's not a perfect movie, but it's highly entertaining and I think it's a ground-breaking action movie. I knew it from the first scene I cut, which was the marriage counselor's office and also the first time Brad and Angelina met. As soon as I saw the first frame and played the take, I said, "My God, this is going to be good!"

It must be hard to reflect on story and plot when you're busy cutting flashy sequences, though.

You have to remember that even with all the action and effects, there is still something intrinsically practical to the story that an audience responds to favorably. My priority in these action films is being with the characters, with their dialogue and interactions. In one action scene with a minivan in *Mr. and Mrs. Smith*, Brad and Angelina are talking about themselves. Their secret lives as assassins are unraveling and they're finally becoming honest with each other. It's action but it's also about the characters. Brad says, "I was married once before," and Angelina slams on the brakes in reaction—that's humor within a life-and-death car chase, which I think is brilliant.

While watching these car chases, I couldn't help but think of an infamous real-life car chase—when O. J. Simpson made his getaway—and wondered how a fictionalized version of that would be made today. Would there be an obligation to do kinetic cutting as in most car chases we see now?

That's a compelling question to think about. I was working at Sony in Culver City at the time and the freeway where the Simpson chase took place is within visual distance. Someone heard about it on the radio, so we went outside and there were all these helicopters overhead and we were basically following the chase in real time. Obviously no cutting there! And it worked. It captivated the country because it was so bizarre. There was also the question: was O.J. going to kill himself in the Bronco? You never knew what to expect. And of course, on TV we had the helicopter POV the whole time. It was reality unfolding. Now if I were directing a film with the O.J. chase, part of me would say: Yes, as is, this is such an iconographic moment emblazoned on the psyche of the American public. But wouldn't you *want to see* O.J.'s reactions inside the Bronco when he held the gun to his head? Wouldn't you want to see the reaction of a driver in another lane who might spot him and say, "Oh my God, that's O.J.

Simpson!" Wouldn't you want to be privy to the dialogue that O.J. and his friend, Al Cowlings, were sharing in the Bronco? Or the police? Or the helicopters? If it were a documentary film, I would never re-create the slow-speed chase, but I would show the actual footage and have O.J. record a voiceover—if he was out of jail, of course!—and describe what was going on. But for a fictionalized version, it's a different context with different expectations.

Would you say that expectations of a film's success are closely tied to the expectations of the personalities involved in making a film?

Well, I would say what it takes to be an editor these days is to learn to work with a disparate group of individuals with unique personalities and to get a consensus on the intent for the film. My work can be tremendously political, so sometimes I feel like a tightrope walker moving between a strong producer, a strong director, a studio, a writer, the actors. I remember once a director with whom I had worked before called me back to do another film. The star-producer was a wonderful comedian and also a very powerful guy in Hollywood. His movies make more money than is imaginable. He also happens to be very loyal to the people who have worked with him for years, so pretty much I, the first AD, and the costumer designer were the only personnel that the director was allowed to bring into the movie. About halfway through photography, the star's postproduction people mentioned that they were bringing in another editor to help out. Fine, I'm a collaborator, no problem. But what I didn't realize was that this editor was beginning to recut the scenes I had already cut for the star, because his editor knew "what he wanted," even before photography had ended. It became very difficult for me to be in the cutting room and hear dialogue from a scene I had worked on being recut just for the star. I believe in the sacred bond between director and editor, and I felt it was a completely disrespectful thing to do to the director. One time I saw the star give his fellow actor direction on how to deliver a line of dialogue. The director said privately to me, "I don't even know why I'm here." Once he realized what was going on, the director went to the studio and asked if anything could be done, but, as I said, the star is one powerful guy. The editor was young and talented and tried hard to fit in, and he told me what he was doing, but I didn't want to see it, I didn't want to hear it. About three weeks later, something happened in the cutting room that made me say, "I can't do this anymore." I talked to my agent, I drove out to the set, and for the first time in my life, I left a project. It was gut-wrenching for me, but the director understood. And there's no ill feeling between me and the other editor—I still see him and he's a great guy. But under those circumstances, I couldn't stay.

It went against your work ethic.

It undermined my whole ethical being. I know that so many people do what I do better, but the one thing I have is my integrity and if I lose that, I'm worthless. The star acquired his success and that's what's important to him. It's not my world and it will never be. What's important to me is the acknowledgment of my peers. If someone picks up the phone and says, "Tronick, I saw your work on *Remember the Titans*," that's my gratification. I'm still in awe of editors and sometimes can't believe I'm in their midst doing what they do.

I suspect meeting the stars has its perks too.

Well, I'm not a celebrity monger, but it is part of the job I love. When I was working on *A Chorus Line,* Princess Diana came to visit Twickenham Studios in England, and she was just striking. When I saw Angelina Jolie for the first time, she took my breath away. I can still remember on *Reds* when I walked into the dubbing stage at Trans Audio in New York and got introduced to Warren Beatty, all I could think in the back of my mind was "Oh my God, this is Warren Beatty, movie star!" When I worked with the Rolling Stones on a Hal Ashby documentary, I used to pick up Mick Jagger from the Hermitage Hotel in my Peugeot 504 to drive him to Todd-AO to mix the movie. And there was the time I argued with Brad Pitt over the ending of *Mr. and Mrs. Smith*! These are extraordinary circumstances that I can't wait to go home and tell my wife and friends about! I'm just a schlub from Sherman Oaks and I'm dealing with film royalty. It's often "pinch-myself" time!

Do the stars hang out in your cutting room?

Oh yes. Actually, the first time Brad came into the cutting room was on *Meet Joe Black* because he was concerned about his performance in a certain scene, and he saw what we had to do to make the scene work and why we chose specific takes. I'll never forget what he said as he left: "My experience in the cutting room is going to make me a better actor."

That's quite a compliment about what an editor can do for an actor—

And for a production designer, a director, a writer, a producer. It doesn't matter what job you have. I consider it imperative that whatever you see yourself doing in film, you should spend time in the cutting room because that's where it all comes crashing down! It's essential. For the most part, editors are treated respectfully because actors know that their performance by and large is in our hands. Well, obviously it's in the director's hands above all, but editors do have influence on how actors come across. The people who understand what we do respect us. Those who don't understand couldn't care less! *(Laughs.)* But if something I say about editing can resonate with someone going to film school anywhere, then to me that's even more gratifying than cutting a scene.

And seeing your work on a giant screen is pretty gratifying too.

It is. This past week, we had the premiere of *The Green Hornet* at Graumann's Chinese Theatre. I was working on the movie till last week, for a year and a half, so I was just Green-Horneted to death. But when I went to the premiere, I allowed myself to appreciate that I was watching my work on a huge screen with a thousand people. I'm sure you realize by now from all your interviews with the fraternity/sorority of film editors that we're not really a "shine-the-spotlight-on-me" kind of group.

Yes, editors have been in the shadows for a while.

But every now and then, I allow myself a certain "Wow, I remember cutting that scene and *now* look at it up here on this huge screen."

Even though editors aren't responsible for shooting the footage or directing the film, they can assemble works of art that become the legacy of filmdom.

Yes, these films are going to be permanent records that future generations will access. And my name is going to be on some of those films! I don't really think about that as I'm working on a film in that context, and I rarely watch my work because I'm too critical. But I do remember watching on TV a film I didn't edit called *An Everlasting Piece* that Barry Levinson made about toupee salesmen in Northern Ireland. Part of the movie takes place in a movie theater where the main kids in the film are watching *Stop Making Sense*, which was Jonathan Demme's film about the Talking Heads concert, which I did help out on. So here comes the end of *Stop Making Sense* that the kids are watching, and the end credits come up and suddenly I see my name! "Special Thanks to Michael Tronick." There I am, seeing my name on a movie that kids in a movie are watching! That's crazy! And it's another chance to allow myself to feel proud.

Bibliography

Apple, Wendy. *The Cutting Edge: The Magic of Movie Editing.* Documentary film. American Cinema Editors (ACE), 2004.

The Art and Craft of Film Editing. Special supplement of *Cineaste* 34, no. 2 (Spring 2009): 27–64.

Barnouw, Erik. *Documentary: A History of the Non-Fiction Film.* Rev. ed. Oxford: Oxford University Press, 1983.

Chandler, Gael. *Cut by Cut: Editing Your Film or Video.* Studio City, CA: Michael Wiese Productions, 2006.

———. *Film Editing: Great Cuts Every Filmmaker and Movie Lover Must Know.* Studio City, CA: Michael Wiese Productions, 2009.

Cinemeditor. Publication of the American Cinema Editors (ACE). (www.ace-filmeditors.org).

Clark, Jim, with John H. Meyers. *Dream Repairman: Adventures in Film Editing.* Crockett, TX: LandMarc Press, 2010.

Cohen, Steven. *Avid Agility: Working Faster and More Intuitively with Avid Media Composer.* CreateSpace, 2010.

Coleman, Lori, and Friedberg, Diana. *Make the Cut: A Guide to Becoming a Successful Assistant Editor in Film and TV.* Burlington, MA: Focal Press, 2010.

Crittenden, Roger. *Film Editing.* London: Thames and Hudson, 1981.

Cunningham, Megan. *The Art of the Documentary: Ten Conversations with Leading Directors, Cinematographers, Editors, and Producers.* Berkeley, CA: New Riders Press, 2005.

Dancyger, Ken. *The Technique of Film and Video Editing: History, Theory, and Practice.* 5th ed. Burlington, MA: Focal Press, 2010.

Dmytryk, Edward. *On Film Editing.* Burlington, MA: Focal Press, 1984.

Eisenstein, Sergei. *The Film Sense.* Translated and edited by Jay Leyda. New York: Harcourt Brace Jovanovich, 1942.

Hanson, Matt. *The End of Celluloid: Film Futures in the Digital Age.* East Sussex, England: Rotovision, 2004.

Hollyn, Norman. *The Film Editing Room Handbook: How to Tame the Chaos of the Editing Room.* 4th ed. Berkeley, CA: Peachpit Press, 2009.

LoBrutto, Vincent. *Selected Takes: Film Editors on Editing.* New York: Praeger Publishing, 1991.

Murch, Walter. *In the Blink of an Eye.* 2nd ed. Los Angeles: Silman-James Press, 2001.

Oldham, Gabriella. *First Cut: Conversations with Film Editors.* Berkeley: University of California Press, 1992.

Ondaatje, Michael. *The Conversations: Walter Murch and the Art of Editing Film.* New York: Alfred A. Knopf, 2004.

O'Steen, Bobbie. *The Invisible Cut: How Editors Make Movie Magic.* Studio City, CA: Michael Wiese Productions, 2009.

O'Steen, Sam, and O'Steen, Bobbie. *Cut to the Chase: Forty-Five Years of Editing America's Favorite Movies.* Studio City, CA: Michael Wiese Productions, 2002.

Pearlman, Karen. *Cutting Rhythms: Shaping the Film Edit.* Burlington, MA: Focal Press, 2009.

Pepperman, Richard D. *The Eye Is Quicker: Film Editing: Making a Good Film Better.* Studio City, CA: Michael Wiese Productions, 2004.

Pudovkin, V. I. *Film Technique and Film Acting.* London: Vision Press, 1970.

Reisz, Karl, and Miller, Gavin. *The Technique of Film Editing.* Reissue of 2nd ed. Burlington, MA: Focal Press, 2009.

Rosenblum, Ralph, and Karen, Robert. *When the Shooting Stops . . . The Cutting Begins. A Film Editor's Story.* New York: Da Capo Press, 1986.

Rubin, Michael. *Nonlinear: A Field Guide to Digital Video and Film Editing.* Gainesville, FL: Triad Publishing, 2000.

Sobel, Jeff. *Sound Editing in Final Cut Studio.* Apple Pro Training Series. Los Angeles: Peachpit Press, 2009.

Staten, Greg. *The Avid Handbook: Advanced Techniques, Strategies, and Survival Information for Avid Editing Systems.* 5th ed. Burlington, MA: Focal Press, 2008.

Thompson, Roy, and Bowen, Christopher. *Grammar of the Edit.* 2nd ed. Burlington, MA: Focal Press, 2009.

Vaughan, Dai. *Portrait of an Invisible Man: The Working Life of Stewart McAllister, Film Editor.* London: BFI Publishing, 1983.

Weynand, Diane. *Final Cut Pro 7: Professional Editing in Final Cut Studio.* Apple Pro Training Series. Los Angeles: Peachpit Press, 2009.

Index

Made in the USA
Monee, IL
03 March 2020